SO-BYG-672

FREE BOOK
GREENWICH
RECYCLING

The
COMPLETE
IDIOT'S
GUIDE TO
the Internet
for Windows

by Peter Kent

que

A Division of Macmillan Publishing USA
201 W. 103rd Street, Indianapolis, IN 46290

International Standard Book Number: 1-56761-609-7
Library of Congress Catalog Card Number: 95-73566

97 96 95   8   7   6   5   4   3   2   1

Interpretation of the printing code: the rightmost number of the first series of numbers is the year of the book's printing; the rightmost number of the second series of numbers is the number of the book's printing. For example, a printing code of 95-1 shows that the first printing of the book occurred in 1995.

Printed in the United States of America

Publisher
Roland Elgey

Vice-President and Publisher
Marie Butler-Knight

Editorial Services Director
Elizabeth Keaffaber

Publishing Manager
Barry Pruett

Development Editor
Heather Stith

Technical Editor
C. Herbert Feltner

Production Editor
Phil Kitchel

Copy Editor
Barry Childs-Helton

Cover Designer
Scott Cook

Designer
Barbara Kordesh

Illustrator
Judd Winick

Indexer
Kathy Venable

Production Team
Claudia Bell, John Hulse, Barry Jorden, Daryl Kessler, Kaylene Riemen, Kristine Simmons, Tina Trettin, Scott Tullis, Paul Wilson

Contents at a Glance

v

Contents

21 FREE Software? Shareware and Freeware 197

22 You'll Have to Pay—Commercial Suites 209

Introduction

Assuming you haven't been shipwrecked on a desert island for the last year or two, you've heard about the Internet. It's this week's big culture and technology story. The Internet provides a whole new world, or at least new improved access to the old one—if you can figure out how to get up and running in "cyberspace."

That's not necessarily easy. Hundreds of thousands of users have been disappointed. They got on the Internet and found themselves back in the '70s. Outside the Internet, you're working in a multimedia, wired, up-to-date, graphical-user-interface 1990s. On the Internet, you're typing commands at a UNIX command line!

Others went after the latest Windows Internet software, only to discover that installing the stuff was a nightmare. Some were lucky and only spent an hour or two. Others gave up in disgust after a couple of days.

Welcome to The Complete Idiot's Guide to the Internet for Windows

There's a better way. Read this book and you'll be up and running on the Internet in about 30 minutes! That's right, 30 minutes.

This book comes with a disk (you noticed, didn't you?). That disk contains Internaut software—a special, award-winning program that's easy to install and easy to use. After you install the program, you'll connect to the Pipeline USA network, a national Internet service provider with numbers throughout the U.S. of A.

Within seconds of connecting you'll be on the Internet, in all its glory. You even get a free one-week trial to play around and see what you think. And you get *all* the major Internet tools—e-mail, mailing lists, newsgroups, the World Wide Web, Gopher, FTP, Archie, Telnet, WAIS, Internet Relay Chat, and more!

It Shouldn't Be Hard!

Why should the Internet be hard? To connect using some methods you almost need a degree in computer networking! All that talk of IP numbers, TCP/IP, login scripts, packet vectors, Van Jacobson compression, maximum transmission units...what is all this? And why do you need to know about it?

You don't, if you use Internaut. I'll bet you have better things to do than turn into a networking geek. When you buy a car you don't have to understand how to *build* one, do you? So why should you have to know how to "build" an Internet connection?

If you've never used the Internet, Internaut will get you up and running so fast you'll never know how hard it is for other people. If you *have* used the Internet before you'll be pleased by the neat Windows interface...and wonder why all the other systems can't be so easy to install.

You Know a Little, Right?

I've made a couple of assumptions. I'm assuming that you know how to use your computer, and that you know how to work in Microsoft Windows. If you don't, read *The Complete Idiot's Guide to PCs* by Joe Kraynak and *The Complete Idiot's Guide to Windows* by Paul McFedries.

I'm not going to explain all the ins and outs of Windows—how to click on buttons, how to use list boxes, and so on. You need to understand those things before we get started.

How Do You Use This Book?

I've broken this book down into several parts. **Part 1, "Connecting to Pipeline USA,"** starts with how to install the Internaut software and connect to Pipeline USA. And once you're connected, you'll learn the basic information you need to get around in Internaut—about the Internaut window, the Internaut "gopher," and setting bookmarks wherever you go (so you can find your way back quickly).

Part 2, "Talking to the World—E-mail and Newsgroups,"
describes how you can use the most popular Internet tools—e-mail,
mailing lists, and newsgroups. E-mail lets you send messages all over
the world—to your friends, family, and colleagues. Mailing lists and
newsgroups help you connect with other people of like interests,
whether you are into scuba diving, S&M, Chinese history, or
nanotechnology.

In **Part 3, "Traveling the World,"** we'll take a look around the
Internet, using tools such as the World Wide Web (if you haven't heard
about this you've been asleep for a few months); Archie and FTP (find
useful computer files throughout the world); Telnet (log in to computers set up to play chess or Go, provide database access, and more);
Internet Relay Chat (get into real-time conversations with other
Internet users, wherever they may be); and WAIS (search publicly
accessible databases).

Part 4, "Beyond Internaut," goes, well, beyond Internaut for
some other ways to connect Microsoft Windows to the Internet—some
easy, some not quite so easy.

I have used a couple of conventions in this book to make it easier
to use. For example, when you need to type something, it will appear
like this:

Type this

Just type what it says. It's as simple as that. If I don't know exactly
what you'll have to type—because you have to supply some of the
information—I'll put the unknown information in italics. For instance:

Type this *filename*

I don't know the filename, so you'll have to supply it. Also, I've
used the term "Enter" throughout the book. (Your keyboard may have
a "Return" key instead.)

If you want to understand more about what you're reading, you'll
find boxes with background information, which you can quickly skip
over if you don't want the gory details. Here are the special icons and
boxes to look for to learn just what you need:

These boxes provide technical tidbits for the truly interested.

These boxes put strange Internet lingo into plain English, warn you about potential pitfalls, and provide helpful tips.

Trademarks

All terms mentioned in this book that are known to be trademarks have been appropriately capitalized. Que Corporation cannot attest to the accuracy of this information. Use of a term in this book should not be regarded as affecting the validity of any trademark or service mark.

Part 1
Connecting to Pipeline USA

Have you tried other Internet software—the ones that make you enter a zillion different configuration numbers and write a login script? (Script sounds okay until you realize it means "program.") Well, installing Internaut and connecting to Pipeline USA is so easy, it doesn't take a lot of thought.

In Part 1, I'll explain how to install Internaut, how to pick the best type of connection method, and how to connect. Then we'll take a quick look at a few basics: how the Internaut window works, and what the "Pathways into the Internet" are. We'll also find out about the Bookmarks system that lets you find your way back to somewhere you visited earlier.

## Chapter 1

The Least You Need to Know

Internaut provides the easiest full-access Internet connection around. It's easy to install, easy to connect, and easy to use. Still, if you've never used the Internet, you'll need to learn a few new concepts. Nothing complicated—no brain surgery, no metaphysics, no "nucular" physics.

Here's a quick summary of some of the things you'll learn. We'll get into detail in later chapters.

1. Internaut is the name of the program you're going to use. Pipeline USA is the name of the online service that Internaut connects to. You may have heard the software referred to as The Pipeline (in computer-magazine reviews, for instance). It was originally known as The Pipeline, but that was the name of the small service provider in New York that owned it, too, so the program was renamed to prevent confusion. Then the service provider (and the program) was bought out by PSINet, who wanted to use the program for a new service, Pipeline USA.

2. Installing Internaut is quick and no hassle—just run the Setup program on the floppy disk. You'll need an IBM-compatible 386 or later, with at least 4MB of RAM (but preferably 8MB) and 3.5 MB of free disk space. See Chapter 2 for more information.

3. The Internaut window is based on an Internet "Gopher." The list in the middle of the window—the **Pathways into the Internet**—is a Gopher menu. Double-click on entries to travel through gopherspace. When you reach a picture, a Web document, a Telnet session, or whatever, Internaut automatically displays the utility you need. See Chapters 4 and 5 for information about using the Internaut components and working in gopherspace.

4. Internaut has a system-wide bookmark scheme. You can set bookmarks on any Internet item—a Web document, Gopher menu, picture, Telnet session, FTP site, whatever—then quickly recall that item from the Bookmarks dialog box. You can even create your own folders, so you can categorize your bookmarks. See Chapter 7.

5. E-mail lets you send messages all over the world; to friends, colleagues, family—anyone you know who's connected to the Internet. Internaut's e-mail system is easy to use. It lets you send computer files across the Internet (using something called UUENCODE), create folders to save different categories of incoming messages, create an address book with oft-used e-mail addresses, and more. See Chapters 8 and 9.

6. A mailing list is a "discussion" group that uses the e-mail system to swap messages between group members. When you send a message to the group, that message goes to every group member. What sorts of subjects do these groups cover? There are thousands of different topics, so pick one—mathematics in Chile, child abuse, effective study methods, tractor restoration, tropical storms. See Chapter 10 for more information.

7. There's another form of discussion group on the Internet called newsgroups. Pipeline USA subscribes to about *11,000* of these groups! Again, just pick a subject—you'll probably find a group related to it. Unlike mailing lists, newsgroups don't use the e-mail system to distribute messages—rather, you need a *news reader*. See Chapters 11 and 12 for more information.

8. Internaut's message-filtering system works in both the e-mail and newsgroup systems. It lets you automate what happens to your messages. You can automatically delete messages from particular people (get rid of those irritating e-mail messages from your boss—and tell him, quite honestly, that you never saw them). You can automatically move messages about particular subjects into a special folder, download some messages (but only see the Subject of others), and so on. See Chapter 13 for details.

9. The World Wide Web is *the* hot topic on the Internet these days. You've probably heard of Mosaic, but Mosaic is simply one of many Web *browsers*, programs that can display Web documents. Internaut has its own Web browser. See Chapter 14 for information on how to use the browser, and where to go on the Web to search for useful documents.

10. Internaut has combined two separate Internet functions into one; it's taken Archie and FTP, and created a utility that will search for computer files—there are millions publicly accessible on the Internet—and transfer them to your computer. See Chapter 15 for more information.

11. Telnet is a system that lets you log onto other people's computers (only those that have been made publicly accessible, of course). Why? So you can search databases (for job listings, for instance), play Chess or Go, or try the many MUD games. See Chapter 16 for details.

12. Finding people on the Internet can be tricky, but Internaut provides various tools to help you. See Chapter 17.

13. Do you want your Internet activity to be a bit more "interactive," to provide more real-time contact with other users? Then you need Talk and Internet Relay Chat. See Chapter 18.

14. Internaut may be the easiest way to get a full-fledged Internet connection up and running, but it's not the only way. In Chapters 19 to 25, I'll take a look at some other methods for connecting your Windows computer to the Internet.

## Chapter 2

Installing Internaut

In This Chapter

➤ System requirements

➤ Installing the software

➤ Checking your SHARE setting

Other computer book authors make you wait until the end of the book before they tell you how to use the stuff on the free disks. Not me (at least not in this book). I want you to break out that disk right now! This chapter explains how to install the Internaut software that's on the floppy disk onto your hard disk so that you can connect to Pipeline USA and get running on the Internet. (If you don't know the difference between Internaut and Pipeline USA, go directly to Chapter 1. Do not pass Go. Do not collect $200.)

Do You Have What It Takes?

First, let's look at what you need to run the Internaut software bundled with this book:

If you are using a video mode with more than 256 colors, you may find that Internaut doesn't run correctly. Try reducing the video mode to 256 colors or less.

An IBM-compatible PC

A 386 processor or later

4MB of RAM (8MB preferred)

About 3.5MB of free hard-disk space

A modem—preferably at least a 9600-bps modem (some of the access numbers run at 28,800 bps)

Microsoft Windows 3.1, 3.11, or Windows 95

That's the minimum. Pipeline USA actually recommends that you be running a 486 with 8MB of RAM or more. The program will run more efficiently that way—but then, all software runs better on a faster system with more RAM. You'll also want a mouse. Although you can perform most mouse actions with the keyboard, you can't perform all of them. Besides, a mouse makes life easier in Windows.

Installing the Software

Want more software? Pipeline USA regularly posts the very latest beta software for their subscribers to download. (*Beta* means, "This seems to work okay, but there are a few details we haven't quite nailed down, so this isn't an official 'release'.") Double-click on the **Closer to Home: Pipeline USA and Account Information** "pathway" once you've logged on to Pipeline USA. (See Chapter 5 for more information about the pathways.)

In the absence of a yellow brick road, follow these steps:

1. Close Microsoft Windows.

2. Reopen Microsoft Windows.

3. Place Pipeline USA Disk 1 in your 3.5-inch floppy drive.

4. At Program Manager, select **Run** from the **File** menu.

5. Type **b:\setup** or **a:\setup** (depending on which drive letter identifies the floppy drive on your computer).

6. Press **Enter**.

7. The installation program begins. When it asks where you want to place the files, you can accept the default (**c:\pipeusa**) or enter a different directory path.

8. Click on **Continue**.

The installation program will load all the files onto your hard disk, and create a Pipeline USA program group in Program Manager.

Using Windows 95?

If you are working with Windows 95, the installation procedure is a little different. Follow these steps:

Having installation problems? You can call Pipeline USA technical support at 703-904-9115.

1. Close all your applications and place the Pipeline USA disk in your computer's disk drive.

2. Click on the **Start** button in the Task Bar.

3. Click on the **Settings** option in the Start menu when it pops up. Another menu will appear.

4. Click on the **Control Panel** option. The Windows 95 Control Panel will open.

5. Double-click on **Add/Remove Programs**.

6. When the dialog box opens, click on the **Install** button. Another dialog box opens.

7. Click on the **Next** button, and Windows 95 will search for the setup program.

8. A text box will appear inside the dialog box, showing the setup program that Windows 95 found.

9. Make sure that the text box shows the correct disk drive. If not, type **a:\setup** into the text box (assuming you placed the disk in drive **a:**).

10. Click on the **Finish** button, and the setup program will start.

    When it asks where you want to place the files, you can accept the default (**c:\pipeline**) or enter a different directory path.

11. Follow the instructions, changing disks when appropriate.

12. The installation program will load all the files onto your hard disk, and create a Pipeline USA cascading menu within the Program menu (which, in turn, is within the Start menu on your Task Bar).

The Least You Need to Know

➤ You need *at least* a 386 with 4MB of RAM, 3.5MB hard-disk space, and a modem to run Internaut.

➤ As always with computers, more is better—a 486 with 8MB of RAM will run Internaut better.

➤ Run **SETUP** on the installation disk to install the program.

## Chapter 3

Reach Out and Touch Someone— Dialing Pipeline USA

In This Chapter

➤ Starting Internaut

➤ Selecting a Pipeline USA telephone number

➤ Connecting to Pipeline USA

➤ Selecting connection options

➤ Finding the latest software

➤ Changing your password

➤ Converting your test account into a full account

Setting up your free demo account on Pipeline USA is quick and easy. You dial into a Pipeline USA 800 number, select a telephone number for your connection, set up your account information, then log off. So let's get connected!

Starting the Program

Let's start the Internaut program:

1. Double-click on the **Pipeline USA** icon in Program Manager. The Welcome to Pipeline USA dialog box appears (you only see this the first time you start Pipeline

USA). If you are using Windows 95, click on the **Start** button on the Task Bar, click
on **Programs**, click on **Pipeline USA**, and click on **Pipeline USA** in the final cascading menu.

2. Click on the **I want to try it FREE for 7 days** option button, and then on the **Go**
button. You'll see the Connect dialog box.

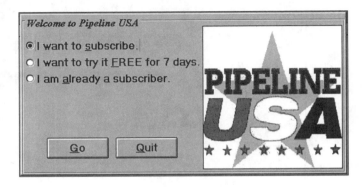

*Click on the second option button then click on **Go**.*

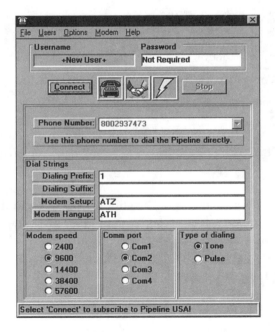

Setting up a modem doesn't have to be difficult.

3. Internaut dials an 800 number. That number is already in the **Phone Number** line. You *may* have to change the **Dialing Prefix**. Include any other necessary numbers: a **9** to get an outside line, for instance, or ***70** or **1170** (whichever is appropriate in your area) to turn off call waiting.

4. Click on the **File** menu and then on the **Set modem initialization string** option. You'll see the Select Your Modem Type dialog box. This shows a list of modems. When you find your modem in the list, **double-click** on it (or click once and press **Enter**). This will enter the correct **Modem Setup** and **Modem Hangup** information. If you don't find your modem in the list, try picking one of the Hayes modems—

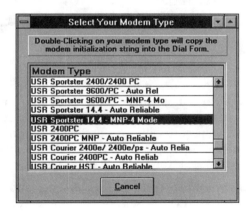

Help! The Help file that is being shipped with Internaut at the time of writing is *way* out of date. I know, because I created the Help system for Pipeline New York, the original Pipeline service. It will be updated eventually, but if you find that it doesn't seem to match what you are looking at...that's because it *doesn't!*

either a "Hayes-compatible" modem, or—if you need a faster speed than is available in the list for these—pick one of the faster Hayes modems.

Select your modem from the list.

You probably won't need to change the **Dialing Suffix**, so you can leave it alone for now. Later, if you run into problems, Pipeline USA technical support staff may advise you to change them. (You can contact them at 703-904-9115.)

5. In the **Modem speed** column, click on your modem speed—the fastest speed that your modem will work with. If your modem's maximum speed is not listed, select the next highest. (Pipeline USA's modems vary from 9600 to 28,800 bps—they are currently in the process of upgrading all areas to 28,800 bps.)

6. In the **Comm port** column, click on the communications port that your modem is connected to. If you're not sure, check your computer's documentation or call the computer's technical support line.

7. Click on one of the **Type of dialing** option buttons. In most cases you will use **Tone**. If you don't have tone dialing, select **Pulse**. (If your phone beeps when you press a button, you have tone dialing. If your phone "click-click-clicks" when you press a button, it's pulse dialing—though your phone lines may allow you to use both tone and pulse dialing. If you're not sure, ask your phone company.)

8. Click on the **Connect** button. The program dials into Pipeline USA—after a few moments you'll see the Signing Up dialog box.

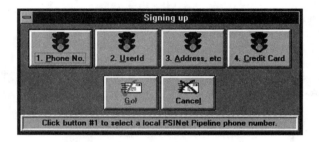

The Signing Up dialog box.

9. Click on the **1. Phone No.** button to see a list of Pipeline USA phone numbers. Scroll down through the list of numbers until you find a number in your area. If you can't find one in your area, check with your long-distance company to find out which area code is cheapest to call. (At the time of writing, Pipeline USA has about 60 numbers around the United States—though they should have around 120 by the time this book hits the bookstores, and 200 by the end of 1995.)

10. Double-click on that number. You'll see a dialog box showing you the number that you have selected. Click on **OK** to select that number (or **Cancel** to return to the list of numbers so you can select another).

11. Click on the **2. Userid** button. You'll see the Select a user name dialog box.

14

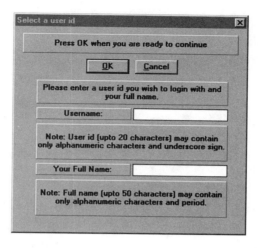

Identify yourself to the system—enter an account name and your real name.

You Got Your I.D.?

Every user on Pipeline USA has his or her own "account." A *User ID* or *account name* identifies the person connecting, so Pipeline USA knows which e-mail to give that person, which newsgroups the person has subscribed to, and so on. User IDs and account names are public knowledge—the *password*, however, is private; it's used to make sure you really are who you say you are. You'll be given a password later in this procedure.

12. In the first text box, type the name by which you want to be known online. This is normally a contraction of your name—if your name is Jane Doe, it might be **jdoe** or **janed** or whatever—but it can be almost whatever you want. There's a 30-character limit for the name; you can use any number or lowercase letter, and underscore characters if you wish.

13. Type your real name into the text box at the bottom, and then click on **OK**.

14. Click on the **3. Address, etc** button to see the Address and Phone Number dialog box. Enter all your information; click on **OK**.

15

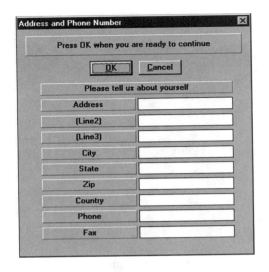

Enter your address and phone information.

15. Click on the **4. Credit Card** button to see the Payment options dialog box.

16. Click on the payment plan you want to use. You'll probably want to start with the **Test drive**. You'll get a free week of service. The other two options are **Timed** (you'll pay a monthly fee of $5 for the first five hours you use, then $1.50 for each hour over that) and **Untimed** (you'll pay $19.95 a month for unlimited use).

17. Enter your credit-card number (you can use MasterCard, Visa, Discover, or American Express), and the expiration date. Make sure you enter the expiration date in the format MMYY—for instance, for 7/97 enter **0797**.

    You *must* enter a credit-card number, even if you are only signing up for the Test Drive. Your card won't be charged until you convert your account from a Test-Drive account to a full account. Pipeline USA wants this information for two reasons. First, when you want to convert your account it can be done very quickly—second, because the only form of billing used by Pipeline USA is credit-card billing. If you don't have a credit card, there's not much point trying out the service.

    If the Payment options dialog box reappears, look in the message area immediately below the **Expiration** text box for some kind of reason—perhaps you entered an invalid number, or maybe the credit-card company rejected the transaction!

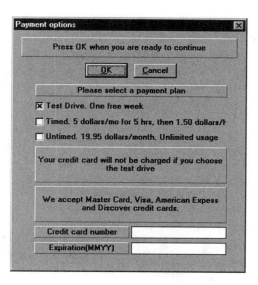

You must enter a credit-card number!

18. Click on **OK** and the information is sent to Pipeline USA. (You'll see a message box telling you to be patient. Click on the **OK** button to remove this message.)

19. Once your information has been approved, your computer should beep, the Go! button will become enabled, and you'll see a message in the status bar saying **Click on the GO! button to finalize the signup!**.

20. Click on the **Go!** button to see the Terms and Conditions dialog box. Read this box, and then click on the **OK** button. (Note that PSI—Performance Systems International, Inc., the owners of Pipeline USA—will not charge anything to your card during the "test drive.")

21. Now you'll see a message box telling you your password. Write this down for now (you can change it later).

22. Click on the **OK** button and you'll see another message, this time telling you your e-mail address (your selected user id@usa.pipeline.com) and your password again. Write down your e-mail address and click on **OK**.

23. Internaut will now log off Pipeline USA. You're almost finished, but not quite.

24. Click on the **Connect!** menu option in the Internaut window. The Connect dialog box appears again. Notice that the number you selected during the account-setup procedure is in the **Phone Number** text box. You may have to change it, though—if it shows a 1 followed by the area code, but you selected a number in your area code,

delete the 1 and the area code. Also, as before, make sure you have the correct **Dialing Prefix** information—a 9 to get an outside line, and *70 or 1170 to turn off call waiting, and so on.

25. Click on the **Connect** button and Internaut begins dialing into the number you selected. You can watch the progress in the status bar at the bottom of the Connect dialog box.

Problems If you have any problems setting up your system or connecting to Pipeline USA, call Pipeline USA's technical support at 703-904-9115.

26. When Internaut connects to Pipeline USA, the Connect dialog box disappears and the e-mail Inbox appears (you'll learn more about this in Chapter 9). If there are any messages in the box, double-click on them to read them. Otherwise shut the Inbox—press **Alt+F4**.

That's it—you're up and running. You can log off now, if you wish (click on the **Goodbye!** menu option in the main Internaut window). Or go on to Chapter 4 to learn how to use Internaut.

Getting the Latest Software

The folks at Pipeline USA are constantly adding new features and improvements to Internaut. You should make sure you have the latest software—in fact, a few of the features I've mentioned in this book are not on the disk that's bundled with the book—they are features that are being added to Internaut, and will be available on the upgraded software.

First, find out what version of Internaut you are using. Select the **Help** menu and then click on the **About Pipeline USA** menu option. A box will appear, showing you copyright information and the program's version number. Close this box, then double-click on the **Closer to Home: Pipeline USA and Account Information** line in the **Pathways into the Internet** (you must be connected to Pipeline USA to do this—see Chapter 5 for more information about the Pathways). In the window that opens, you'll find an entry that will lead you to the software updates.

Changing Your Password

It's a good idea to change your password now and again. To do so, double-click on the **Closer to Home: Pipeline USA and Account Information** pathway, and then on **Change my Password** entry in the window that appears. You'll see a dialog box into which you must type your current password, followed by the new password. Note that you can use up to eight characters, that at least one must have a character other than a letter (a number or a punctuation character), and that you can't include spaces.

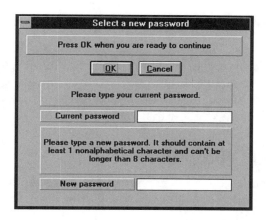

Change your password periodically.

A Few More Connect Options

I should say a few more things about the Connect dialog box. The first thing is that you don't have to display all the modem information all the time. If you open the **Options** menu in the Connect dialog box, and then select **Advanced Options**, the box shrinks, leaving you with everything down to the Connect and Stop buttons. You can always replace the other information by selecting the menu option again.

You can also tell Internaut to display your password. So that nobody can look over your shoulder and see your password Internaut normally shows asterisks when you type the password. But if you open the **Options** menu and select **Hide password**, removing the check mark from that option, the asterisks are replaced by the actual characters.

Don't want to type your password each time? Then open **Options** menu and select **Remember password across sessions**. Internaut will remember the password, and fill in the **Password** text box for you each time. You won't want to do this if your copy of Internaut is on a system that you share with someone, of course, such as a work computer. Only save the password if you are sure your computer is safe.

Password Won't Work? You enter your password and try to log on, but Internaut won't connect? Perhaps you entered your password incorrectly. The *case* of the password is important. If you were given the password **qjq12y**, you can't enter QJQ12Y or qJq12Y, for instance. Enter each letter in the correct case.

19

Finding More Phone Numbers

How do you find another Pipeline USA telephone number? Perhaps you are off on a road trip, and want to keep in touch. Or maybe you're just moving to another area? Well, you can find the telephone-number list online. Log on to Pipeline USA, double-click on the **Closer to Home: Pipeline USA and Account Information**, then on the **Current list of dialup points** entry in the window that appears.

Converting Your Account

After seven days, your account will expire. At that point you will see a dialog box appear when you log on to Pipeline USA. This box will inform you that your demo account has finished, and ask whether you want to subscribe. Follow the instructions in this box.

The Least You Need to Know

> ➤ Double-click on **Pipeline USA** icon to start the program.

> ➤ Select **I want to try if FREE for 7 days** option button, then click on the **Go** button.

> ➤ Set up your modem, then click on **Connect**.

> ➤ When you connect to Pipeline USA, click on each button in the Signing up dialog box in sequence, and enter the information.

> ➤ When Internaut logs off, click on the **Connect!** menu and make sure the number in the Phone Number text box is entered correctly.

> ➤ The Connect Options let you view your password; you can tell Internaut to remember the password for you.

> ➤ Make sure you upgrade your software to the latest version.

> ➤ When your demo account's seven days have finished, you'll be informed and given the opportunity to subscribe.

## Chapter 4

Window on the World—the Internaut Components

In This Chapter

➤ The Internaut menus

➤ The Internaut buttons

➤ Closing Internaut

➤ Internaut's integration and multitasking

So you're in, and you're looking at the Internaut window, wondering what to do next. Actually you're probably looking at the Inbox window—every time you open Internaut the Inbox window (which shows you e-mail messages you've received) opens automatically, even if you have no incoming e-mail. (Select the **Autostart at Login** command on the **Options** menu to stop this from happening.) For now, though, let's close this window—select **Exit** from the **File** menu, or press **Alt+F4**. We'll come back and look at e-mail later, in Chapter 8. (If you already have incoming mail, you may want to skip forward to Chapter 8 to figure out what to do with it—or here's a quick bit of info: double-click on an entry in the top of the **Inbox** window to read the message.)

Internaut's Front End

Let's start by taking a look at the Internaut window and its various components.

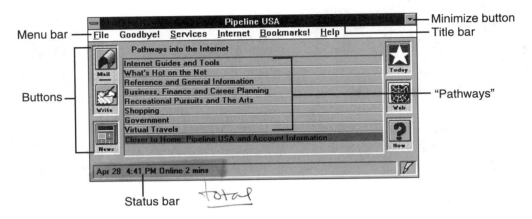

Where do we go from here?

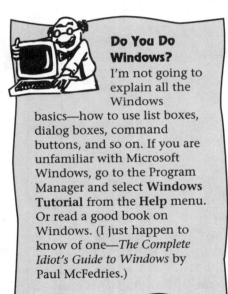

Do You Do Windows?

I'm not going to explain all the Windows basics—how to use list boxes, dialog boxes, command buttons, and so on. If you are unfamiliar with Microsoft Windows, go to the Program Manager and select **Windows Tutorial** from the **Help** menu. Or read a good book on Windows. (I just happen to know of one—*The Complete Idiot's Guide to Windows* by Paul McFedries.)

So what are all these components? Read on:

Title bar   Doesn't do much for us—just tells us we're connected to Pipeline USA.

Menu bar   Typical Windows menus with loads of commands to help us get around in the Internet.

Minimize button   Minimizes Pipeline USA window (that is, reduces it to an icon at the bottom of your screen).

Buttons   Click on one of these to use a particular service.

"Pathways"   The "Pathways into the Internet" is what's known as a "gopher" menu—and you'll learn more about it in the next chapter. Basically, it's a way to travel through the Internet to information on every conceivable subject.

Status bar   This shows the time and date—which is handy for many Internet users, as they have a tendency to lose track of the day and week—and the number of minutes you've been online.

What's on the Menu?

Let's take a look at the menu options, and what they can do for you.

File|Create new user   Use this command to set up a new user account (after you've subscribed), providing Internaut with your username and real name. See Chapter 3.

File|Options and preferences   This command opens a dialog box where you'll set up a variety of Internaut options, from what the program should do when e-mail arrives to how to handle World Wide Web images. See Chapter 7.

Menu Conventions
I use a convention in all my books to describe using menus. Instead of saying, for instance, "Open the File menu and select the Exit command," I just say, "Select "**File|Exit**." It saves paper, ink, and hassle.

File|Printer Setup   Use this to set up your printer to print text or figures you discover in Internaut.

File|Viewer Setup   Use this to set up "viewers" for your Web browser. Viewers are programs that display and play various kinds of file formats that you'll run into on the World Wide Web. See Chapter 14 for more information.

File|Display picture file   Use this to open a file on your hard disk.

File|Show Packet Transmission Form   A special dialog box used to track data transmission problems—you'll only use this if instructed to do so by technical support.

File|Show floating window list   A list of all the windows you have open. A very useful way to jump to the Internaut window you need. The list remains "on top", so it's always available.

File|Exit   Use this to close Pipeline. If you are online at the time, you'll be asked if you really want to disconnect. You can also press **Alt+F4** or **Ctrl+X** to close.

Goodbye!   This menu was the Connect! menu, remember, until you logged onto Pipeline USA. Click on **Goodbye!** to log off.

Services|Mail: open mailboxes   Opens the Mail window. You'll learn about this in Chapter 9.

Services|Mail: write a letter   Opens the Composer window, so you can write a message to someone. See Chapter 8.

Services|Open address book   Use this to go directly to the address book. See Chapter 9 for more information.

Services|News: open Usenet forums   Opens the News window, from which you'll read your newsgroup message. This has nothing to do with the news in the real-world sense, by the way (newspapers, journalists, and so on). Rather, in Internet-speak, it means discussion groups. Don't worry, you'll learn more in Chapter 11.

Services|Send queued Mail and News   If, for some reason, your e-mail or newsgroup messages are not sent, but remain in the mail system's Outbox, you can use this command to "force" them out.

Services|Today's News and Weather   This opens the Today text file, which tells you a little about today's weather! Sometimes it contains useful information about new services and goings-on, too.

Services|Talk (chat with someone)   This command lets you "talk" with someone. Well, it's not real talking—you type, and they type back. Still, a lot of people really get into it, and you can learn about it in Chapter 18.

Internet|World Wide Web   Heard of Mosaic? The current media hype about the Internet seems to be focusing on the World Wide Web and Mosaic, a "browser" that lets you travel around the Web. Well, Internaut has a browser, too—see Chapter 14.

Internet|Get files ("FTP" and "Archie")   There are millions of computer files—programs, documents, pictures, music, and more—just waiting for you on the Internet...*if* you know where they are and how to grab them. This command's the one you need—see Chapter 15 to learn how to use it.

I Know a Shortcut   When you open a menu, some of the options have keyboard shortcuts. For instance, pressing **Ctrl+I** is the same as selecting **Internet|Chat (IRC)**, **Ctrl+P** is the same as **File|Display picture file**. You can find them on the tear-out card at the front of this book, too.

Internet|Chat (IRC)   Do you like idle chatter and mindless prattle? Then Internet Relay Chat is the place for you! (Okay, I'm sure you can find intellectual discussions in IRC, too—somewhere.) Chapter 18 explains how to use this.

Internet|Find someone on the Internet   It's hard to track down other Internet users sometimes. This command leads you to a database of newsgroup users—and may help you find someone's e-mail address (if they use newsgroups). See Chapter 17.

Internet|Search all Gopherspace (Veronica)   A *gopher* is a large rodent, true. But on the Internet it's a huge menu system. And Veronica is a special tool to help you search Gopherspace, this huge network of menus. You'll see how in Chapter 6. (This menu option may not be available in your software, but will probably be added soon.)

Internet|Connect to another system (Telnet) Would you like to log on to a computer half way around the world and play games or search a database? Then you need Telnet and Chapter 16.

Internet|Gopher anywhere Here's a shortcut through the gopher system I just mentioned. Select this command, type a gopher "address," and away you go. Again, you can find more info in Chapter 6.

Bookmarks! If you spend much time on the Internet, you'll eventually get lost. Or rather, you'll find that you can't find your way back to where you once found yourself. Bookmarks let you keep a record of where you've been, and help you quickly jump back there. See Chapter 7.

Help|Contents Select this to see the Internaut help file (the original of which was written by yours truly).

Help|"How do I?" This currently displays a picture of the Internaut window—click on parts of the window to see what they do.

**Offline/
Online** Offline is techie jargon for "not connected." You are offline before you dial into Pipeline USA. **Online** means that you *are* connected to Pipeline USA.

Help|About Pipeline USA Displays the About box, which shows the program version number and copyright information.

Note that you can use some of these commands at any time. **Service|Mail: Write a letter**, for instance, will work whether you are connected to Pipeline USA or not. Others, of course, won't work if you're not connected. There's no point in starting the World Wide Web, for instance, when you are *offline*.

Buttons for Those Who Prefer the Mouse

Now for the buttons. All the buttons, with the exception of the last one, are duplicates of menu commands. They simply speed up your work by letting you click once instead of twice. The last button, **How**, displays a menu of documents you can read to help you learn more about Pipeline USA.

Displays the Mail window (the same as **Services|Mail: open mail-boxes**—see Chapter 9)

Displays the Composer window (the same as **Services|Mail: write a letter**—see Chapter 8)

Displays the News window (the same as **Services|News: Open Usenet forums**—see Chapter 11)

Displays the Today file (the same as **Services|Today's News and Weather**)

Opens the Web browser (the same as **Internet|World Wide Web**—see Chapter 14)

Displays a list of useful informational documents

You're going to learn about all these different tools later in this book.

Closing Internaut

To close the program, you can **double-click** on the **Control menu** (that little box in the top left corner), press **Alt+F4**, press **Ctrl+X**, select **Exit** from the **File** menu, or select **Close** from the **Control** menu. Enough choices for you? (This is a Windows convention, by the way—giving users loads of ways to get out of a program. If I were a dedicated Macintosh user, I'd probably make a joke about how Windows users *need* loads of ways to get out. I'm not, so I won't.)

If you happen to be online when you try to close the program, you *may* see a message box asking if you really want to close your connection. Click on **OK** to close both the connection and the program. You *won't* see this message if you use the double-click, Alt+F4, or Control-menu-Close options.

If you just want to log off Pipeline USA, but keep the program open, simply click on the **Goodbye!** menu option or press **Alt+G**.

Fitting It All Together

Internaut has garnered some great reviews from the computer and Internet press. Why? Mainly, I believe, because of the way Internaut integrates all the Internet tasks into one system. If you've worked with any other Internet graphical user interfaces, you may be aware of how they comprise a collection of tools. Systems such as Internet in a Box, SuperHighway Access, InterAp, and so on—we'll look at these in Chapter 23—are not so much a single program, as a *collection* of programs. They each have a Web browser, FTP tool, e-mail program, newsgroup program, gopher client, and so on.

Internaut has these programs too, but they are much more tightly integrated. If you've read the earlier chapters in this book, you've already seen that integration at work, and you'll see more examples later. One form of this integration is the use of system-wide Bookmarks. The Bookmarks dialog box can take you to Web pages, gopher menus, text documents, FTP sites, Telnet sessions, and more.

Then there's the way the gopher system itself is integrated with the other tools, as you see in Chapter 5. Double-clicking on items in gopher will bring up FTP, picture, text, Telnet, and Web tools. And the same in the Web browser—clicking on Web links can, in certain situations, bring up FTP, gopher, and Telnet tools. The Internet is no longer a mass of unrelated tools; it's all linked together.

It's true that many Internet programs seem to be moving to a closer integration of tools. But none has taken this to the degree that Internaut has.

Do It All at Once—Multitasking

There's another important issue to consider—the way Internaut can handle several operations at once. The Internet runs something called TCP/IP (Transmission Control Protocol/Internet Protocol), and most of the fancy Internet programs that are available for PCs and Macs run on TCP/IP. One great advantage of such software is that it can *multitask*—while one program is doing one thing on the Internet, another can be doing something else. The problem is that setting up the TCP/IP connection between your computer and your service provider's computer is quite complicated.

As you've already seen, Internaut's setup is quite easy, as easy as using a basic dial-in terminal Internet account—a non-TCP/IP account. (If you've tried to set up a TCP/IP connection, entering configuration data and writing a login script, you'll appreciate just how easy Internaut is.) These dial-in terminal accounts are very common on the Internet, but they don't allow you to run the fancy software that everyone wants these days. Rather, dial-in terminal users are stuck at the command line, typing UNIX commands and selecting from text-based menu systems.

Even though Internaut is easy to set up, it's far more sophisticated than a dial-in terminal account. In fact, it has one of the great advantages of a complicated TCP/IP system—the ability to multitask.

Internaut uses a special communications protocol called PinkSlip™. This protocol was designed specially for Internaut. It's not exactly the same as TCP/IP, but from the user's point of view, it's very similar. Because of PinkSlip™, Internaut can do many things at once.

Protocol The techie term **protocol** is simply a fancy way of saying "the way the computers talk to each other."

You can be downloading a file from an FTP site, transferring a picture you found in a gopher menu, and reading your newsgroup messages, all at the same time. This is a great benefit. Rather than waiting for a large file to transfer, then going to the gopher menu and transferring the picture, then going to your newsgroups, you can do it all at once.

If you use the Internet a lot, you'll soon realize the benefit of this system. After a while the idea of running just one operation at once will seem archaic.

Working in Windows 95

Internaut will work in Windows 95, which is due to be released sometime after this book goes to print. Windows 95 varies from Windows 3.11 in a few important ways, so I'd better give you a few quick pointers. First, notice from the figure below that the buttons in a window's title bar are different in Windows 95.

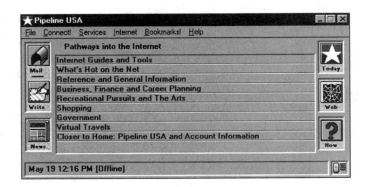

Yes, it'll run in Windows 95!

28

The manner in which you work with Windows has changed slightly in Windows 95. Here are a few basic techniques:

 Maximizing a window   Click on the button with a picture of a square, in the top right corner.

 Restoring a window to its previous size   Click on the button with two squares in the top right window (this button only appears if the window is maximized).

 Minimizing a window   Click on the line button in the top right corner.

Sizing a window   Place the mouse pointer over the border or corner, and drag it.

 Closing a window   Click on the X button in the top right corner. You can also double-click on the Control menu (the icon in the top left corner of the window), select Close from the Control menu, press Alt-F4, or, in some cases, select a Close or Exit command from the window's File menu.

Switching between windows   Press and hold Alt while you press Tab—you'll see the application bar. Continuing holding Alt and pressing Tab to select the window you want. You can also move the mouse pointer to the Task Bar, then click on the button representing the application you want to view.

Notice also that the old Control menu icon (on the left side of the title bar) has been replaced with the program's icon, though you'll find if you click on the icon the menu is still there.

Working with the Task Bar

Windows 95 uses a new feature called the Task Bar. This remains on your screen, and contains several elements: a Start button that opens the Start menu, a button for each open window, a clock, and several small icons representing special utilities (your modem and an MSN menu, for instance).

You can configure the Task Bar to work in a variety of ways; I suggest you experiment to find the one most convenient for you. To modify the Task Bar, click with the right mouse button on the bar and select **Properties** from the menu that pops up. In the dialog box that appears (see the following figure), you'll find these options.

Always on top   Select this and the Task Bar will be on top of other applications—you won't have to minimize them to get to it. This may sound inconvenient, but I combine it with the following option.

Auto hide   Select this to hide the Task Bar. It won't appear until you move the mouse pointer over the Task Bar and touch the edge of the display area. If you turn on the Always on top feature, the Task Bar will appear even if you have another application maximized.

Show small icons in Start menu   Reduces the size of the icons shown in the Start menu. Useful if you add lots of items to this menu.

Show Clock   You can remove and replace the digital clock that appears on the right end of the Task Bar.

Here's what I find most convenient. I turn on the **Always on top** and **Auto hide** options, and move the Task Bar to the top of my screen—you can do that by pointing to a blank area on the bar and dragging it up (you can also place it on the sides of your screen). Because I often run lots of applications, I also enlarge the size of the Task Bar—point at the border and drag the border out to extend the bar.

Working with the Task Bar takes a little getting used to. With these settings, the bar won't appear when you move the mouse pointer over it—you have to move the mouse pointer all the way across the bar and touch the bottom edge of the screen (or top edge if the bar's on the top). So you have to be careful when clicking on a menu in a maximized window not to move the pointer up to the menu bar too quickly, or you'll overshoot the menu bar, hit the edge of the screen, and display the Task Bar. (Click in the application to remove the Task Bar.)

There's another way to get to the Task Bar—press **Ctrl+Esc**. The bar appears, and the Start Menu opens. (I've set up my programmable keyboard to use this; I press F1 to open the Start menu, F3 to open my Start menu and then open the Programs menu, and so on. If you have a programmable mouse you could do something similar.)

The Least You Need to Know

➤ The Internaut menus lead you to a number of Internet tools.

➤ Remember to look at the keyboard shortcuts on the tear-out card.

➤ The buttons are, in most cases, duplications of commands in the menus.

➤ The How button leads to a collection of documents with more information about Pipeline USA, Internaut, and the Internet.

➤ Log off Pipeline USA by clicking on **Goodbye!**

➤ Close the program using **Ctrl+X** or selecting **File|Exit**.

➤ Internaut is a tightly integrated multitasking system. You can carry out multiple operations at once.

Pathways to the Internet—Working with Gopher

If you've used the Internet for awhile, you may be familiar with the term *gopher*. Of course, even if you *haven't* used the Internet, you're familiar with the small rodent that digs around in the dirt. "Gopher" also sometimes refers someone who "goes fer" stuff (though the spelling is different)—a plumber might call his assistant a "gofer," for instance.

Well, in the true Internet tradition of choosing cute or funny names, the developers of a giant Internet menu system decided to call it the Internet gopher—because they just happened to be at the University of Minnesota (and the team's mascot is a gopher), because the menu system is used to "dig" around in the Internet, and because you can use it to "gofer" stuff.

The main Internaut window is actually based around a gopher menu—each of the **Pathways into the Internet** lines you can see are gopher menu items. They are pathways, though, in the sense that you can follow them deep into *cyberspace*—or *gopherspace*, I should say. This chapter shows you how.

Cyberspace

You haven't heard the word *cyberspace* yet? Oh, then you've been spelunking in Outer Mongolia for a few years. Cyberspace is that area reached by computer communications programs when "traveling" around on the Internet or other online systems. *Gopherspace* is that particular area navigated through gopher menus.

What's All This, Then?

Using the gopher—or pathways, if you prefer—is simple. Just double-click on one of the entries. Or, use the arrow keys to move the highlight to the pathway you want to follow, then press **Enter**. Another window will open. In this window, you'll find more menu options—but you'll also find information or links out of the gopher system.

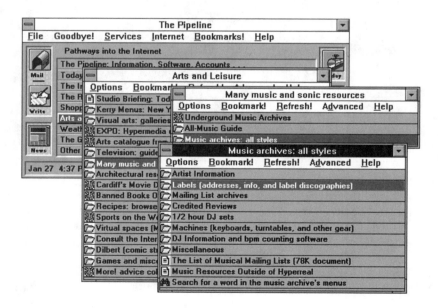

Just double-click to follow the pathways through gopherspace.

As you travel through gopherspace, more and more of these windows pop up. Look in the left column of each line, though, and you'll see that next to each entry is a small picture—the picture indicates what will happen when you select that entry. Let's take a quick look:

 Select this and another gopher menu will open.

 Select this to read a document.

 Select this to enter information.

 Select this to search for information.

 Select this to view a picture.

 Select this to transfer a file to your computer.

 Select this to open the World Wide Web browser.

 Select this to run a Telnet session, so you can connect to another computer or run a UNIX program.

We're going to take a look at each of these in turn. But first, a quick convention. I'll be telling you to look for various things in the "pathways" now and again. I'm going to separate each step in the path that you have to take with a vertical line (|). For instance, I might say, "follow the pathways to **Arts and Leisure|Many music and sonic resources| Underground Music Archives**." By double-clicking on each of those entries in turn (**Arts and Leisure** first, then **Many music and sonic resources** in the gopher menu that appears, then **Underground Music Archives** in the next gopher menu), you'll find yourself at the famous IUMA (Internet Underground Music Archives) World Wide Web site. (That's a great place to find samples from unknown bands, by the way, along with some not-quite-so-unknown ones, too.) Note also that these pathways may change, so the ones you find may be slightly—or not-so-slightly—different from the ones in this book.

Using the Gopher Menus

When you click on an entry with the folder icon, another gopher-menu window opens. What can you do in here? Well, you can double-click on an entry, of course, to go to yet another gopher menu or to view some kind of file. But you'll notice a number of menu options in here that help you work with all of these entries.

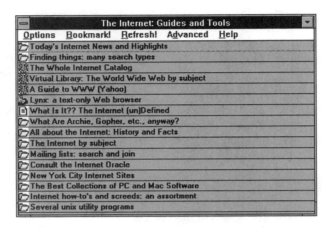

A Pipeline gopher menu—a pathway into the Internet.

Options menu   If you don't like the way these windows look, change them. You can use this menu to select a different font, and to change the background and foreground (text) colors. When you change these, you are changing the program defaults—from now on, all gopher menus will use these colors and font.

Set the Maximum
You can tell Internaut the maximum number of entries in one of these gopher windows, and the maximum number of windows to leave open at any time. See Chapter 7 for more information.

Bookmark!   Click on this if you find an entry you want to add to your Bookmarks list, so you can quickly return later. (You'll learn more about bookmarks in Chapter 7.) Note that you are adding the highlighted entry (click on an entry first) to your bookmarks, not the window you are viewing. (To add the window, you'll have to back up to the previous window, select the entry that took you to the window you want to add, then use the Bookmark! command.)

36

PrevPage and NextPage   You won't always see these, but if you do happen to get into a very long gopher menu, Internaut may not display all the entries. Instead it puts the PrevPage and NextPage entries onto the menu bar, so you can move through the list.

Refresh!   Some gopher menus change frequently, so if the window has been open for a little while, the information displayed is out of date. Click on **Refresh!** to grab the latest information.

Close that Window!
These windows can be a bit much, if you let them. When you've finished with a window, close it—use **Alt+F4**, or select **Close** from the **Control** menu or **File|Exit** in the windows that have a **File** menu.

Advanced|Dblclick selected items   This is a handy option when you want to select several items from a menu at once. Rather than double-click on each one, one after the other, simply select them all and then select this menu option. You can highlight multiple entries several ways: by holding the **Ctrl** key down while you click on them, by dragging the mouse pointer across several while holding the mouse button down, by clicking on one and holding the **Shift** key while you click on another, and by holding the **Shift** key down while you press the **up** or **down arrow**.

Advanced|AutoRefresh   This option simply automates Refresh for you, so you don't need to remember to use the Refresh! command. You'll see a dialog box which lets you set a Refresh period every minute, two minutes, five minutes, fifteen minutes, or hour.

Reading the Documents

When you double-click on an entry with the document icon, you'll open a text file. You'll see the text displayed in a window. (Usually this will be a simple Internaut text window. If the file is very big, though, it will be placed in a word processor—probably Windows Write. You can use the Options and Preferences dialog box to define which word processor should be used—see Chapter 7.)

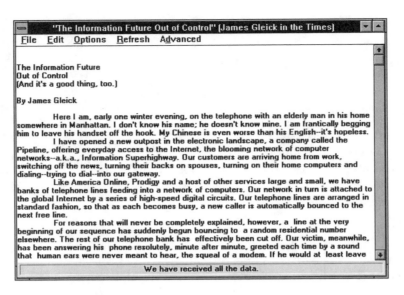

You'll find thousands of online documents.

You can read this stuff, of course—use the scroll bar, **PgUp**, **PgDn**, and **arrow** keys to move through it. But there are a few more things you can do, too:

File|Save to a File   Use this command to save the document in a text file—then you can log off and read it offline, saving you connect charges.

File|Forward this by mail   Found something interesting you'd like to send to someone else? Select this and the Composer window opens (see Chapter 8) with the document inside it. Add notes of your own and send it off.

File|Print   Paperless office be damned—you've got to have a paper copy. Use this command to print it.

File|Start Web (selected URL)   If you find a document that contains a URL—a sort of World Wide Web "address"—highlight the URL and then select this command to start the Web browser. See Chapter 14 for more details.

File|Exit   This closes the window.

Edit|Cut   You can cut pieces from the document, so you can paste them to an e-mail message or word processor.

Edit|Copy   This simply copies the text, rather than removing it.

Edit|Paste   You can paste text into the document—perhaps you want to combine pieces from two documents, and then print or save them.

Edit|Find This command lets you search for a word in a document.

Edit|Repeat search This one repeats the search.

Options|Color Use this menu to change the text or background color. Remember that when you do so, you are changing the program defaults—the next document window will look the same as what you choose here.

Options|Font Select your preferred document font—again, you are changing the program defaults.

> **Mark Your Place**
> Are all these pathways—having to remember how to get to each place—getting you down? Don't worry. In Chapter 7 you'll see how to set bookmarks to your favorite places, bypassing the pathways.

Options|Display as Text|As is This displays the document in its original format. That's not always what you want, though; often documents on the Internet are formatted in quite narrow columns.

Options|Display as Text|Word Wrap + Header Removal This reformats the text, so if the original is narrow, it now spreads across the window. Also, if the document is originally from an e-mail or newsgroup message, the header information (all the garbage that says where the document came from and the path it took) is removed.

Options|Display as Text|Word Wrap This is the same as the previous command, without removing the header.

Refresh Some documents (in a few rare cases) may be updated periodically. Click on **Refresh** to make sure you have the latest.

Advanced|Autorefresh Use this command to set an interval for refreshing the contents of the window automatically.

In some cases you won't go directly to a document when you double-click on a document-icon entry. Instead, you'll see a small dialog box that asks for information. You'll type the information and click on **OK**, and *then* you'll see the information.

Entering Information

When you click on an entry with the pencil icon, you'll see some kind of dialog box into which you will type something. These are usually used to configure your account in some way—to change the password, add personal information, and so on. For instance, if you want to change your password, go to **Closer to Home: Pipeline USA and Account Information|Change My Password**.

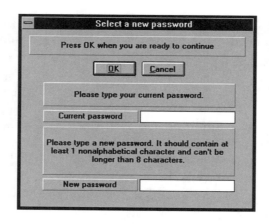

The pencil icon leads to some kind of dialog box—in this case where you change your password.

Search for Information

The Internet has so much information, it's hard to know how to find stuff sometimes. So there are loads of tools for searching for information. When you click on an entry with the binoculars icon, you'll see a dialog box into which you'll type something you want to search for.

Adjusting the Picture
Picture doesn't look too good? You may have to change your computer's video mode to accommodate 256 colors or more. See your Windows documentation.

For instance, go to **Internet Guides and Tools| Finding things: many search types|Find people: search News postings**. A dialog box opens. You can type someone's name, then click on **OK**, and a search begins—a database of people who have sent messages to newsgroups (see Chapter 11) is being searched, and eventually you'll get an e-mail message back with the results.

View a Picture

There are loads of pictures on the Internet, and Internaut has a built-in "viewer." When you double-click on one of the picture-icon entries, this viewer opens automatically. For instance, go to **Reference and General Information|Weather Anywhere|The latest Weather Service satellite maps**. Then double-click on one of the picture-icon entries. The picture will be transferred (it may take a few minutes), then up will pop the picture viewer, with one of the weather maps inside.

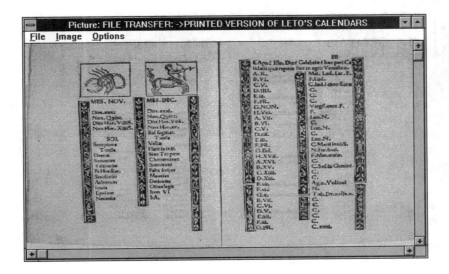

Internaut's built-in picture viewer.

What sort of pictures can you load into this viewer? You can use .GIF and .XBM—formats commonly used on the World Wide Web—.BMP, .PCX, .JPG, or .PCT. If you want to see a full list of the graphic-file types that it works with, open the picture viewer and look in the **File|Save As** cascading menu.

Once you open the picture, there are a number of things you can do to it:

File|Save   You can save the picture onto your hard drive—you've got loads of options. Save as various types of .TIF file, .BMP, .EPS, .JPG, and so on. (So which do you want to use? Depends on the program you plan to put the picture into. The .BMP, .PCX, and .TIF Uncompressed are compatible with most programs these days.)

File|Forward this by mail   You can send a picture to another Internet user with this command. You'll see the Composer window—add some notes and click on **Send**. To get technical about it, the file is attached to the e-mail message as a UUENCODED file—see Chapter 8 for more information.

View Your Own Pictures
You can also use the Viewer to open a file on your hard disk. Use the **File|Display picture file** menu command from the main Internaut window.

You Need Permission
Remember, just because you find it on the Internet doesn't mean it's yours. You can load it onto your hard disk, and view it, but you probably can't publish it without permission.

41

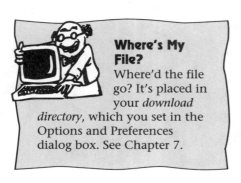

Where's My File?
Where'd the file go? It's placed in your *download directory*, which you set in the Options and Preferences dialog box. See Chapter 7.

File|Copy picture to Clipboard   This copies the picture to the Windows Clipboard, so you can then paste it into another Windows program.

File|Print   You guessed—this one prints it.

File|Exit   Yep, it closes the window.

Image|Zoom In   Use this to get a closer look at the picture.

Image|Zoom Out   Use this one to move out a little way.

Image|Rotate   Rotate the picture with this command—perhaps you plan to print or save it.

Grab a File

No online service would be complete without the capability of downloading software—programs, pictures, documents, sounds, and everything else. When you double-click on a file-icon entry, you are preparing to transfer a file to your computer.

For instance, go to **Internet Guides and Tools|The Best of PC and Mac Software| SIMTEL archives for PC files|4Dos**. You'll see a number of disk-icon entries. Each one represents a file. Double-click on one of these and you'll see the Enter File Name dialog box.

Saving a file from a gopher menu.

If the file is a picture, you could click on the **Display as picture?** check box. This tells Internaut to transfer the file to your hard disk, then display it in the picture viewer.

Open the World Wide Web

The *World Wide Web* is a giant hypertext system—documents all over the world, linked together. Click on a text link on one document, and you'll find yourself reading another, one that may be on another computer, even on another country or continent.

42

Well, there are links from gopher menus to the World Wide Web. And when you double-click on a Web-icon entry, the World Wide Web browser opens and displays the document. You'll learn more about this in Chapter 14.

Run a Telnet Session

Telnet is a system that allows you to connect to another computer, somewhere on the Internet. Why? To run programs on that computer. Perhaps you'll be playing a game—Chess, for instance, or Go. Maybe you'll be searching some kind of database—a jobs database, or some type of research database.

Whatever it is, when you double-click on a phone-icon entry in a gopher window, a Telnet window opens. For instance, if you go to **Internet Guides and Tools|Finding things: many search types|Library and other resources (Hytelnet)**, you'll be connected to a system that lets you search for Telnet information. (No, it's not pretty. But then, you're logged onto another computer now, and the information is simply being fed through Internaut and Pipeline USA. You'll learn more about Telnet in Chapter 16.)

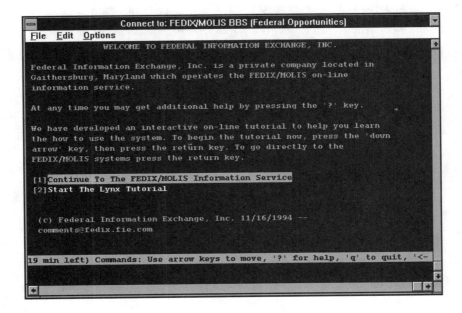

Connecting to FEDIX through a Telnet session.

Well, that's basic gophering for you. There's more advanced stuff we can go into, but not here. Move on to the next chapter for information about going directly to a gopher server and searching gopherspace.

Keeping Track of It All!

With all these windows flying around, it's difficult to keep track. There are a couple of things you can do, though. First, try the **File|Show floating window list** command. You'll see a small window, with a list of all your open Internaut windows. This list stays visible all the time, even when you are working in another application. Click on the window's **title bar** to bring all your Internaut windows to the front. And double-click on an item to bring that particular window to the front.

The other thing you can do is to select **File|Options and Preferences**, click on the **General** tab, and change the **Most lists to show at once** number. This is the number of gopher menus that will be open at any one time. For instance, if it's set to **5** and you already have five open, the first one closes automatically when you open another.

The Least You Need to Know

> ➤ A gopher is a menu system that helps you find your way around on the Internet.

> ➤ The Internaut's "Pathways into the Internet" system is a gopher.

> ➤ Double-clicking on an entry in a gopher menu selects another form of information.

> ➤ Each type of information is identified with a small picture in the left column.

> ➤ An entry may take you to another gopher menu, a text document, a picture, a file-transfer dialog box, a Telnet-session window, a World Wide Web browser, or a dialog box into which you enter information.

## Chapter 6

Searching Gopherspace

In This Chapter

➤ Going directly to a gopher server

➤ Other links to gopher servers

➤ Using Veronica to search gopherspace

➤ Using Jughead to search Pipeline USA's gopher server

Gopher Shortcut

So far you've seen how to travel through Pipeline USA's gopher—but what if there's a gopher server somewhere you want to reach? Let's say you have one of those giant Internet directories everyone and their dog is publishing these days. You look up NATO, and find that there's information about that subject at the wiretap.spies.com gopher server (this gopher server has lots of interesting stuff, actually). So—how to get there?

Anatomy of a Gopher System

Any gopher system comprises two parts; a gopher server, which contains a list of menus and connections to various files, and gopher clients, the programs (such as Internaut) that can view these menus. There are gopher servers all over the world. When you start Internaut you are viewing Pipeline USA's gopher server. When you use the **Internet|Gopher anywhere** command you are connecting to another server.

Select **Internet|Gopher anywhere** and you'll see a dialog box. Type **wiretap.spies.com** into this dialog box and click on **OK**. In a few moments a gopher window will pop up, showing the wiretap.spies.com main gopher menu.

Did you notice the **Add this command to my Bookmarks menu** check box? Let's say you think you'll want to travel to wiretap.spies.com again. Click on this check box, then when you click on the OK button, a bookmark is added. Next time you want to go there you won't need to use the Internet|Gopher anywhere command; you'll be able to select from the Bookmarks dialog box—which you'll learn about in Chapter 7.

Mind you, if you don't add a bookmark and want to go back to a gopher site you looked at previously, you'll find the gopher server address in the drop-down list box inside the **Gopher to** dialog box. Just click on the **down arrow** to the right of the text box, then select a destination site from the list.

There are a couple of other ways to get to a gopher server. Double-click on **Go to Internet Guides and Tools** in the main Internaut window. You'll see a gopher menu that contains several ways to find gopher servers, such as these:

All the World's Gophers   A list of the world's gopher servers—organized by country.

Gopher Jewels   A listing of subjects—pick a subject to find a gopher with related information.

Internet Gophers by subject   Pick a subject, and you'll find a useful gopher.

The Famous Minnesota Gopher   Gophers, remember, originated at the University of Minnesota. This takes you to the home of the gopher.

Spies on the Net: Wiretap   I told you there's loads of neat stuff at Wiretap—so much that Pipeline USA added a link directly there.

Gopher Anywhere   This is the same as the **Internet|Gopher anywhere** command. You'll see a dialog box into which you'll type a gopher server address.

Yes, but Where Is x? Searching Gopherspace

There's another way around gopherspace, too. You can search for a subject you are interested in. There are two tools you can use—Veronica and Jughead. That's right, two well-known cartoon characters—friends of Archie's, in fact. (You'll meet Archie in Chapter 15.)

These are actually acronyms, though clearly the names came first and the acronyms were forced to fit. Veronica means *Very Easy Rodent-Oriented Net-wide Index to Computerized Archives*. Jughead means *Jonzy's Universal Gopher Hierarchy Excavation And Display* tool.

 There's an important difference between the two. With Veronica you can search all of gopherspace—gopher servers all over the world. With Jughead you can only search one gopher server—Pipeline USA's server, the Wiretap server, or whatever—at a time. So let's start with Veronica.

Very Easy Ronica

First, a little background about Veronica. When you search gopherspace using Veronica, you are not searching gopherspace directly—that is, Veronica doesn't go out across the Internet looking at all the gopher servers for what you want. Rather, it goes to what's known as a *Veronica server* (and there are only a few of those). A Veronica server is like a giant index to gopherspace. Periodically—every few weeks or so—the Veronica server does a search of gopherspace and stores the results. When you use Veronica, you are searching what the server found last time.

Now, this means a couple of things. First, it's not totally up to date (though it's probably close enough for most purposes). Second, you may not get through. That is, you try to run a Veronica search, and get a message saying that the server is too busy. If that happens, you can always try another server.

There's another thing to consider—the type of search. There are two types. An *all titles* search searches for *all* information stored in gopher servers—menu names (a *menu* is, in effect, the same as a directory), telnet connections, FTP connections, filenames, and so on. A *directory titles* search looks only at the menus, not at the files, so it will find fewer entries.

To do a Veronica search, select **Internet|Search all Gopherspace (Veronica)**. (Or follow the pathways to **Internet Guides and Tools|Finding things: many search types|Search titles in Gopherspace using Veronica**. You'll see a window that contains a couple of documents, with detailed information about searching using Veronica—double-click on **Search the Internet with Veronica now**.)

47

A dialog box pops up; type a word, then click on **OK**. For instance, type **books** to search for entries related to books. Internaut then carries out its Veronica search. When (or if) it finds something, it will display the results in a gopher window.

Let's Get Complicated—Advanced Veronica

We can get really fancy with these searches. There are a number of ways to limit the search and get exactly what you want.

A Matter of Case
It makes no difference whether you type your search statements in uppercase or lowercase— **BOOK AND ELECTRONIC** is the same as **book and electronic.**

First, you can use *Boolean operators*: AND, NOT, OR, (, and). For instance, if you search for **book and electronic**, Veronica will search for items that contain both the words **book** and **electronic**. (Actually, if you leave out the word **and**, Veronica will assume that's what you mean: **book electronic** is the same as **book and electronic**.)

If you search for **book not electronic**, Veronica will look for all items containing the word **book**, but *not* the word **electronic**. So if it found something like *The electronic book archive*, it would ignore it.

If you search for **book or electronic**, Veronica will find all items that contain any item that has the word **book** in them, and all items that have the word **electronic** in them.

As for the parentheses, these can be used to "nest" statements. For instance, **(book and archive) and (book and electronic)** would tell Veronica to find all items that contain both the words **book** and **archive**, and all the items that contain the words **book** and **electronic**.

Is that enough for you? Well, there's more. You can actually tell Veronica which types of items you want to search. You do this by adding **-t** followed by a code. For instance, **book electronic -t1** will search for the words **book** and **electronic**, but only find gopher "directories" (menus). If Veronica finds (for example) an entry that points to a document, it ignores the entry. You can use these codes:

0	text file
1	directory (gopher menu)
2	CSO phonebook server (a system that lets you search for Internet users)
4	BinHexed Macintosh file
5	DOS binary archive file of some kind, such as .ZIP or .ARC files

6	Unix UUENCODED file (see Chapter 12 for information about UUENCODING)
7	Index-Search server, a system that lets you search for information
8	Telnet session
9	binary file of some sort
s	mulaw sound file of some sort (a Unix sound file)
g	.GIF graphic file
M	An e-mail file in MIME format
T	A tn3270 session, similar to a Telnet session

It's All MIME

MIME (Multipurpose Internet Mail Extensions) lets you send computer files through the e-mail system. Currently most e-mail programs in use on the Internet don't work with it, though. The Internaut e-mail system uses UUENCODE instead of MIME. See Chapter 8.

For instance, let's say you are only interested in finding .GIF files and text documents. You could enter **madonna -tg0**. This says, in effect, "Look for all gopher entries that have the word **madonna,** and that point to .GIF files and text files."

Here's another way to restrict a search. Use the **-m** switch. For instance, adding **-m400** to a search tells Veronica to find the first 400 entries that match, then stop. Typing **book -t1 -m100** says, "Find gopher menu entries with the word **book,** but stop when you get to 100."

There's more you can do with Veronica searches—take a look at the documents in **The Internet: Guides and Tools|Finding things: many search types|Search all gopherspace (Veronica)** menu.

Finding Another Server

What if the server Internaut uses is busy? That's quite a common occurrence these days. You can, if you wish, go to another gopher and search from there. For instance, select **Internet Guides and Tools|All the World's Gophers by Place and Subject**. When you get to a gopher server, look around for an entry that says something like, "Search all gopherspace with Veronica." You may have to dig around a little, going through a level or two before you find it. For instance, follow this pathway: **Internet Guides and Tools|All the World's Gophers, by Place and Subject|United Kingdom|ALMAC BBS|Veronica|Select a server "by hand."** You'll see a window with all sorts of Veronica choices. First, notice that some of the entries say *via* something, as in *via NYSERNET*, *via PSINet*, *via University of Pisa*. These are the different servers. If PSINet is busy, try the University of Pisa, for instance.

Also, notice that some entries say *Find GOPHER DIRECTORIES*, while others say *Search Gopherspace*. The first will search only for gopher directories (menus), the equivalent of doing a -t1 search. The second searches all of gopherspace, searching for any kind of gopher entry—menus, documents, files, and so on.

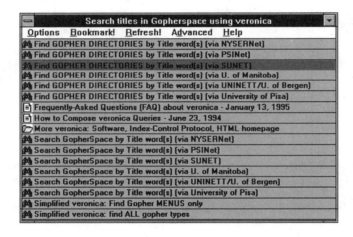

A Veronica gopher menu.

Jonzy's Universal Gopher HEAD

Now it's Jughead's turn. *Jughead* is very similar to Veronica, but instead of searching a Veronica server, which indexes all of gopherspace for you, Jughead simply searches a single gopher server. Now, gopher servers are actually linked to one another. Double-clicking on a link in one server may take you across to another server somewhere else in the world. Jughead, however, stops at that point. It searches all the entries in the server you are working on, but it won't jump across gopherspace when it finds a link that takes it out of that server.

To get to Pipeline USA's Jughead, follow this pathway: **Internet Guides and Tools|Finding things: many search types|Search our gopher and onward (Jughead)**. You'll see a simple dialog box into which you can enter a search string. You can use Boolean operators—as we saw with Veronica—but you can't use the -t switch to limit the search to certain gopher-entry types. If you want to find more detailed information about searching with Jughead, search for **?help**. You'll get the Jughead documentation.

Finding Stuff on Pipeline USA's Server
Jughead is very handy for finding something you've noticed while looking around in Pipeline USA's gopher server, but can't remember where. Place the highlight on the **Search our gopher and onward** entry; click on the **Bookmark!** menu option to add it to your bookmark system. See Chapter 7 for more information.

The Least You Need to Know

➤ A gopher server is a system that maintains a menu. Internaut is a gopher *client*, which can use those menus.

➤ There are gopher servers all over the world.

➤ Use **Internet|Gopher anywhere** to go directly to a gopher server.

➤ Select **Internet Guides and Tools** from the main Internaut window, and then any of the **Gopher** entries, to find more gopher servers.

➤ Use **Internet|Search all Gopherspace (Veronica)** to do a Veronica search through gopherspace.

➤ Go to **Internet Guides and Tools|Finding things: many search types|Search our gopher and onward (Jughead)** to use Jughead to search Pipeline USA's gopher server.

## Chapter 7

The Way You Want It— Bookmarks and More

In This Chapter

➤ Setting bookmarks

➤ Using Internaut's existing bookmarks

➤ Creating bookmark folders

➤ Setting Internaut general options

➤ Setting e-mail and newsgroup options

➤ Diagnostics and maintenance commands

As with any program, when you first get Internaut you'll probably find that it's not set up quite the way you want it. You'll find, for instance, that there are really interesting Internet sites that you want to visit often, but that are not easy to get to through Internaut—you have to follow through a convoluted pathway, or dig through the World Wide Web or whatever to get there, when you want to go directly. Well, there's a quick fix for this problem—bookmarks—and there are fixes for other issues, too. In this chapter we're going to look at how to configure Internaut to run the way you want it to run.

A Direct Link—Bookmarks

The Internaut *bookmark* system provides a direct link to wherever you want to go. It's a system-wide feature; you can place bookmarks on World Wide Web sites, entries in gopher menus, Telnet sites, and so on. Let's start by looking at how to set a bookmark on something—it's really very simple. (We'll be looking at some of these Internet tools—such as Web documents and FTP sites—later in this book.)

In a gopher menu Highlight the entry you want to set the bookmark on, and click on **Bookmark!** on the menu bar. (Note that you are adding the highlighted entry—not the current window—as a bookmark.)

In a Web document Click on **Bookmark!** on the menu bar to add that document to the bookmarks.

A directory in an FTP site Highlight the directory and click on **Bookmark** in the menu bar.

A Telnet session When you use the **Internet|Connect to another system (Telnet)** command, enter the Telnet address and then click on the **Add this command to my bookmarks** check box.

Various dialog boxes A number of commands use dialog boxes into which you type some kind of information. These dialog boxes often have an **Add this command to my bookmarks** check box. Click on it to add the dialog box as a bookmark.

When you use one of these commands, a bookmark is automatically placed in the Bookmarks window, where you can move or modify it.

Using Bookmarks

To see the Bookmarks window, click on **Bookmarks!** on the menu bar in the Internaut main window. When the Bookmarks dialog box opens, you'll see a single "folder"—the Bookmarks folder. The Bookmarks folder is like the "root directory" on your hard disk. All the bookmarks and other folders are placed inside this folder.

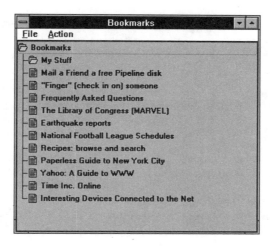

The Bookmarks window is your shortcut through the Internet.

You'll find that you already have a number of bookmarks set for you. There are bookmarks to these items:

1. **Mail a Friend a free Pipeline disk**   This opens a dialog box into which you can type a name and address. Pipeline USA will send the latest release of Internaut to that person.

2. **"Finger" (check in on) someone**   Displays the Finger dialog box, which lets you get information about other Internet users. (You'll learn more about this in Chapter 19.)

3. **Frequently Asked Questions**   A gopher menu taking you to documents that answer your FAQs (that's Internet jargon for Frequently Asked Questions) about a variety of subjects related to Internaut, Pipeline USA, and the Internet.

4. **Earthquake reports**   Displays a text document from the Pacific Northwest Seismograph Network.

5. **National Football League Schedules**   Takes you to a Telnet session in which you can find any scheduled game.

6. **Recipes: browse and search**   Displays a gopher menu with links to recipes—from Appetizers and Beverages, all the way to Tex-Mex, Truffles, and Veggies.

7. **Paperless Guide to New York City**   A World Wide Web directory of New York.

8. **Yahoo: A Guide to the WWW**   A great directory of World Wide Web sites. A good start when looking for information on the Web.

Closing the Window When you use the Bookmark window to go to a bookmark, the window doesn't close automatically. If you want to close it, use **Ctrl+X** or **File|Exit**.

9. **Time Inc. Online** Pathfinder, the Time Inc. Web page, with information from *TIME*, *Entertainment Weekly*, and *Money*.

10. **Interesting Devices Connected to the Net** This takes you to a World Wide Web document with links to strange devices connected to the Internet: telephones, pizza "servers," robots, hot tubs, refrigerators. Really, no kidding. If you want to know the temperature of Paul Haas' hot tub, this is where to look. (It was about 100 degrees Fahrenheit when I looked. I don't know what good that does me.)

To use any bookmark, simply double-click on it.

Customizing Bookmarks

As you can see, using bookmarks is easy. But you can customize the bookmark system to make it suit your needs:

Creating a new folder You may want to create several different folders—for business, music, art, travel, and so on. You can create a *main level folder* inside the Bookmarks folder or a *subfolder* inside another folder. Select **Action|Add folder**, type a folder name, and click on **OK**.

Moving bookmarks into a folder When you create bookmarks using the Bookmarks! menu option (or the **Add this command to my bookmarks** check box), they are placed inside the Bookmarks folder. You can move them into a folder you have created by clicking on the bookmark, holding the mouse button down, and dragging the bookmark onto the folder.

Changing Bookmark names When you create a bookmark, Internaut creates the bookmark name for you, and you may not like what it picks. To change the name—to make it more descriptive—click on the bookmark, select **Action|Edit Entry**, type a new name into the **Description** text box that appears, then click on **OK**.

Deleting Items To delete a folder or bookmark, click on it and select **Action|Delete Entry**.

You can also create a bookmark "by hand," though this is not necessarily easy. If you click on the folder you want to place the bookmark into, then select **Action|Add Bookmark**, you'll see the Add a new item dialog box.

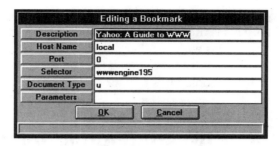

Creating or editing a bookmark by hand—not always easy.

This dialog box requires you to enter information using the correct format for gopher addresses, which is easy if you know this format, but not so easy if you don't:

Description   A description of the Internet site.

Host Name   The gopher server hostname (for instance, **ashpool.micro.umn.edu**, or, in some cases, **local**).

Port   Usually **70** if the bookmark is being set on a gopher site, but in some cases it will be different—use **0** for a Web site, for instance. If you know you need a different port number, you can enter it here.

Selector   Local commands. For instance, if you are placing a bookmark on a Web site, use **wwwengine195**. If it's a gopher site, it's the path through the menus (such as **1/fun/Recipes**).

Document Type   The gopher document type—we looked at these in Chapter 6 (0 = text, 1 = directory, and so on).

Parameters   If the gopher document type you're using requires a parameter, enter it here. For instance, if it's a Web site you're going to, you would enter the *URL* (Universal Resource Locator), the Web "address."

This is not simple stuff. If you want to explore it a little further, I suggest you use the **Action|Edit Entry** command to see how the existing bookmarks are set up. Otherwise, just set bookmarks using the Bookmark! menu option and the check box.

Sharing Bookmarks

Internaut has a nice system for sharing bookmarks. You can export your bookmarks to a file and send that file to another person (see Chapter 8 for information about sending files). The recipient can then import the bookmark file, or merge it with his existing bookmark file.

Use the **File|Export Bookmarks** command to save your bookmarks in a .BT file (a Bookmark Table file). This is the file that you'll send to your friend or colleague. To replace your current bookmarks with another bookmark file, use the **File|Import Bookmarks** command (you may want to save your existing bookmarks first, so you can return to them), or add a new list of bookmarks to your existing ones, using the **File|Merge Bookmarks** command.

Any Way You Want It—Configuring Internaut

Let's look at the ways you can configure Internaut to work the way you want. Open the **Options and Preferences** dialog box. You can do this by selecting **File|Options and preferences** from the main Internaut window, or **Options|Other Options** from the mailbox or newsgroup windows (see Chapter 9).

Notice the tabs at the top of the dialog box. Clicking on a tab opens an area. Let's look at each in turn.

General Options

Click on the **General** tab, to see the General options:

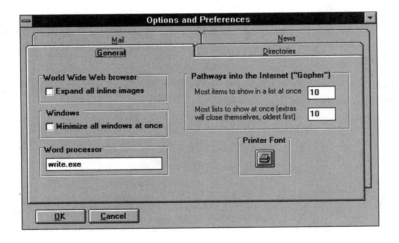

The Internaut General options.

Expand all inline images   Many World Wide Web documents (see Chapter 14) contain pictures. Unfortunately, these can take a long time to transfer across your phone lines. If you clear this check box, Internaut won't transfer the pictures, speeding things up. If you decide you want to see the pictures, you can change the selection in the browser itself.

Minimize all windows at once   If this is selected, when you minimize one of the Internaut windows, all other Internaut windows will be minimized too. I don't like this, personally, but you may.

Most items to show in a list at once   This sets the size of a gopher list (see Chapter 5). A small number will make lists appear more quickly. If a gopher list has more items than the number you set, you'll see the NextPage menu option—and clicking on this will load the next batch of entries.

Most lists to show at once   This tells Internaut how many gopher windows should be open at any time. Once you exceed this number, Internaut closes the window that was opened the earliest.

Word processor   If you open a large document—perhaps you find a large document in a gopher menu, for example, or a large document in a newsgroup or your e-mail inbox—Internaut places it in a word processor. By default, that is Windows Write, though you can use any Windows word processor you wish. Remember to include the full path (the directories and filename) if the program is not in your Windows directory, or is in another directory in your DOS PATH statement (which you'll find in your AUTOEXEC.BAT file, which you'll find in the root directory of drive C:).

Printer Font   When you click on this button, a typical Windows Font selection dialog box appears. Select a font family, style, and size—this is the font that will be used when you print from document, e-mail, and newsgroup windows.

Mail Options

Click on the **Mail** tab to see the options that affect the way in which the e-mail system functions:

Tell Internaut how to handle your e-mail in the Mail area.

Beep   If this is checked, Internaut beeps your computer each time an e-mail message arrives.

Show message   If this is checked, a message box pops up to let you know when an e-mail message arrives.

Confirm deletions   If this is checked, each time you try to delete an e-mail message you'll see a message box asking you to confirm that you really want to do so.

Save outgoing mail   If you want to save a copy of each e-mail message you send, select this. Internaut will put a copy in the **Sent mail** box (see Chapter 8). You'll be able to override this setting when you send a message, so just select this if you want *most* of the outgoing messages saved.

Quote letter in reply   It's common on the Internet to "quote" messages when you reply to them. That is, the reply contains some of the text from the original, so you can respond directly to comments, and so the recipient can see what he said. If you select this option, your reply to a message will contain the original text. If you *don't* select this option, you can still copy text automatically from the original to the reply by highlighting the text before clicking on the **Reply** button.

Display: Fonts and Colors   These buttons let you set the font used in the mail windows, *and* in the *newsgroup* windows. The **T.O.C.** buttons refer to the Table of Contents—the lists of e-mail and newsgroup messages. The **Body** buttons refer to the actual message text. So click on the **Body Fonts** button to change the type of font used to display the message, but the **T.O.C. Fonts** button to change the font

60

used to display the list of messages. The **Foreground Color** buttons set the text color; the **Background Color** buttons set...yes, the background color.

Use signature   A *signature*, in the world of the Internet, is a short message—three or four lines, usually—placed at the end of an e-mail message. For instance, your signature may contain your full name, telephone number, company name, e-mail address, and so on. Some people put poetry there, or some strange comment ("Barney eats children" is my favorite). If you want your signature to be sent out at the end of each e-mail or newsgroup message you send, click on this check box. (You'll be able to remove the signature from a particular message if you wish.)

Signature text box   This is where you type the message you want to appear in your signature. It can be as large as you want, though many people are offended by very long signatures—stick to three or four lines.

News Options

To modify the way you work with newsgroups (see Chapter 11), click on the **News** tab:

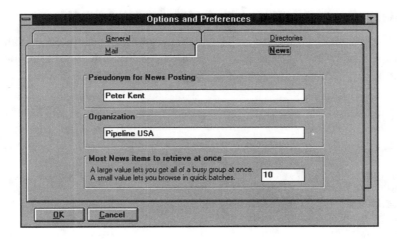

Just a few News options.

Organization   Type the name of your company or organization, if you wish. This appears at the top of a message sent to a newsgroup.

Most News items to retrieve at once   This *incrementer* box option tells Internaut how many messages to retrieve from a newsgroup at once. Some busy newsgroups have hundreds of messages. This lets you limit how many of them you grab, so you don't wait too long. (You'll learn how to go back and get more messages in Chapter 11.)

Download Directory

Click on the **Directories** tab to set your *download directory*. This is where the files you download will be placed. By default Internaut sets up a download directory for each account created. These are the PIPEUSA\USER*USERNAME*\DOWNLOAD directories. However, you may want to set up a different directory; something more convenient, for example, might be a DOWNLOAD directory in your root directory, or perhaps PIPEUSA\DOWNLOAD. Simply type the new path into this text box.

A Little Help—Diagnostics and Maintenance

There are a few special commands that are available to help you manage Internaut. Most you'll never use...but you never know. One really useful command is **File|Show floating window list**. It displays a small "always on top" window, which lists your open Pipeline windows.

These others are for when things go wrong:

Changing Your Newsgroups   To modify the font, text color, and background color used in the newsgroups, change the e-mail settings; these affect both the e-mail and newsgroup systems.

File|Show packet transmission form   This displays a dialog box that shows what's happening when Internaut and Pipeline USA transmit information to and fro. You'll probably use this one only if technical support asks you to do so.

File|Send queued mail and news   On rare occasions, you may find that for some reason the e-mail and newsgroup messages you tried to send didn't actually go anywhere. (You've looked in the Outbox and there are still messages in there—they should be sent right away, as long as you are online.) This command is a way to "force" the messages out.

The Assistance File Analyzer

There's also something called Assistance. This is a program you'll find in your Pipeline USA program group that analyzes all the files you need to run Internaut—and makes sure you have the correct ones. Why wouldn't you have the correct ones? Well, thanks to the wonderful way Windows shares and manages certain files, you may find that a program you install *after* you've installed Internaut loads a shared file that Internaut uses (a *dynamic link library* file, for instance). That may not be a problem...except that some programs may have *earlier versions* of these shared files, versions that Internaut won't work with.

The program looks at all the files when you double-click on the **Rescue** icon. Then it tells you which files, if any, are not the correct ones. You can then call technical support and find out how to fix the problem.

The Least You Need to Know

➤ Use the **Bookmarks!** menu option and the **Add this command to my bookmarks** check box (you'll find them throughout Internaut) to add bookmarks.

➤ Use the **Bookmarks!** menu option in the main Internaut window to view your bookmarks.

➤ Double-click on a bookmark to go to the referenced site.

➤ You can create folders to categorize your bookmarks. Use **Action|Add Folder** in the Bookmark window.

➤ Set a variety of system options in the **Options and Preferences** dialog box. Press **F2** in the main Internaut window, or the mail and newsgroup windows.

➤ Use **File|Show floating window list** to help manage your Internaut windows.

Part 2
Talking to the World—
E-mail and Newsgroups

Sometimes on the Internet the world will come to you—you don't even have to go out exploring. When the Internet was first formed, this wasn't supposed to happen. The Internet was planned as a system for exchanging computer files and letting someone in one part of North America log onto a computer in another part.

But, according to Internet "historians," the people actually creating the Internet had slightly different ideas from the people paying the bills—they realized that the Internet provided a wonderful new form of communication. So they snuck in a few programs that would let someone in North America send messages to someone in another continent. These are great systems. They're fun, interesting, and addictive.

Sending Messages (All Over the World)

E-mail is... never having to pay postage. The great thing about e-mail is—well, there are lots of great things about e-mail:

➤ It's cheap. I'll show you how to write your e-mail before you connect to The Pipeline, then send it automatically while you do something else online.

➤ Wherever you send e-mail—Johannesburg, Japan, Juneau—it's always the same price.

➤ It's easy. No calling and finding the person isn't in, or the receptionist doesn't speak your language—just send it and let the recipient respond at leisure.

➤ You can take e-mail and place it in a computer file. Great for submitting magazine articles, chapters of your latest book, or memos to colleagues.

➤ You can e-mail computer files as well.

There are plenty more good reasons to use e-mail, as you'll soon find out. In fact, when people find that e-mail *isn't* of use to them, it's usually because they don't know anyone else who uses e-mail. But the world is going e-mail, and pretty soon we'll all know people using it. Already families keep in touch with e-mail—sure, it may be less personal than phone calls, but it's much cheaper, so it tends to be more frequent. Rather than getting a call every few weeks, you get a message every day or two. Companies keep in touch with e-mail, friends keep up long-distance relationships with e-mail, writers keep in contact with editors with e-mail. It's a great tool. And, not surprisingly, Internaut provides a handy way to handle your electronic mail.

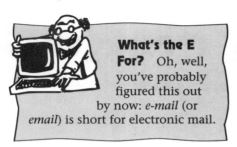

What's the E For? Oh, well, you've probably figured this out by now: *e-mail* (or *email*) is short for electronic mail.

Who can you send e-mail to (or receive e-mail from)? Anyone with a connection to the Internet. That means people with connections through Internet service providers, or through their companies, schools, or government departments, but also people with accounts on other systems—CompuServe, GEnie, PRODIGY, America Online, and thousands of small bulletin boards. As long as you have the person's e-mail address, you can send them e-mail. (Yes, finding an address can be a problem, one that we'll "address" in Chapter 17.) So, without further ado, let's take a look at Internaut's mail facility.

What's Arrived Today? The Inbox

Each time you start Internaut, you'll see the Inbox. This opens automatically, whether e-mail has arrived or not (if you don't want the Inbox to open each time, select **Options**, **Autostart at login** to remove the check mark from this menu option). The Inbox has two parts. At the top is a list of messages (Internaut calls this the *Table of Contents*). Below this list you'll see a message—click on the message you want to read.

Right now, however, I don't want to get into the Inbox; I want to show you how to send e-mail (that way you can send a message to yourself, so you'll have something to see in the Inbox). We'll come back to the Inbox in Chapter 9.

Your Link to the World—Sending E-mail

There are several ways to start an e-mail message:

➤ Click on the **New** button at the bottom of the Inbox.

➤ Click on the **Write** button in the main Internaut window.

➤ Select **Services|Mail: write a letter** in the main Internaut window.

➤ Press **Ctrl+E** in the main Internaut window.

There are a few other ways to get to the Composer window; actually, they're spread around Internaut—when you reply to an e-mail message, forward the message, post a newsgroup message, or reply to a newsgroup message, you'll see this window. (See Chapter 11 for information about newsgroups.) Whichever method you use, you'll see the Composer window.

> **Customize Your Mail** You can change the background color, text color, and font used in both the Table of Contents and message. Press **F2** to see the Options and Preferences dialog box. See Chapter 7 for more information.

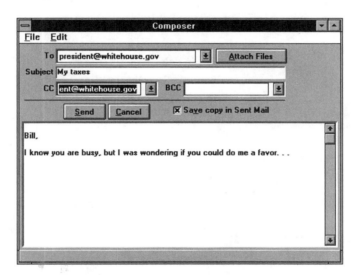

The Composer window—your first step with e-mail.

Let's look at the different parts of the window:

To   Type the e-mail address of the person you want to send the message to. If you have created an address book, you can press **F4** or click on the **arrow** button to open a list of addresses. You can also press the **down arrow** to move through the list (see Chapter 9 for more information about the address book). We'll look at e-mail addresses in detail in a moment.

> **Do It Offline**
> Don't write your e-mail while you're online— you'll be paying connect time and you can just as easily write messages offline. If you are online now, log off (click on **Goodbye!**), then open the **Composer** window.

69

Attach Files button If you want to send a computer file along with the e-mail message, click on the **Attach** button. But see Chapter 9 first for more information.

Subject Type a subject into this box. Remember the "Table of Contents" in the Inbox? One of the columns was the Subject line, so you can quickly see what your messages are about. Of course, you don't have to use a subject if you don't want one. If you don't, the message isn't sent the first time you click on the **Send** button—a **No Subject** indicator appears in the Subject line instead, to warn you. (If you click **Send** again, the message is sent.)

CC This means *carbon copy*. You can type another e-mail address into this box to send a copy to another person. Again, if you have created an address book, you can select from the list. If you want to send several copies, though, you'll have to type each address, leaving a comma between each one and the next. For instance: **barney@bedrock.com,fred@bedrock.com**.

Using an Alias
You can create a mailing list, allowing you to send a message to many different people by entering one e-mail *alias*. I'll explain that when we look at the address book.

BCC This means *blind carbon copy*. This works just like the CC field, except that the original recipient of the message, and the people in the CC field, will not know that the person in the BCC field got a copy (the e-mail message "header" will contain a Cc: line showing who got a CC copy but will not include the BCC address).

Save copy in Sent Mail If this check box is selected, a copy of the outgoing message is placed in the Sent Mail box. (To see the Mail options, press **F2** when you're in the Inbox or main Internaut window—you can set the default for this check box by checking or clearing the **Save outgoing mail** check box.)

large text area The large empty area is where you type your message. If you created an e-mail *signature*, you'll see the signature in this area—type your message above the signature. (We looked at how to create a signature in Chapter 7.)

Send button When you have finished typing your message, click on this button. If you are online, the message is sent right away. If you are not, the message is placed in the Outbox (see Chapter 9), and will be sent as soon as you log on.

Cancel button Use this button to cancel the letter.

Why not send a message to yourself? Simply type your e-mail address into the To box, type a Subject, type some kind of nonsense into the text area, then click on **Send**. Ah, but what *is* your e-mail address?

About E-mail Addresses

Let's have a quick look at e-mail addresses. Here's my Pipeline address: **peterk@usa. pipeline.com**. The first part (**peterk**) is my username, the name given to my pipeline account. The second part (**pipeline.com**) is the *domain name*, the name given to the service provider, Pipeline. By putting them together, with the @ sign between, we get an Internet address.

> **Net Phonetics**
> In Internet-speak, my e-mail address (peterk@usa.pipeline.com) would be pronounced "peter k at usa dot pipeline dot com."

Actually you don't need to use the domain name when you send e-mail to someone else on the same system. For instance, if you want to send a message to the Pipeline staff, you don't have to enter **staff@usa.pipeline.com**; all you need to do is use **staff** as the address. So you can send e-mail to yourself just by entering your username on the To line.

If you are sending e-mail somewhere else, to another service provider in New York, a company in Denver, or a college in Hong Kong, you'll need the complete e-mail address—username and domain name.

How About CompuServe? AOL?

Do you have friends with accounts on CompuServe, AOL, PRODIGY, or some other online service? Can you exchange e-mail? Absolutely! In most cases you'll simply add something to the end of your colleague's system ID or username. Follow the instructions in this table:

Service	Procedure
America Online	Add **@aol.com** to the address
Applelink	Add **@applelink.appl.com**
AT&TMail	Add **@attmail.com**
BITNET	Add **@host.bitnet**
CompuServe	Replace the comma in the CompuServe ID with a period, then add **@compuserve.com**. For instance, 12345,1234 would be 12345.1234@compuserve.com.
Delphi	Add **@delphi.com**
GEnie	Add **@genie.geis.com** to the address

continues

Service	Procedure
MCI Mail	*firstname_lastname*@**mcimail.com** (use the name without a hyphen or a number)
Prodigy	Add **@prodigy.com** to the address
UUCP	Add **@host.uucp**

How do these systems send e-mail to you? Well, it varies, so your colleagues will have to inquire with their service's support people. But in general it's pretty simple. With America Online, for instance, they simply type your Internet address as normal (*username*@**pipeline.com**). With CompuServe, what the user types depends on which program is in use. A NavCIS user, for instance, simply types the Internet address; other CompuServe programs require the user to precede the Internet address with **INTERNET:**.

More Than Just Text—E-mailing Computer Files

Eventually you'll have a reason to send someone a computer file. You don't just want to send a message, you want to send a word processing file, a picture, a spreadsheet, some music, or whatever else you can shove into the packages of bits and bytes we call computer files. There are three ways this magic can be done on the Internet, two of which Internaut can use (you need to understand all three, though):

➤ If the file contains nothing more than text, you can place it inside the text message.

➤ You can UUENCODE a file and then place it inside the message—you could use this for word processing files, music, or whatever.

➤ You can send it using a MIME-enabled e-mail program—again, this can be used for word processing files, music, spreadsheets, and so on.

Internaut can use the first two methods, not the third. You need to be aware that the third method exists, because if you ever want to send a file to someone on the Internet outside the Pipeline system, or want to receive a file from them, you'd better know which method they plan to use. So let's look at each method in turn.

Inserting Text

If the file you want to send is simple ASCII text, you can insert it inside the message. What is ASCII text? It's letters, numbers, and a few special characters (?, &, %, and so on). Word processors do not usually create ASCII text (unless you specifically tell the program to save the file as ASCII, or as Text). If a file has special formatting—bold, italic, paragraph formats, and so on—it's not ASCII. But if the file comes from a text editor such as Windows Notepad, then it's ASCII, and can be placed inside an e-mail message.

Here's how to put the text directly into your message. Create the message in the normal way, then place the cursor inside the text area, exactly where you want to place the text you are going to insert.

Click on the **Attach Files** button. In the Insert or Attach dialog box, click on the **Copy the text of a file into the current letter** option button, then click on the **OK** button. You'll see a typical Windows Open dialog box. Find the file you want to send—probably a .TXT file—and double-click on it (or click once, and then click on the **OK** button). You'll see the text inserted into the message.

> **ASCII** ASCII means the *American Standard Code for Information Interchange.* It's a standard way for computers to use bits and bytes to represent characters.

Magical Conversion—UUENCODE

The second method of attaching files is to UUENCODE them. This means that Internaut will convert the file to ASCII text. Even if the file is music or a picture, once it's been "encoded" it's just a jumble of letters, numbers, and special characters. This jumble is then sent with the message.

What happens at the other end? Well, the message must be "decoded." If you are sending the message to another Internaut user, or are receiving one from another Internaut user, it's no problem, because Internaut will automatically UUDECODE for you. Also, some other e-mail programs can recognize UUENCODED files and decode them.

Most of the e-mail programs in common use *can't* automatically decode such files, though. That means the recipient will have to decode the file. No problem, everyone knows how to do that, right? Well, not exactly. You may have to tell the recipient how to decode the file. There are a couple of things you can tell them. First, you can say that they can use the UNIX UUDECODE program. This is available on virtually all UNIX machines (most

> **Insertion Trouble** The file wasn't inserted into the document—instead you saw the message OK, C:*path**filename* is attached at the bottom of your Composer window. What happened? Internaut decided that the file *isn't* ASCII text, so it used the other attachment method, UUENCODE. Or perhaps Internaut *did* insert the file—but you didn't see text, you saw garbage. The file wasn't ASCII, but Internaut couldn't figure it out.

Internet host machines are UNIX computers). All the user has to do is save the message you send him in a file—he'll have to read his e-mail's documentation to figure out how to do that. Then he goes to the UNIX shell and types **uudecode** *filename*. For instance, if he called the file he created **sound**, he would type **uudecode sound**. That will convert the file back to its original format. (For non-UNIX machines, tell the recipient to ask his system administrator how to decode.)

The other way the recipient can convert is to use a UUENCODE/UUDECODE program for the personal computer he is working on. If he's got a PC, he could use a DOS or Windows UUDECODE program. In fact, *Wincode* is a very good little Windows program. It's available all over the Internet. (Tell your friend to use Archie to find it and FTP to grab it—we'll look at these in Chapter 15.)

Now look at how to attach an encoded file. Again, start creating your message, then click on the **Attach Files** button. This time select **Send a file as an attachment**, and click on **OK**. When you select the file you want to send, Internaut converts it to ASCII, and places a message in the status bar of the Composer window saying **OK, C:***path******filename* **is attached**. You won't see the text itself. In fact, Internaut will actually send *two* messages, the one you attached the file to, and a separate message that contains the UUENCODED file itself. This is handy because it lets you type a message, attach the file, then send both at the same time.

What happens at the other end? Other Internaut users will see two messages. One will contain the text you typed into the first message. The other will contain something like this:

> **You have received a file, which has been saved as**
> **C:\\INTERNET\\PIPELINE\\DOWNLOAD***filename*

Internaut has automatically decoded the file for you, and placed it in your download directory. Use File Manager to go to that directory and move or open the file.

Non-Internaut users will also get two messages, but in the UUENCODED one they'll see a huge jumble of text—this is the text they must save in a file and UUDECODE. In some cases they may see several messages—if it's a very long UUENCODED file, it may have been broken into several pieces. The recipient will have to save each message, then either use a UUDECODE program that can decode several separate files into one original (Wincode can do this), or else use a text editor (or word processor) to "paste" the pieces together manually, save it as one file (an ASCII file), then decode it. Whew! (Some e-mail programs can recognize incoming UUENCODE messages and convert them automatically.)

A UUENCODE file sent from Internaut—tell your buddy to save and UUDECODE it.

What happens if someone sends a UUENCODED file from a non-Internaut system to *you*? Again, you'll see two messages; one tells you the file has been converted and saved in your download directory, and the other shows the actual message (UUENCODED garbage and all). That's useful, because sometimes people write messages and then insert the UUENCODED stuff below the message.

So What Can't It Do? MIME

There's another method for transferring files through the Internet e-mail system. It's called MIME, Multipurpose Internet Mail Extensions. There's a problem with this system, though: most e-mail programs in use are either not working with MIME, or *trying* to use it but not doing it very well. If you send a MIME file attachment to someone who doesn't have a "MIME-enabled" e-mail program, they'll just get garbage. (So if anyone wants to send you a file, make sure they're not using MIME—they must UUENCODE.)

Anyone can use UUENCODE—with a little effort, it's true, but anyone receiving a UUENCODED file can decode it if they try. But if they don't have a MIME e-mail program, the file's no good to them—so Internaut uses only the UUENCODE system. Maybe they'll add MIME later.

The Least You Need to Know

➤ To send an e-mail message, click on the **Write** button in the main Internaut window, or on the **New** button in the Inbox.

➤ Don't write e-mail while connected to The Pipeline. Rather, write it offline, and Internaut will send it when you connect.

➤ An e-mail address comprises a username, an @ sign, and a domain name, as in **president@whitehouse.gov**.

➤ You can send e-mail to most online services—CompuServe, GEnie, America Online, PRODIGY, and others.

➤ Internaut lets you insert a text file into a message, or "attach" a UUENCODED file—a file that has been converted to ASCII text.

➤ Internaut does not send or receive files using the MIME system.

## Chapter 9

Here It Comes! Incoming Mail!

In This Chapter

➤ Viewing the Inbox

➤ How Internaut transfers messages

➤ Holding messages—viewing only the From and Subject lines

➤ Working offline to save money

➤ Reading the messages

➤ Other operations—saving, printing, deleting, and more

➤ Working with the address book

➤ Mail folders and mailboxes

All About the Inbox

If you sent an e-mail message to yourself, sooner or later it will end up in your Inbox. While you are online and the Inbox is open, Internaut will check periodically (every minute or so) to see whether any e-mail has arrived for you. (You can tell it not to; just use the Options|Automatic Updates command in the Inbox.)

If it has, Internaut transfers the message to your Inbox. You may see a message box telling you that e-mail has arrived, and your computer may beep—that depends on how you set up your mail options (see Chapter 7).

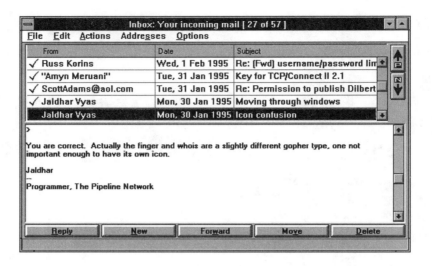

The Inbox is where you'll read and respond to your e-mail.

Getting to the Inbox

If you want to go and view your incoming e-mail at some point when the Inbox has *not* opened automatically, click on the **Mail** button in the Internaut main window. Or select **Services|Mail: open mailboxes**, or press **Ctrl+M**. You'll see the Mail dialog box. This shows you a list of all your mail boxes—right now all you'll see are the Inbox, Outbox, and Sent Mail boxes, but you'll learn (later in this chapter), how to create your own boxes.

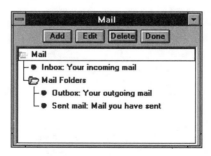

The Mail dialog box.

So double-click on the **Inbox** entry, or highlight it and press **Enter**. The Inbox will open.

What's All This, Then?

If you have received a message, you'll see a line in the Table of Contents at the top of the Inbox—this shows you who the message is from (okay, so it's from you, we know that), and what it's about (the Subject line). You'll also see the date that it was sent. Now, what happens depends on what you have set in your mail *filters*.

You see, when Internaut finds out that you have e-mail waiting, it looks at your filters. You can see these by selecting **File|Filter rules for this folder**. I'm not going to discuss these in detail right now—we'll look at them in Chapter 13. But suffice it to say that when you first start Internaut they are set up to transfer only the From and Subject lines, for instance, so you can see what the message is about (or who it's from), before transferring the entire message.

Check Your Mail Now! To make Internaut check immediately to see whether you have e-mail waiting, use the **Actions|Update Table of Contents** command in the Inbox. Note, however, that even if you send e-mail to yourself, sometimes it can take a while to get "through the system" and back to you.

Here's what happens in the e-mail Inbox with its default set up:

1. Internaut finds out about pending e-mail.

2. It places the red dot and the From and Subject information into the Table of Contents.

3. You read the From and Subject information. If you decide you want to transfer the message, you double-click on it.

4. Internaut changes the red dot to a black dot, and begins transferring the message.

5. When the message is on your computer's hard disk, Internaut replaces the red dot with an envelope icon.

6. You click on the message and begin reading. The envelope icon is replaced with a check-mark icon.

Save Money—Work Offline

Why work offline? To save money, of course, by spending less time online. There are two things you may want to do:

➤ Grab all your e-mail messages automatically, then log off and read them offline.

➤ Grab the From and Subject lines, log off, review the lines, decide which messages you want to view, then log back on, grab them, and log off again.

How Big Is It? How can you tell whether a message is small or large? When you click on the entry in the Table of Contents, look in the status bar at the bottom of the Inbox—you'll see a message telling you how large the message is (how many characters it contains).

You might want to combine the two methods. You may want to grab all the small messages automatically—they won't take long, anyway—but only grab the From and Subject information from the long messages.

Internaut is set up to grab only the From and Subject lines, so you can use the second method without any effort. Log on, grab the information, log off, then review the From and Subject lines. Double-click on the ones you want to download, and delete the others. Log back on and Internaut will grab the messages.

Why would you *not* want to read your e-mail? Well, if you subscribe to mailing lists, for instance, you may get large amounts of mail, only some of which really interests you (you'll learn about mailing lists in Chapter 10). So why not just review the Subject line, and only download the ones you want?

If you want to download all your mail automatically (or if you want to download some automatically and others not), you have to do a little more work. You'll need to set up your filters properly—I'll explain how to do that in Chapter 13.

Now you'll go into the Inbox, and what will you find? You'll see the Table of Contents lines, but the messages may have different icons—the ones Internaut transferred will show the envelope icon, but the ones for which Internaut grabbed only the Table of Contents line will be indicated with the red-dot icon. Read the Subject lines, decide which ones you want to transfer, and double-click on them. Internaut will replace the red dot with a black dot. Log back on, and Internaut will grab the messages you indicated. (To remove the ones you *don't* want from the Table of Contents, click on them and click on the **Delete** button at the bottom of the window.)

So, to summarize, here's what all these icons (plus one more) mean:

✳ When Internaut first finds out about waiting e-mail, it places a red dot in the left column.

◉ The black dot means you've marked the message for retrieval (by double-clicking on the message). Internaut will get it next time you log on.

✉ Once Internaut has transferred the message, it uses an envelope icon. Click on the message to read it.

○ If you don't mark a message for retrieval, and don't delete it, it will be marked with a white dot after you log on again.

✓ The check mark shows that you've read the message.

Enough Already, Let's Read

Okay, enough of that—now that you've got your messages, you can read them. Simply click on a message, and view it in the lower area of the window. You can use the **down arrow** to move down through the list, or simply click on each in turn.

There are some other ways to move through the list, too. The **N** button in the top right corner is very useful. Click on it to move down the message you are reading, then, when you get to the bottom, to move to the top of the next message.

You can sort the messages in the Table of Contents, by the way—use the **Options|Sort by** command. You'll see a cascading menu that lets you re-sort all the messages by date, author, or subject.

What exactly will you see in the message area? Probably just the message. But try this: select **Options|Show full headers**. Now you'll see a whole load of garbage at the top of the message. What is all this? The *message header*—stuff that shows you where the message comes from, and how it got to you. Much of this information is of no interest to you, but some is useful. For instance, you'll be able to see the e-mail address of the person who sent the message, and if the message was copied (CC) to anyone else, you'll see that information, too. Plus, you'll see the date and time it was sent.

Here's another thing you can do to the message: you can select **Options|Reformat messages (word wrap)**. Use this when you notice that a message's lines are confused, short lines followed by long lines. This happens sometimes because the Internet's mail system doesn't handle line breaks very well. In some cases, turning on word wrap will eliminate the problem.

Finding Messages

The Inbox has a handy little tool for finding messages. Select **Edit|Find (sender or subject)** to see a small dialog box into which you can type a name or subject. When you click on **OK**, Internaut looks through the From and Subject lines, and moves to the first one it finds that contains the word you typed. You can then use **Edit|Repeat find**, or press **F3**, to move to the *next* match.

You can take this a step further. Use the **Edit|Find and mark all** command to search for *all* the messages that match the word you type, then select them all. Once you select them, you can print them all at once, save them all to a file, delete them, or whatever. Which leads us to another subject.

Select Them All Select all your messages at once by using the **Edit|Find and mark all** command. Leave the text box empty; click on **OK**.

There's another way to select multiple messages—directly, using the keyboard or mouse:

➤ Click on one message, hold the **Shift** key down, move down the list, then click on another.

➤ Hold **Ctrl** while you click on different messages.

➤ Hold the mouse button down and drag the pointer across the messages.

➤ Hold the **Shift** key down while you press the **down arrow** or **up arrow**.

What Can We Do with the Messages?

What, then, can you do with a message itself? You mean you thought you could just *read* it? No, there's more!

Save it in a file   Select **File|Save (to file)** to place it in a text file.

Print it   Select **File|Print**.

Place it in a word processor   Select **File|Start word processor** or press **F5**, and your word processor will open with the e-mail message loaded inside. Which word processor? The one set up in the General area of the Options and Preferences dialog box—by default this is Windows Write (see Chapter 7).

Reply to the message   Click on the **Reply** button if you want to respond to a message. If the **Quote letter in reply** check box is selected in the Options and Preferences dialog box (see Chapter 7), then the entire original message is placed in the reply. If you select some of the text first, however, click on **Reply**; only the selected text is placed in the reply (even if the **Quote letter in reply** check box is *not* selected).

Forward the message   Click on the **Forward** button to place the message in a new one—you'll have to enter a To e-mail address. If you select a portion of the message, only the selected portion is placed in the new message.

Delete the message   Click on the **Delete** button to get rid of a message. (Accidentally deleted a message? See the **Action|Get latest articles** command later in this chapter.)

Move it to another folder   Folder? What folder? Well, mailbox, really. Oh, we haven't covered that yet, but there are different mailboxes to hold your mail, and you can shift a message to another one. We'll take a closer look later in this chapter.

Forget it! Write a new one   Want to write a new message? Click on the **New** button.

Run the Web browser   Huh? Remember I told you that Internaut integrates various Internet functions. Well, if you find a *Web URL* (a sort of Web address) in an e-mail message, you can select it and then use the **File|Start web (selected URL)** command to open the browser and go to that Web site. See Chapter 14 for more information.

So What's the Actions Menu?

The Actions menu provides a few alternative methods for getting the Table of Contents line, getting messages, and deleting messages.

Update Table of Contents   This tells Internaut to check if any e-mail is waiting for you on the Pipeline system. Internaut checks automatically every minute or so, anyway (if the Options|Automatic Updates command has been selected).

Get selected articles   You can select messages in the Table of Contents (the ones with red dots), then select this command. That will tell Internaut to go grab the messages (immediately if online, or the next time it connects if offline). This is the same as double-clicking on each one.

Erase selected articles   Select several messages, then select this command to delete them.

Also notice the **Options|Always erase seen articles on exit** command. This tells Internaut to erase all your e-mail when you leave the Inbox. If you use this command, you'd better remember to move messages to another box (you'll see how later in this chapter) before leaving.

Saving a Little Time—the Address Book

Those Internet addresses can get a little clunky, so make use of the Address Book. As you've seen, you can just select from a list of names to enter an e-mail address, so you'll save a lot of time, hassle, and mistyping.

In the Inbox—or any of the other mailboxes—select **Addresses|Open address book**. (You can also use the **Services|Mail: Open address book** command from the main Internaut window.) You'll see, yes, the Address Book. To add a new address, click on the **New** button. The box expands. Now you can type information into the text boxes at the bottom. Start by typing the **Alias**—this is the text you want to appear when you select the drop-down list box from the **To** box in the **Composer** window (see Chapter 8). You don't want to see some clunky Internet address—you want to see a real name, don't you?

An *alias* is a common term on the Internet for a name that takes the place of the e-mail address. Rather than selecting the actual e-mail address, you select the nickname—the alias—because it's easier to remember.

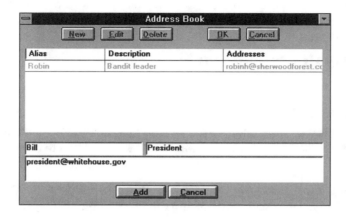

The Address Book, in "add" mode.

In the next box type some kind of **Description**. The strange thing about the Internet is that many users meet loads of new people, more than they'll ever remember. It helps to have a short description to remind you who each person is.

Finally, in the last box, type the e-mail address of the person, then click on the **Add** button, and you've just added someone to the Address Book.

Multiple Mailings Made Easy—Mailing Lists

Okay, yes, I'd noticed—that last text box *is* kinda large, isn't it? In fact, you could get several e-mail addresses in there, couldn't you? In fact, you can get *hundreds* of addresses in there, if you try!

Why? Well, what a great way to create a mailing list! You can assign dozens, even hundreds of e-mail addresses to one e-mail alias. Which means you can send several, dozens, or hundreds of messages by selecting just one name in the To box.

Perhaps you have a group of colleagues you want to send e-mail to, a daily or weekly update memo. Perhaps you plan to replace your Christmas family letter with a family e-mail. Or maybe you are going to create an electronic newsletter. These can all be accomplished with a simple mailing list.

Adding Addresses from Messages

Here's a quick way to add an address to your address book—click on a message in the Inbox Table of Contents, then select **Addresses|Add sender to address book**. The alias is added to your address book automatically. Of course, there's no description—to add one, open the address book, click on the new entry, and then click on the **Edit** button.

Creating Mailboxes

Spend a little time on the Internet, and you'll find your e-mail building up. Now, someone else might think many of the messages you get are trivial, but you know they're important. So important, in fact, that you can't bear to delete them—you just don't know when you might need them!

An Empty Alias In some cases the **Alias** (nickname) text box will be empty. This field is only filled in if Internaut is able to find the person's name on the From line; not all mail systems will send the name (some send only the e-mail address). Type in the person's name.

But you'll find your Inbox getting *very* cluttered. So why not organize all those messages—create a few mailboxes to hold messages of different types. You could have one box for messages from family, one for those from business associates, one for messages from your tractor-restoration mailing list, and so on. (We'll get to mailing lists in Chapter 10.)

Actually you can create *two* types of "containers" for your messages, folders and mailboxes—a folder contains mailboxes. So you might have a folder for family-related messages, and within that folder you'll have a box for Mom, a box for Dad, a box for Mad Uncle Fred, and so on.

Let's start by creating a new folder. Begin by clicking on the **Mail** button in the main Internaut window, to see the Mail window. You'll notice that you already have one folder: **Mail**. This contains the Inbox—which you've seen already—as well as the **Outbox** and the **Sentmail** box. The **Outbox** is where mail you write offline is held until you connect to The Pipeline (when it's taken out and sent). The Sentmail box contains copies of the mail you have already sent—provided you selected the **Save copy in Sentmail** check box in the **Composer** window (see Chapter 8).

Archiving Here's another way to organize your messages: "archive" them. Periodically select blocks of messages, and use the **File|Save (to file)** command to place them in a text file. Then delete them from the mailbox.

Now, when the Mail dialog box opens, click on the **Add Folder** button. In the **Adding a Folder** dialog box, type the name of your folder (**Family**, for instance). Then click on **OK**...and you've created a folder.

Now, let's place a mailbox inside the folder. Click on the new folder in the **Mail** dialog box. Then click on the **Add Group** button. Type a folder name (**Mad Uncle Fred**, or whatever). Click on the **OK** button, and you've just created a mailbox.

Creating folders and mailboxes.

That's pretty much it; you can edit a folder or mailbox (click on it, and then click on the **Edit** button), or you can get rid of one with the **Delete** button. But now let's look at how to use a mailbox.

Moving Messages to Mailboxes

Let's say you get a message from Mad Uncle Fred, and want to move it into his mailbox. How do you do that? There are two ways.

First, let's assume you are in the mail Inbox, and have just read the message. To move it, click on the **Move** button. You'll see the Select Folder dialog box. Simply double-click on the **Mad Uncle Fred** mailbox, or click on it once and then click on the **OK** button. The message is moved.

The other way to transfer messages is to use the *filters*. These let you give Internaut precise instructions about what to do when it receives e-mail. So you could tell it that whenever it gets a message from Mad Uncle Fred, it should automatically transfer it to the Mad Uncle Fred mailbox. I'm not going to explain how to do this here (it's a little complicated), but don't panic, I've given it a complete chapter—see Chapter 13.

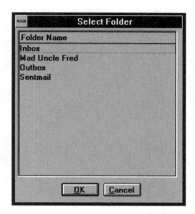

The Select Folder dialog box over the Inbox.

The Least You Need to Know

➤ To view the Inbox, click on the **Mail** button in the main Internaut window, then double-click on the Inbox entry.

➤ Internaut transfers only the From and Subject line automatically.

➤ Log on, grab your mail or the From and Subject lines, then log off. Work with your mail offline to save money.

➤ Double-click on a message to read it.

➤ Use the menus and buttons to save, print, move, delete, reply, forward, and open in a word processor.

➤ The address book lets you save addresses and create mailing lists.

➤ Create mail folders and mailboxes to categorize your e-mail. Then use the **Move** button or filters to transfer messages.

## Chapter 10

E-mail Heaven— Mailing Lists

> ## In This Chapter
>
> ➤ What's a mailing list?
>
> ➤ Using Internaut's search-and-subscribe system
>
> ➤ Finding directories of LISTSERV and other mailing lists
>
> ➤ Subscribing to lists yourself
>
> ➤ Coming soon—automated mailing-list searches

Not getting enough e-mail? Too many hours in the day? Boy, do I have a solution for you! Get on a few mailing lists.

We mentioned the term *mailing list* earlier, in Chapter 9. At that point I was referring to the way you could use the address book to send an e-mail message to loads of people at the same time: create a mailing list with a single "alias," then send the message to that alias.

But *mailing list* has another meaning. The term is often used to refer to special "discussion groups" (sometimes known as "forums" in other online services) that operate through the e-mail system—using, not surprisingly, a system very similar to the one we looked at when you created your own mailing list. This chapter explains how to find and subscribe to mailing lists.

How These Things Work

First, find a mailing list you're interested in—let's say you're interested in renovating old tractors, or in the Workshop on Wood for Energy in the Tropics, or the Film Music Discussion List, or one of literally thousands of other discussions. Subscribe to the mailing list you're interested in (I'll explain how in a moment) and you'll start receiving messages. Anyone who is a member of the mailing list can send a message *to the list*—that message is sent out to everyone on the list automatically. That way, everyone on the list gets to see every message.

Now, this may sound clumsy, but it actually works quite well. These "discussions" are often very interesting—you can learn a lot, "meet" loads of interesting people, and even have some fun. Unfortunately, the system works *so* well that you may find the number of hours in the day quickly shrinking, with unimportant chores—bathing, eating, picking up the kids from school—getting less and less attention. So be careful out there!

What's a LISTSERV?

You'll often hear mailing lists called *LISTSERVs*, or *LISTSERV groups*. But a LISTSERV is simply one type of mailing list. (LISTSERV is a program that administers a mailing list.) So although all LISTSERVs are mailing lists, not all mailing lists are LISTSERVs.

What sorts of subjects can you find? You'll find mailing lists like these:

ABORIG-L   (ABORIG-L@UALTAVM.BITNET) Aboriginal religion course by Dr. Earle H. Waugh

ACADEMIC   (ACADEMIC@BRUFMG.BITNET) Forum de Ciencia Computacional

DOHMEM-L   (DOHMEM-L@ALBNYDH2.BITNET) New York State Department of Health Memoranda

DRSEVENT   (DRSEVENT@DARTCMS1.BITNET) Dead Runners Society events and encounters

DS-H   (DS-H@NIHLIST.BITNET) Major handicap issues in the ICIDH

JAZZ-L   (JAZZ-L@TEMPLEVM.BITNET) Jazz lovers' list

JOBPLACE   (JOBPLACE@UKCC.BITNET) Self-directed job-search techniques and job placement

JOHNLITR   (JOHNLITR@UNIVSCVM.BITNET)
Dialogue concerning the Fourth Gospel

PALEOLIM   (PALEOLIM@NERVM.BITNET)
Paleolimnology forum

TOLKIEN   (TOLKIEN@JHUVM.BITNET) J. R. R.
Tolkien readers

UNCJIN-L   (UNCJIN-L@ALBNYVM1.BITNET)
United Nations Criminal Justice Information
Network

UNIX-WIZ   (UNIX-WIZ@NDSUVM1.BITNET)
UNIX-Wizards Mailing List

UNMETHOD   (UNMETHOD@GWUVM.BITNET)
UN University Millennium Project Discussion
List

> **Trying a Newsgroup Instead** So you can't find the subject you want? Try a newsgroup instead. Newsgroups are very similar to mailing lists—they, too, are discussion groups, but they deliver the messages in a different way, and there are thousands more available. See Chapter 11.

Get the idea? Pick a subject, any subject, and you'll probably find a mailing list related to that subject. There are thousands, with more being added every day.

Finding a List and Subscribing

The first step is to find and subscribe to a mailing list. You can start by getting lists of mailing lists; save them to your hard disk so you can read through them and look for interesting stuff—or even use your word processor's search feature to find something.

To get the latest list of Bitnet LISTSERV mailing lists—perhaps the most common type—write an e-mail message. Address the message to **listserv@bitnic.educom.edu**. In the *body* of the message (not the subject), write **list global**. You'll get a number of e-mail messages automatically, but I warn you, they're *big* (currently over 600 kilobytes total). Select them all in the Inbox, and use the **File|Save (to file)** command to put them in a text file.

There's another list of over 1,200 (non-LISTSERV) mailing lists. You can get this by using FTP (which you'll learn about in Chapter 15). Go to the **rtfm.mit.edu** FTP site, and look in the **/pub/usenet/news.answers/mail/mailing-list** directory. You'll find more than a dozen text files. Also, you may want to get hold of the "How to Find an Interesting Mailing List" document, by Arno Wouters. Send e-mail to **listserv@vm1.nodak.edu**, and put **GET NEW-LIST WOUTERS** in the body of the message; or FTP to **vm1.nodak.edu** and look in the **new-list** directory for **new-list.wouters**.

Quick Retrieve Set these FTP sites as bookmarks, and put the e-mail addresses in your address book, so you can quickly retrieve the latest lists.

Once you have your lists, find the mailing lists you are interested in. Then send e-mail to the ones you want to subscribe to. There are two types of mailing lists: one is automated, and the other is manually administered. Some very small mailing lists are set up to be administered by a real person—that person will add your name to the list. Such lists are often private; subscribers have been invited to join. Other lists use special programs—*mailservers*—to add your name to the list automatically when you subscribe. These are often (though not always) public lists, open to anyone.

Subscribing to manually administered mailing lists is often as simple as sending a message to the administrator, providing your e-mail addressing, and asking to join the list. You can often reach an administrator by sending e-mail to *listname*-**request @hostname**.

To subscribe to an automated list, you often send e-mail to the mailserver program. In the body of the message you would enter **SUB *firstname lastname***. (That's *your* first and last name, of course.) To unsubscribe, you would use the word **SIGNOFF** instead of SUB.

Note that the address of the list administrator and that of the list itself is usually—in most cases, but not always—different. The list may be **biglist@bighost**, and that's where you would send your e-mail when you want to post messages to the list. But when you want to subscribe, unsubscribe, and do other administrative functions, you would normally e-mail to **biglist-request@bighost**.

Working with LISTSERV groups is a little different, though they, too, have two e-mail addresses. Let's take a look at the LISTSERV address. It's made up of three parts: the group name itself, the LISTSERV *site*, and **.bitnet**. For instance, the address of the group College Activism/Information List is **actnow-l@brownvm.bitnet**. **Actnow-l** is the name of the group, and **brownvm** is the name of the site.

A *site* is a computer that has the LISTSERV program and handles one or more LISTSERV groups. In fact, a site may have dozens of groups. The brownvm site, for instance, also has the ACH-EC-L, AFRICA-L, and AGING-L forums, among about 70 others.

To subscribe, you'll send a message to **listserv@*site*.bitnet** with the following text in the *body* of the message (not the subject).

SUBSCRIBE *group firstname lastname*

For instance, if I want to subscribe to the **actnow-l** list at the **brownvm** LISTSERV site, I could send a message (to **listserv@brownvm.bitnet**) like this:

SUBSCRIBE actnow-l Peter Kent

Notice that you send the message to **listserv@*sitename*.bitnet**. Also, the SUBSCRIBE message only contains the name of the group, not the entire group address.

You may (or may not) receive some kind of confirmation message from the group. Such a message would tell you that you have subscribed, and provide background information about the group and the different commands you can use.

After you subscribe, just sit back and wait for the messages to arrive. Or send your own—simply address mail to the full group address (in the preceding case, to **actnow-l@brownvm.bitnet**).

Coming Soon—Automated Search

Pretty soon, perhaps by the time you read this, you should find that Internaut has a special automated-search feature. As you've seen, the existing method of finding a mailing list can be a bit of a pain. First you have to track down the mailing list you want—you have to send e-mail to a special server, or grab some files from an FTP site somewhere. Then, when you find the list you want, you have to send a message to the list, in exactly the right format, to subscribe to the list. Internaut's new feature will simplify this process, though: let's see how.

First, you'll have to find the **Mailing lists: search and join** gopher menu somewhere—I can't tell you where, because at the time of writing it wasn't there, so look around a little. In this menu you'll see a list of mailing list searches.

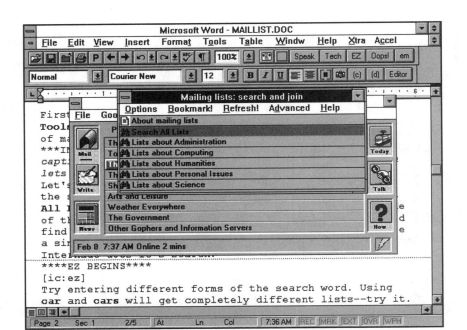

The **Mailing lists: search and join** *gopher menu lets you search for a subject that interests you.*

Let's say you want to find out about a mailing list on the subject of *cars*. You can double-click on the **Search All Lists** entry, if you wish—or maybe you could try one of the specific categories. (But I'm not sure where we'd find cars, so we'll use the All Lists entry.) You'll see a simple text box. Type **cars** and click on **OK**, and Internaut does its search.

Assuming Internaut finds something, you'll see a list of the mailing lists in a gopher menu. Double-click on one you want to join, or just know more about, and you'll see the Mailing List Information dialog box.

Try entering different forms of the search word. Using **car** and **cars** will get completely different lists— try it.

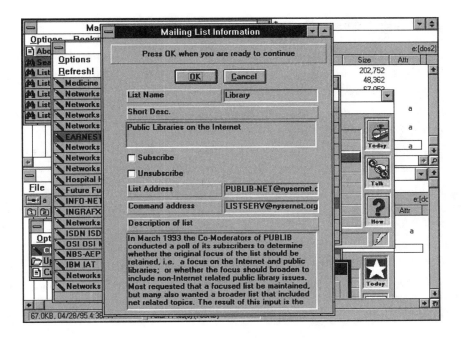

The Mailing List Information dialog box helps you subscribe to a list.

The **List Name** and **Short Desc.** boxes provide an overview of the list, but the **Description of list** will usually give you more information. Notice also the **List Address** and **Command Address** text boxes. These are e-mail addresses. The List Address is the one that you'll be sending your messages to. The Command Address is only used for administrative purposes—it's the address that requests to subscribe and unsubscribe are sent, requests for help, and so on.

Now, to subscribe to the list, simply click on the **Subscribe** check box, then click on the **OK** button. (Notice the **Unsubscribe** button—when you've had enough of a mailing list, return here, click on the Unsubscribe button, and click on OK.) Internaut will send a message to the mailing list to subscribe to the list. Soon you'll start getting messages in your Inbox from that list. You'll probably receive an introductory message, telling you what the list is all about and how to send commands to the list. (We'll get into the commands in a moment.)

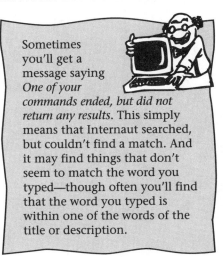

Sometimes you'll get a message saying *One of your commands ended, but did not return any results.* This simply means that Internaut searched, but couldn't find a match. And it may find things that don't seem to match the word you typed—though often you'll find that the word you typed is within one of the words of the title or description.

The Least You Need to Know

➤ A mailing list is a discussion group based on the e-mail system.

➤ A LISTSERV list is a common form of mailing list—LISTSERV is a program that manages mailing lists.

➤ To see the latest list of LISTSERV lists, send e-mail to **listserv@bitnic.educom.edu**, with **list global** in the body of the message.

➤ To see a list of other mailing lists, go to the **rtfm.mit.edu** FTP site, and look in the **/pub/usenet/news.answers/mail/mailing-list** directory.

➤ To subscribe to a LISTSERV group manually, send e-mail to the LISTSERV site (**listserv@***site***.bitnet**). Use the messages **SUBSCRIBE** *groupname yourfirstname yourlastname*.

➤ To send messages to the LISTSERV group, send e-mail to the group at the site (***group***@***site***.bitnet**).

➤ To subscribe to other forms of mailing lists you often send e-mail to the "request" address: *listname*-**request@***hostname*. Use the message **SUB** *yourfirstname yourlastname*.

➤ To send messages to the group, e-mail to *listname***@***hostname*.

➤ By the time you read this, Pipeline USA may have added their special automated mailing-list search facility.

## Chapter 11

Newsgroups—from Anarchy to Zymurgy

In This Chapter

➤ What are newsgroups?

➤ The danger of newsgroups

➤ Newsgroup subjects and hierarchies

➤ Creating folders and boxes

➤ Subscribing to newsgroups

We're getting onto dangerous ground now—newsgroups. These are addictive, and should only be approached by the strong-willed. Before we get into their more problematic aspects, let's discuss what newsgroups are, and what they can do for you.

First, don't be confused by the word *news*. Although a few newsgroups do carry hard news—reports about what's going on in Congress, foreign affairs, and so on—most are far from the world of the *Washington Post* and the evening news.

The word *news*, in Internetspeak, refers to discussion groups. These are similar to the mailing lists we looked at in Chapter 10, with one significant difference—the messages are delivered in a different way. Rather than receiving messages in your e-mail inbox, newsgroup messages are sent in huge blocks to service providers or system administrators who subscribe to them. These services or administrators store the messages somewhere on a hard disk connected to their host computer. Then anyone with a connection to the system can use a special program—called a *newsreader*—to read the newsgroup messages.

There are literally tens of thousands, perhaps hundreds of thousands, of newsgroups around the world. Not all of these get transmitted across the Internet—many are local groups of interest only to people connected to the systems where they originate. But thousands of newsgroups are transnational groups—people all over the world read messages from these groups and post their own messages. Pipeline USA, for instance, currently has over 11,000 newsgroups for you to choose from!

Handle with Care!

You'd think nothing could be more harmless than sitting in the comfort of your own home or office reading messages from people on a subject that interests you. But here's the danger—newsgroups can be addictive.

People sometimes ask me which newsgroups (and mailing lists, and CompuServe forums) I read. I get the impression that they ask expecting me to reel off a dozen or two discussion groups, but there's a problem: I simply don't have time to keep up with a couple-dozen newsgroups.

Now, I *have* been a regular reader, and that's why I'm not anymore—I found it hard to limit my reading. Once into a group, whether it's about working on the Internet, Middle Eastern politics, or movies, I have trouble reading just one or two messages. And when I read a message or two that I find interesting, I have trouble not responding. And by the time I've read all the messages and responded to a handful, it's late morning and I haven't got any work done.

So, I limit my activity in such discussion groups. I do have a regular mailing list I read, and if I want to find a particular piece of information (or simply have time to goof off), I delve into the newsgroups. But I treat newsgroups and the like with the respect they deserve—be careful, or you'll find yourself being sucked in!

Not Just Geeks

If you've never used a newsgroup (or a mailing list, or some other form of online discussion group), you may not be aware of the power of such communications. This sort of messaging system really brings computer networking alive, and it's not just computer nerds sitting around with nothing better to do. (Check out the alt.sex newsgroup—these people are not your average introverted propeller-heads!) I've found work, made friends, found answers to research questions (much quicker and cheaper than going to a library), and read people's "reviews" of tools I can use in my business. I've never found a lover or spouse online, but I know people who have (and anyway, I'm already married).

So, What's Out There?

You can use newsgroups for fun or real work. You can use them to spend time "talking" with other people who share your interests—whether they happen to be "making and baking with sourdough" (see the **rec.food.sourdough** group), kites and kiting (**rec.kites**), or S&M (**alt.sex.bondage**). Or you can do some serious work online: find a job at a nuclear physics research site (**hepnet.jobs**), track down a piece of software for a biology project (**bionet.software**), or find stories about police work in the San Francisco area for an article you are writing (**clari.sfbay.police**).

USENET Groups

Newsgroups are often known as *USENET groups* (after the computer network on which they originate). Not all newsgroups are USENET groups; some, for technical reasons, are not true USENET groups, even though they are distributed along with the USENET groups. These are known as *alternative newsgroups*—not to be confused with the *alt* newsgroups, a category of USENET group. Was that confusing enough?

Here's just a tiny fraction of what's available:

alt.ascii-art   Pictures created with ASCII text characters—such as Spock and the Simpsons.

alt.comedy.british   Discussions on British comedy, in all its wonderful forms.

alt.current-events.russia   What's going on in Russia right now. (Some messages are in broken English, some in Russian, but that just adds romance.)

alt.missing-kids   About missing kids.

alt.polyamory   A newsgroup for those with multiple lovers.

alt.sex   Discussions on Hillary Clinton's sexual orientation, nude beaches, and anything else related to sex, marginal or otherwise.

bit.listserv.down-syn   Discussions about Down's Syndrome.

comp.research.japan   Computer research in Japan.

misc.forsale   Goods for sale.

rec.skydiving   A group for skydivers.

sci.anthropology   People interested in anthropology.

sci.military   Science and the military.

soc.couples.intercultural   Interracial couples.

If you're looking for information on just about any subject, the question is not, "I wonder if there's a newsgroup about this?" It should be, "I wonder what the newsgroup's *name* is, and does my service provider subscribe to it?"

Anarchy and Zymurgy?

The title of this chapter refers to *anarchy* and *zymurgy*. Was I just looking for a nice "A to Z" chapter heading—or are there really newsgroups covering these subjects? The answer is "yes" to both of these questions. Try **alt.anarchism** and (for zymurgy, the study of fermentation as it relates to brewing) **alt.beer**, **rec.food.drink.beer**, and **rec.crafts.brewing**. Clearly, beer is more popular than anarchy.

Updating Your List

When you first install Internaut, the program's list of newsgroups is not complete. You can use the list if you like, but if you want to make sure you have the entire list—between 11,000 and 12,000 different groups currently—log onto Pipeline USA and follow the pathways to **Account Administrivia|Update newsgroup lists**. Highlight all the entries in the gopher menu that appears, and select **Advanced|Dblclick selected items**; the new lists will be transferred to your computer. (For a faster download, you can just double-click on the list categories you are interested in.)

You may want to update your list periodically to make sure you have the latest lists. Note also that when you go into the **Adding newsgroups for folder** dialog box (which we'll look at in a moment), you'll see an entry in the newsgroup list that says **Get_The_Latest!!! Download the latest USENET newsgroups from the Pipeline USA**. This is simply a reminder that you don't have the latest list.

Starting News

Let's get down to work then, and see how to read the newsgroups that The Pipeline subscribes to.

To begin working with your newsgroups, click on the News button in the main Internaut window, or select **Services|News: Open Usenet forums**, or press **Ctrl+N**. You'll see the News dialog box.

You already have a number of newsgroups set up in the News dialog box.

This dialog box lets you create folders you can use to categorize your newsgroups (and you can add newsgroups to those folders). You'll see that you already have a number of newsgroups set up for you—Internaut has *subscribed* to these newsgroups automatically. Notice that the newsgroups have small dots in front of their names: If it's a white dot, it means there are currently no messages in the newsgroup "inbox," though you can tell Internaut to get some for you (as you'll see in Chapter 12). If it's a red light, there are messages you haven't looked at. If it's a black box, there are messages you've already read.

Don't Read Them All!
Don't try to keep up with all the newsgroups that have been set up for you—they're just a starting point. Only the most hardened Internet geek has any hope of keeping up with loads of newsgroups. It helps if you're independently wealthy and don't have to work.

Adding Your Own

These groups are all very well for a small taste of what's available, but you'll want to add your own. You can add your own folders, and your own news "boxes." A box can contain a newsgroup, or be set up so you can store messages from the newsgroups, as we'll see later in this chapter.

Creating a new folder in the Box management dialog box.

To create your own folder, click on the **Add Folder** button. Type the name of your folder—**My Stuff, Fun, Automobiles, Food**, or whatever other subject category you want to create. Click on **OK** and Internaut creates your folder.

Now add a newsgroup. Click on your new folder, then click on the **Add Group** button. You'll see the Adding Newsgroups dialog box.

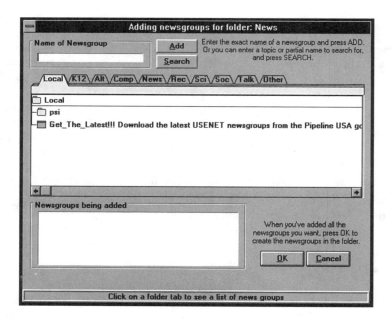

Type the name of the newsgroup you want to add, or select from the list.

You can type a newsgroup name, if you know it, into the **Name of Newsgroup** text box. Then click on the **Add** button and the name is placed in the **Newsgroups being added** list box at the bottom of the dialog box. Most of the time, you'll probably just select from the list of newsgroups.

Now you've got two ways to find a newsgroup. You can type a word into the **Name of Newsgroup** text box and then click on the **Search** button. Internaut will search its list for any matches. For instance, I typed **film** and clicked on **Search**; Internaut found seven newsgroups: **aus.films, bit.listserv.film-l, convoy.film+video, no.film, pronet.film-video-tv, uchi.films, zer.z-netz.freizeit.filme.**

What are all of these? Well, in most cases there's a question mark after the name of the group. That means Internaut has no information about the subject matter—it simply knows that the word *film* appears in the name. In one case, though, there's a short description. The bit.listserv.film-l entry is followed by **Film making and reviews list.** This is actually a mailing list (you can tell because **bit.listserv** refers to a mailing list type), with a "gateway" to the newsgroup system. (For information about mailing lists, see Chapter 10.)

As for the others, how do you know what they are? You may be able to figure it out from the names. It's a good bet that the aus.films newsgroup is about Australian films, and that the zer.z-netz.freizeit.filme group is in German. But ultimately the only way to really find out is to subscribe.

The other way to find a group is to view a list. You'll notice tabs across the dialog box below the Search text box. Each tab represents one category of newsgroup. Let's take a quick look at how newsgroups are named. Newsgroup names look much like host addresses, a series of words separated by periods. This is because, like hosts, they are set up in a hierarchical system (though instead of going right-to-left, they go left-to-right). The first name is the top level. These are the top-level USENET groups:

In Town   These are local newsgroups, related to The Pipeline and New York.

Clarinews   Clarinet's newsgroups from "official" and commercial sources—mainly UPI news stories and various syndicated columns.

Alt   "Alternative" subjects, often subjects that many people would consider "inappropriate" or pornographic. Or just weird. Or simply interesting stuff, but the newsgroup has been created in an "unauthorized" manner to save time and hassle.

Comp   Computer-related subjects.

News   Information about newsgroups themselves, including software used to read newsgroup messages and information about finding and using newsgroups.

Rec   Recreational topics—hobbies, sports, the arts, and so on.

Sci   Science—discussions about research in the "hard" sciences, as well as some social sciences.

Soc   A wide range of social issues, such as discussions about different types of societies and subcultures, as well as sociopolitical subjects.

Talk   Debate about politics, religion, and anything else controversial.

Other   Stuff. These are newsgroups that are not true USENET groups. Many are local groups, though they may be distributed internationally through USENET—don't worry about that, it doesn't matter.

Such newsgroups are known as *alternative newsgroups hierarchies*. In this area you'll find other categories, such as these:

bionet   Biological subjects.

bit   A variety of newsgroups from the Bitnet network.

biz   Business subjects, including advertisements.

brasil   Groups from Brazil (it's spelled with an "s" in Portuguese).

courts   Related to law and lawyers.

de   Various German-language newsgroups.

fj   Various Japanese-language newsgroups.

gnu   The Free Software Foundation's newsgroups.

hepnet   Discussions about high-energy and nuclear physics.

ieee   The Institute of Electrical and Electronics Engineers' newsgroups.

info   A collection of mailing lists formed into newsgroups at the University of Illinois.

k12   Discussions about K-through-12th-grade education.

relcom   Russian-language newsgroups, mainly distributed in the former Soviet Union.

vmsnet   Subjects of interest to VAX/VMS computer users.

Now, to view a list of newsgroups, click on one of the tabs. Internaut will load the list (it may take a few seconds, especially in the case of the Other tab).

Once the list has been loaded, you'll see a couple of folder icons—the first is simply a duplicate of the tab—don't do anything with it. Double-click on the second folder to open the list of newsgroups. (If you clicked on the **Other** tab you'll see many more folders, each one representing a hierarchy of newsgroups. Double-click on any one that catches your eye.)

104

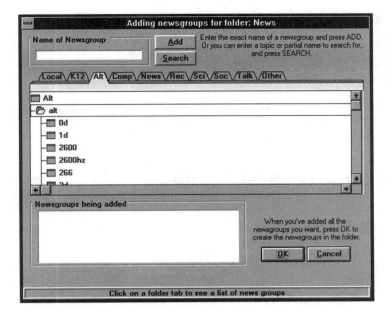

Looking through the Alt list.

This opens up the category. You'll now see a lot of gray-box icons, and some more folder icons. In general, the gray boxes represent the actual newsgroups. The folder icons represent subcategories. Double-click on a folder to open up the subcategories, and the folder icon to select the newsgroup you want to subscribe to. (Sometimes the gray boxes also have subcategories—a "branch" opens up when you double-click.)

Newsgroup Hierarchies

Newsgroup hierarchies can have several levels, each divided by a period. For instance, the *alt.binaries* category has several subcategories. There's *alt.binaries.pictures* and *alt.binaries.sounds*, for instance. Within these subcategories are newsgroups, and even more subcategories. For instance, you'll find the *alt.binaries.pictures.fine-art* subcategory, which contains the *alt.binaries.pictures.fine-art-d*, *alt.binaries.pictures.fine-art.digitized*, and *alt.binaries.pictures.fine-art.graphics* groups.

Once you have the groups you want in the **Newsgroups** list box, click on **OK** and Internaut subscribes to the group for you. (Notice that you can remove entries from this list—click on the entry and a **Remove Selected Newsgroups** button appears.)

Adding an Archive Box

Here's another type of box you can add—an archive box. If you find newsgroup messages that you want to keep, you can transfer them to an archive box; you'll see how to do this in Chapter 12, and when we discuss filters in Chapter 13.

To create one of these archive boxes, click on the folder into which you want to place the box, and then click on the **Add Group** button. Type a name (**Archive**, **Save**, or whatever), click on **Add**, and then click on **OK**.

The Least You Need to Know

➤ A newsgroup is a discussion group—there are over 11,000 available on Pipeline USA.

➤ Be careful—newsgroups are addictive, and can suck up your time like the Pentagon sucks up your money.

➤ Newsgroups are grouped into *hierarchies*, as a way of organizing them into different areas of interest.

➤ Start the newsgroup system by clicking on the **News** button in the Internaut window.

➤ Click on the **Add Folder** button to add a new folder.

➤ To subscribe to a newsgroup, click on your new folder, and then click on the **Add Group** button.

The Daily News— Reading Your Newsgroups

Off to Work—Reading Newsgroup Messages

Okay, it's time to read. First, connect to The Pipeline, then open the **News** dialog box, and *double-click* on the newsgroup you want to read. That group's window will open. At first the window will be blank, except for a folder at the top. But if you click on the folder and press **Ctrl+N**—or **Actions|Update Table of Contents**—Internaut will get a list of the messages in the newsgroup. In a few seconds, assuming the group has messages waiting, you'll see a list of folders and messages within those folders.

Actually, there are two different views. The type I've just described might be termed a "threaded view," because it displays message *threads*. A thread is a series of linked messages—someone posts a message, someone else responds, someone else responds to that, and so on. This view (the one I recommend) will be used if you select **Options|Sort by|Subject**. A similar view is used for **Options|Sort by|Author**, though each folder contains messages from a particular person, rather than messages in a particular thread.

If you select **Options|Sort by|Date** or **Options|Sort by|Author**, you'll see a very different type of window—each message will appear on a separate line, in the same way messages are displayed in the e-mail Inbox. This isn't very convenient for newsgroups, though, because you really want to see a thread, so you can quickly read responses.

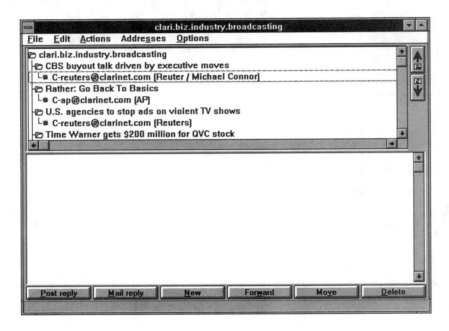

Mail call!

What are the folders? These represent what are sometimes known as *threads*; one person sends a message, someone else sends a response, another person responds to that, and so on. These messages are grouped together in one folder.

The messages themselves have a red dot next to them. That means you haven't yet downloaded the messages—all you've got are the message headers. Click once on a message and then look in the status bar at the bottom of the window. You'll see information about this message: the size, in characters, the person who sent it, and the time and date it was sent (in GMT, Greenwich Mean Time).

If you want to read a message, double-click on it. Or select several at once (hold **Ctrl** while you click on them, or hold the mouse button down while you drag the pointer over them), then select **Actions|Get selected articles** or press **Ctrl+G**—or double-click on the item.

GMT
Greenwich Mean Time is the time in Greenwich, England, where there's a very old observatory. As the Internet stretches across all 24 hourly time zones, GMT provides a handy way to show a time.

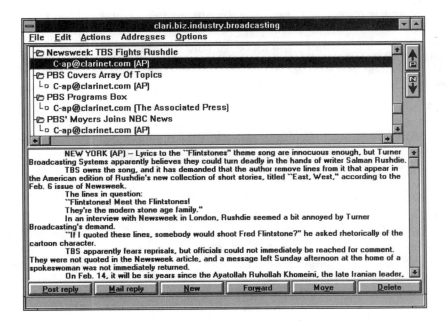

Catching up on the latest news.

You'll see the red dot turn black. That tells you that Internaut is transferring the message. Once it has it, the black dot turns into either a black check mark (if the message is highlighted—the check mark means that the message has been displayed in the lower panel of the window), or into an envelope icon (meaning it's ready to be read—just click on it).

Don't Just Read—Respond!

Yes, there's more. You could just *lurk* (that's the term for reading messages in a newsgroup without taking any part in the discussion). But once you get a feel for what's going on in a group—and decide whether you want any part of it—why not get involved?

There are three ways to send messages to a newsgroup and newsgroup participants:

Reply directly   Click on the **Post reply** button if you want to respond to the message you are viewing with a message to the newsgroup.

Reply to the author   Click on the **Mail reply** button if you want to send e-mail directly to the person who wrote the message. Your message won't be sent to the whole newsgroup.

Start a new discussion   Click on the **New** button if you want to send a new message, unrelated to any previous message.

Message Lag
There's a lag in newsgroup messages. Newsgroups are sent around the Internet each day—your service provider only receives an update once a day. So if you send a message to a newsgroup, don't expect to see it turn up in the newsgroup window for *at least* a day, probably more.

Whichever of these three procedures you use, you'll see the Composer window—which you learned about in Chapter 8, of course.

Note that you can also use the **Forward** button to send the message you are reading to another person via e-mail. You can also use the **Move** button to move the message into an archive newsgroup box that you've created. You can even move the message to another newsgroup box, but I can't imagine why you'd want to! The Move procedure works in the same way as in the e-mail system (see Chapter 9). You can also remove the message using the **Delete** button.

Newsgroup Management

Newsgroups can be surprisingly complicated. You see, somewhere on The Pipeline's system is a huge block of text files containing all the newsgroup messages. You probably don't want to see all these messages, or your newsgroup boxes would fill up. So you need a way to decide which messages you see. You've already learned how to retrieve just the messages you want, but there are other ways to manage messages:

Clear the list and get a new one   Use **Actions|Delete all, update (Ctrl+U)**. Internaut removes the entries from the list, and grabs a few more from the newsgroup, however many you set in the Options and Preferences dialog box as the **Most news items to retrieve at once** (see Chapter 7).

Clear the list but *don't* get more   Use the **Actions|Delete all, no update** command to clear the list without getting more messages.

Get more messages, but don't clear the list   To get more messages, but retain what's in the list, use **Actions|Update Table of Contents** or **Ctrl+N**.

Clear the list and get the latest messages   Use the **Actions|Get latest articles** command.

Read articles related to the current one   Select the **Actions|Get all articles with this subject** command, and Internaut searches for messages with the same subject.

Find old messages   To go back through the newsgroup use the **Actions|Get articles since** command. In the dialog box you'll see, enter a date in the format mm/dd/yy. It may take a little while, and you can't go back too far—perhaps only a couple of weeks.

Open and close the folders in the list   Select **Options|Expand article tree** (**Ctrl+E**) to open or close folders, hiding and exposing the message names.

Erase the articles you've read   Use **Actions|Erase seen articles**.

Erase selected articles   Highlight the articles you want to delete, then select **Actions|Erase selected articles**.

Get all the articles that you *haven't* selected   Why would you do this? Perhaps you want most of the messages, but you know there are one or two you don't want. Select the one or two you *don't* want, then select **Actions|Get unselected articles**.

Grab a few articles at a time   If you press **F2** you'll see the Options and Preferences dialog box. You can enter the number of news messages to grab at a time in the **Most news items to retrieve at once** text box. Now, if you close the dialog box and then select **Options|Automatic Updates**, Internaut will grab that number of messages every couple of minutes. For instance, if there are 100 messages waiting, and you set Most news items to retrieve at once to 15, Internaut will grab the first 15, then another 15 a couple of minutes later, then another 15 a bit later, and so on.

Deleted Messages Deleted a message and then regretted it? You can get it back using the **Actions|Get articles since** command.

111

Erase all the articles that are *not* selected   Use the **Actions|Erase unselected articles** command.

If You've Used E-mail...

...you'll be right at home here. A lot of the commands are the same as in the e-mail system (so see Chapters 8 and 9). For instance, you can save a message to a file, place it in a word processor, highlight a Web URL and launch the Web browser. You can also search the list of messages for a particular person or subject, search and select all matches, even open the address book or add someone's address to the book.

You'll also notice that the **Options** menu lets you sort messages, show full headers, and word wrap the message.

A Few More Options

The newsgroup window has a few more options. There's an **Options|Always erase seen articles on exit** command. This simply means that if you've read a message, Internaut will delete it when you close the window.

Also, you can use the **Options|Other Options** command (or press F2) to get to the Options and Preferences dialog box. We looked at this in Chapter 7; it lets you enter the **Organization** name that will appear in your message headers when posting messages to newsgroups, change the number of messages that Internaut will retrieve at one time, and also enter a Pseudonym, a name that will appear in the From line of your newsgroup messages.

Finally, remember that when you modify the fonts and colors used in the e-mail windows (see Chapter 7), you will also change the newsgroup-window formats.

Working Offline

As with e-mail, you can work with your newsgroup messages offline, if you want to. Log on to Pipeline USA, grab your message headers, log off, then read the headers and decide which ones you want to download. Double-click on the ones you want—the dots will turn to black. Then, if you wish, you can use the **Actions|Erase unmarked articles** menu option to remove the ones you *haven't* double-clicked on. Then log back on and Internaut will grab the messages you requested.

It's Magic!—Pictures (and Sounds) from Text

You'll often find pictures in the newsgroups, and (less commonly) other forms of media such as sounds. Of course, newsgroups are based on text—remember those huge text files flying around the Internet I mentioned earlier?

So how can newsgroups contain pictures—people UUENCODE them, of course! We discussed this in Chapter 8—it's the system that Internaut uses to send computer files across the Internet.

First, where can you find these pictures? Well, any newsgroup can have a UUENCODED message, if someone decides to send one. But there are newsgroups that "specialize" in this sort of thing, in particular the *alt.binaries* newsgroups. You'll find newsgroups such as these:

alt.binaries.clipart

alt.binaries.multimedia

alt.binaries.pictures.cartoons

alt.binaries.pictures.erotica.blondes

alt.binaries.pictures.fine-art

alt.binaries.pictures.tasteless

alt.binaries.sounds.midi

alt.binaries.sounds.erotica

alt.binaries.sounds.tv

alt.binaries.sounds.utilities

There's all sorts of interesting stuff in this area—but be warned, much of it is what might be termed tasteless. And one man's erotica is another man's pornography (and many of these pictures are *very* graphic... or so I've been told).

Converting to the Real Thing

Let's say you want to view one of the cartoons in **alt.binaries.pictures.cartoons**. You'll view the message as usual, but you'll see that much of the message is full of garbage text, the same sort of thing we saw in Chapter 9.

Now, figure out if the message contains an image, or if the message is simply one of several messages that contain the image. For instance, you may see three messages with these Subjects: *filename*.jpg 1/3, *filename*.jpg 2/3, *filename*.jpg 3/3. This means that the image has been UUENCODED, then broken into three pieces and put into three messages (because it's so large—some e-mail programs choke when they get very large messages).

These messages have to be strung together and *then* UUDECODED. We'll get to that in a moment. Right now, though, let's look at the simpler situation, a single message containing a UUENCODED image.

You have to actually get the message from the newsgroup—that is, you can't simply click on a message in the list, you must double-click or use **Actions|Get selected articles** to transfer the message to your computer (you must see the actual message displayed in the bottom panel of the window).

Important!

Make sure the **Options|Reformat messages (word wrap)** option is *turned off*! If there's a check mark next to this menu option, Internaut will reformat the UUENCODED message, and you won't be able to decode it!

Next, make sure that at the top of the encoding is a line like this:

```
begin 644 valien.jpg
```

This shows you that you've got the beginning of the UUENCODING, and the filename that will be used (in this case VALIEN.JPG).

Next, go to the bottom of the message and make sure there's a line with the word **end** by itself. If you see a message saying **Press F5 to see the rest of this article**, that means it was way too long to fit in the window, so you won't be able to mail it to yourself. (You'll have to save it, but we'll come to that in a moment.)

Now, e-mail the message to yourself—click on the **Forward** button, type your username in the **To** box, and click on **Send**. When the e-mail system receives the UUENCODED message, it creates two messages—remember how this worked before? You'll see one message telling you that the file has been converted and downloaded onto your hard disk, and another with the text from the file.

This doesn't work correctly all the time, for a variety of reasons. Sometimes the UUENCODED part of the message was created using a non-standard program and

Internaut can't figure out how to decode it. Sometimes what you thought was a single-message image turns out to be simply one part of a multi-message image (remember to look for the **begin** and **end** lines).

Now, what can you do if the file is too long (you saw the **Press F5 to see the rest of this article** message at the bottom) or if it's just one part of a multi-part message? Then you have to get a UUENCODE/UUDECODE program—I recommend Wincode. This is a simple Windows program for decoding files. You can find it all over the Internet—search for the word **Wincode** using Archie (see Chapter 15).

To prepare your files for Wincode, save them onto your hard disk as text files; use **File|Save (to file)**. If you are saving several files that make up a single image, save them with an incrementing number—**picture1.uue**, **picture2.uue**, and **picture3.uue**, for instance. (You don't have to use the UUE extension, but Wincode likes it.)

Now, in Wincode, use the **File|Decode** command to convert the picture. You'll see a dialog box in which you'll select the file you saved—if it's a multi-part picture, select the first file in sequence (**picture1.uue**, for instance).

How Do You View These?

Now that you've got the pictures (or sounds), how do you use them? You may have a program that can work with that file format. If not, see Chapter 14 for information on finding "viewers."

The Least You Need to Know

➤ To view a newsgroup, double-click on the name in the News dialog box.

➤ To get messages listings, use **Actions|Update Table of Contents** or press **Ctrl+N**.

➤ To retrieve a particular message, use **Actions|Get selected article** or press **Ctrl+G**.

➤ To get pictures and sounds from messages with UUENCODE inserts, get the **Wincode** program.

➤ Occasionally you'll be able to e-mail files to yourself and let Internaut's e-mail system UUDECODE them, but this often won't work.

## Chapter 13

Message Wizardry— Automated Message Management

In This Chapter

➤ The Filter Rules dialog box

➤ The default e-mail filter rule

➤ The rule components

➤ Quick rules

➤ Creating your own rules

➤ Examples

Time for a little fun. This book has been too simple so far; it really hasn't *stretched* you. Well, that's going to change. We're going to play with *filters*. It's not brain surgery, but you will have to pay a little more attention, so sit up and read carefully.

Filters are used to *do something automatically* with incoming e-mail and newsgroup messages. Filters can do all sorts of things: move messages to folders when they arrive, automatically delete messages from a particular person (your boss, ex-spouse, obnoxious colleague), throw away very large messages, save a message on a particular subject to a text file, and so on.

This filtering system works in both the e-mail and newsgroup system, in pretty much the same way—there are just a few more options when you're working in the newsgroup system. So you can use filters to manipulate newsgroup messages, mailing list messages, and plain old everyday e-mail messages.

The Filter Rules Dialog Box

Let's take a look at where this happens. Each separate mailbox or newsgroup box has its own filter rules. So open a newsgroup window or your Inbox. Then select **File|filter rules for this folder**. You'll see the **Filter Rules** dialog box.

Now, the first time I looked in here, I was pretty confused, but don't worry, it's really simpler than it appears. This filtering thing just takes a bit of effort.

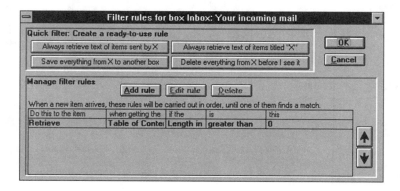

The Filter Rules dialog box—simpler than it looks.

First, look at the four large buttons in the **Quick filter** area. These buttons help you create four common types of filter. We'll come back to those in a little while.

Below them, in the **Manage filter rules** area, is a table with several headings—and, perhaps, a rule. To get an idea of what's going on, take a look at these headings and a sample rule.

Current filter rule:

Table 13.1   Filter Rule Example

Heading	Rule	Description
Do this to the item	Retrieve	This tells Internaut *what* you want to do with the message. In this case you want to *retrieve* (get) the message.
when getting the	Table of Contents	This states *when* Internaut should carry out the operation—in this case, when it gets the Table of Contents (that is, when it gets the list of messages from The Pipeline).

118

Heading	Rule	Description
if the	Length in chars	This tells Internaut what condition to look at. In this case, Internaut looks at the length of the message, in characters.
is	greater than	This tells Internaut what to look *for*; in this case it looks at the message length to see if it is greater than the value in the final box.
this	0	This is the value upon which the final decision is made. In this case, if the message length is over 0, Internaut carries out the procedure.

So what does the rule mean? "When you get a list of messages from Pipeline USA, look at the length of each message, and if the message is more than 0 characters long, retrieve the message."

What's 0 characters? All messages have more than 0 characters, don't they? Yes, and that's the point of this rule—to transfer your e-mail messages to the Inbox automatically. Without this rule, Internaut would grab the Table of Contents information—the From and Subject—but leave the messages where they are. This rule tells Internaut to go ahead and transfer both the Table of Contents information *and* the messages themselves.

The E-mail Default

You can use this rule to modify the e-mail default. When you first install Internaut, it's set up so that it *won't* automatically download your e-mail messages. Rather, it grabs the Table of Contents lines—then, if you want to read a message, you have to double-click on that message. This rule tells Internaut to download all your e-mail automatically.

You can see how easy it is to modify this rule to transfer small messages, but leave big ones behind—simply change the 0 value to some number—say, 2,000 characters—and change "greater than" to "less than." That way any messages with less than 2,000 characters are transferred; larger messages are not. (You'll see in a moment how to actually change something.)

What's the use of such a rule? It's especially handy when you work with mailing lists, or as a newsgroup rule. Rather than transfer (*pay* to transfer) every huge message that arrives in your Inbox or gets posted to your favorite newsgroups, just grab the Table of Contents lines for the big ones—and *then* decide if you want the whole message.

Other Rule Components

Before we go on, let's see the other rule components we could use. For each of the headers, there are several options you can choose; let's look at each column in turn.

The "Do this to the item..." Column

These are the operations that Internaut can carry out:

Append to (disk file)   Internaut places the message in a text file. You specify the filename in a text box that appears when you create the rule—but you won't see the filename after you save the rule. Internaut saves the message to the *end* of the file (so it can contain more than just one message). Note, however, that the message itself is then deleted, so you may not realize you've received one.

Delete   Internaut deletes the message.

Move to (another box)   Internaut moves the message to the box you specify when you create the message—again, the box name won't appear in the table.

Just skip remaining rules   Exempts the message from subsequent rules (this needs more explanation, and you'll get it later in this chapter).

Retrieve   Internaut automatically retrieves the message, not just the Table of Contents information.

The "when getting the..." Column

These are the situations in which the operation is carried out:

Full text   When Internaut retrieves the entire message—if a previous rule told it to do so, that is.

Table of Contents   When Internaut retrieves the Table of Contents information.

Either   When getting the Table of Contents information or the full text.

Note that not all three of these options are available all the time; it depends on what you chose in the **Do this to the item** box.

The "if the..." Column

This is the item that Internaut must look at:

From line   The From line, showing who the message came from.

Subject line   The Subject line, showing what the message is about.

Length in lines   The message length, in lines.

Length in characters   The message length, in characters.

Newsgroups   The name of the newsgroup (this rule would be used if messages are being transferred—by a filter rule—from a newsgroup to an archive box).

Date   The message date.

Cc line   The Cc line, to see who else the message has been sent to.

To line   The To line, to see who the message was sent to.

Full text   The actual message text—so you can search a message for a particular word.

Headers   The message header—the gobbledygook that appears at the top of the message, showing routing information.

The "Is" Column

This is the condition Internaut will look for:

contains   Tells Internaut to look to see whether the item in the **if the...** column contains the text in the **this** column.

is contained by   Internaut checks to see whether the item *contains* what is in the **this** column.

is   Internaut checks to see whether the item exactly matches the **this** box.

greater than   Internaut checks to see whether the item is larger than the value in the **this** column.

less than   Internaut checks to see whether the item is *less* than the one in the **this** column.

The "this" Column

This column contains something you type—a username, date, line length, character size, or whatever.

The Phantom Text Box

In a couple of cases you'll see another text box next to the first drop-down list box. This only appears if you select the **Move (another box)** or **Append to (disk file)** choices in the first drop-down. (You can double-click in this box to open the Select Folder or Save As dialog box, so you can pick a folder or file, instead of typing it.)

Now You Understand It All—Entering Rules

Now that you know what it's all about (don't worry, you'll see some more examples in a moment), let's look at how you actually enter the rule.

To create a rule, click on the **Add rule** button. The dialog box expands. At the bottom you'll now see four drop-down list boxes and a text box. Select the items from the lists in the first four columns, then type a value into the text box and click on **OK**.

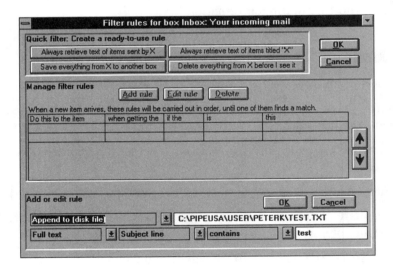

Create your own rules—it's really quite simple.

Editing the rule is much the same—click on the rule in the table, then click on the **Edit rule** button. The **Delete** button, you won't be surprised to find out, deletes the rule. What's less obvious, however, is that you can drag rules around in the table with the mouse. Or you can highlight the rule and move it around with the big arrow buttons on the right side of the box.

Quick-and-Easy Rule Creation

Here's the easiest way to create a rule—use one of the large buttons at the top. Rather than messing around in the rule table, you can click on a button; Internaut asks you for one piece of information and then creates the rule for you.

These are the rules you can create this way:

Always retrieve text of items sent by X   This tells Internaut to retrieve any messages from a particular person automatically. Internaut will ask you for the name of the person sending the message—type the e-mail address of that person. Here is the rule that Internaut creates:

Do this to the item...	Retrieve
when getting the...	Table of Contents
if the...	From line
is...	(contains)
this...	*name*

Always retrieve text of items titled X   Internaut will always grab a message if the Subject contains the text you specify. This is the rule it creates:

Do this to the item...	Retrieve
when getting the...	Table of Contents
if the...	Subject line
is...	(contains)
this...	*word*

Save everything from X to another box   Internaut automatically gets a message from a particular person, and transfers it to another mailbox. You'll be asked for the e-mail address of another user, and will then see the Select Folder dialog box so you can select a folder to place the messages into. This is the rule created:

Do this to the item...	Move to (another box)
when getting the...	Table of Contents
if the...	From line
is...	(contains)
this...	*name*

(You won't see the box name in the table, though.)

Delete everything from X before I see it   This one's nice. If you're getting hate e-mail, or just being bothered by some minor irritant you don't want to hear from, let Internaut automatically delete e-mail from the jerk before you even see it! You'll be asked for the e-mail address of the person. This is the rule you'll see:

Do this to the item...	Delete
when getting the...	Table of Contents
if the...	From line
is...	(contains)
this...	name

Skipping Rules

Earlier you saw that Internaut lets you create rules that skip other rules. The purpose? To exempt some messages from certain rules. Perhaps you want to delete very large messages. But there's one person that you sometimes get large messages from *that you want to get right away!* You can exempt that person from the rule. So you would set up two rules, like this:

Do this to the item...	Skip remaining rules
	Delete
when getting the...	Table of Contents
if the...	From line
	Length in lines
is...	greater than
this...	name
	1000

So, when Internaut looks at a message, first it looks at the name. If the name matches, it skips the next rule. If there's no match, Internaut looks at the next rule to see whether it matches—and if it does (if the message is over 1,000 lines long), it deletes the message.

Examples

Here are a few things you might want to do, and how to do them:

Stop all messages from transferring—you only want to see the Table of Contents line.

This is actually the default condition—if there are no rules in the rule table, Internaut transfers the Table of Contents line only.

124

Retrieve all messages.

To retrieve all your messages (not just the Table of Contents line) automatically, try this:

Do this to the item...	Retrieve
when getting the...	Table of Contents
if the...	Length in chars
is...	Greater than
this...	0

Stop all but long messages.

You want to transfer short messages (let's say 50 lines or less) automatically, but not long ones:

Do this to the item...	Retrieve
when getting the...	Table of Contents
if the...	Length in chars
is...	Less than
this...	50

Transfer messages from a mailing list into a particular box.

The easiest way to do this is to use the **Save everything from** X button, and enter the mailing list e-mail address. You'll end up with a rule like this:

Do this to the item...	Move to (another box)
when getting the...	Table of Contents
if the...	From line
is...	(contains)
this...	*listname*

Save messages about a particular subject in a text file.

Easy—try this:

Do this to the item...	Append to (disk file)
when getting the...	Table of Contents
if the...	Subject line
is...	(contains)
this...	*word*

125

Save Your Rules You haven't actually saved your filter rules until you click on the dialog box's **OK** button. *Don't* press Esc to close the box!

A text box will appear below the first drop-down list box—type a filename in there. Or double-click in the text box to open the Save As dialog box, so you can select a file. Remember, however, that the message is deleted from the Inbox or newsgroup as soon as it's saved in a text file.

The Least You Need to Know

➤ Filter rules tell Internaut to carry out an operation when grabbing the Table of Contents lines or the full message.

➤ You can make Internaut retrieve a message automatically, delete it, save it in a text file, or move it to another mail box.

➤ There are four large buttons that help you create the four most common types of filter rules.

➤ Use the **Add rule** button to create your own rules—select from the drop-down list boxes, and enter information into the text box.

➤ Make sure you use the **OK** button to save your filter rules.

Part 3
Traveling the World

E-mail, mailing lists, and newsgroups are all very well, but sometimes you have to go out and find what you need—you have to "travel" around the world, finding the information you're after. You can use utilities such as the Web browser (read a World Wide Web document), Archie (find a computer file you need), FTP (transfer the file back to your computer), Telnet (log onto someone else's computer to play a game or search for information), WAIS (search hundreds of databases), finger (view information on earthquakes, storms, sports, or coffee pots), and more. In Part 3, we'll look at these types of Internet tools. We'll also be looking at Internet Relay Chat, which lets you get into a little keyboard "conversation"—with one person or many.

NO, I DON'T MISS THE INTERNET!!

MAROONED WITH A COMPUTER GEEK

## Chapter 14

MALL BROWSER

WEB BROWSER

What's Worthwhile on the World Wide Web?

In This Chapter

➤ Why you *don't* need Mosaic

➤ Starting the Internaut Web browser

➤ Using links to get around

➤ The history list and bookmarks

➤ Caching and reloading

➤ Downloading files

➤ Adding viewers

The World Wide Web (also referred to as the *Web*, *WWW*, and *W3*) is probably the most exciting Internet tool—it's certainly getting plenty of attention in the press, and it's the "most wanted" tool among new users. They've heard about the Web, and they want to try it. Problem is, getting on the Web is difficult for many users, because installing the necessary software can be tricky. That's no problem for you, though, because Internaut has a built-in Web browser, and it's closely linked to the rest of the Internaut system, as you'll see.

What Is the Web?

The World Wide Web is a giant *hypertext* system. Have you ever used a Windows Help file? Or an encyclopedia or book on a CD? Such systems contain documents—topics or chapters or whatever you want to call them—that contain *links*. The most common form of link is a *text link*: click on a word and you jump to another document with related information. Links can also be other things—pictures, menu options, or buttons. Whatever their form, they get you from one document to another.

The Web is special, of course. When you click on a link in a Web document, you may end up reading a document from the other side of the world, or viewing a picture from the other side of the continent. And the Web is huge—thousands of sites, containing tens of thousands of documents and files.

The Web is often called *Hypermedia*, and in a sense it is. Web documents contain not only text, but graphics too, and sometimes even video. A Web document may contain links to any kind of computer file: graphics and video (in any format), sounds, .ZIP archived files—anything. And links may point to other Internet resources; the things we've just spoken about: FTP and gopher sites, WAIS servers, Archie, finger—almost anything that runs on the Internet can be accessed through the Web.

Browser A browser is a program that can view World Wide Web documents. It's sometimes also known as a Web *client*.

What's the relationship between the Web and the Internet?, I'm sometimes asked. The Internet is the hardware structure—the lines connecting computers all over the world. The Web is a software system that lies on top of this hardware. It comprises three main components— *documents* (the information you want to get to), *servers* (programs that administer the documents, and send them out when requested), and *browsers* (programs that users work with). A user uses a browser command to request a document from a server, and the server sends it out across the Internet, back to the browser.

You Don't Need Mosaic

First, let me clear up some confusion—you don't need Mosaic in order to use the World Wide Web. Mosaic is a well-known program from the National Center for Supercomputing Applications. It was the first good graphical browser (a browser that can display pictures), and for a while it didn't have much competition. For that reason the names *Mosaic* and *World Wide Web* have become almost synonymous in the mainstream press.

But now Mosaic is simply one of many Web browsers—there are a couple-dozen Windows and Macintosh browsers available, and Mosaic is by no means the best.

Starting Internaut's Browser

To cruise around on the World Wide Web, you need to run the Internaut browser. You can start this program in several ways:

> ➤ *Double-click* on an entry in the **Pathways into the Internet** that references a Web document.

> ➤ Highlight a URL in a newsgroup or e-mail message, and press **Ctrl+W**.

> ➤ Double-click on a Web entry in your Bookmarks dialog box.

> ➤ Select **Internet|World Wide Web** from the main Internaut window.

> ➤ Press **Ctrl+W** at the main Internaut window.

 ➤ Click on the Web button in the main Internaut window.

> **URL** A URL is a *Universal Resource Locator*, a Web "address." It usually begins with **http://**. For instance, **http:// www.stones.com/** is the URL for the Rolling Stones' Web page.

In the first three cases, the Web browser opens and your session begins—you'll see (after a while), the document you selected. In the last three cases, though, the Web window opens and displays the Pipeline USA Web page. If you want to go to a particular Web page, you can now click inside the large text box you see at the top of the window and type the URL of the Web page that you want to view.

Truckin' Around the Web

Now it's time to move around on the World Wide Web. Let's find a Web page to start with (later in this chapter I'll give you a few good starting points). Press **Ctrl+W**, type **http:// nearnet.gnn.com/wic/**, and press **Enter**. You'll soon see a Web page titled *The Whole Internet Catalog*.

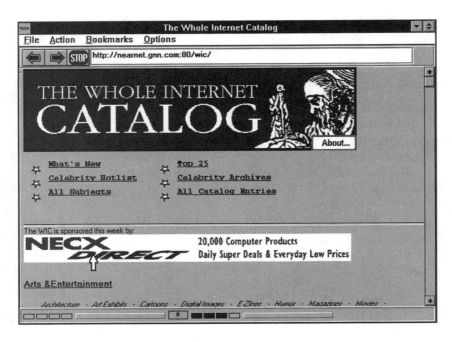

The browser—you're ready to surf the Web.

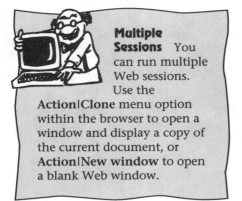

Multiple Sessions You can run multiple Web sessions. Use the **Action|Clone** menu option within the browser to open a window and display a copy of the current document, or **Action|New window** to open a blank Web window.

This is a pretty good place to start exploring the Web; it has "pointers" to all sorts of Web pages. Internaut uses a new browser technique: when it transfers a document, it starts displaying part of it before the entire document has been received. This speeds things up by letting you begin reading sooner. It means, however, that Internaut will keep adding things to the browser while you're reading—pictures will appear as you read. This sometimes makes the document jump around a little; use the scroll bar to get back to where you were reading.

Notice also the progress bar near the bottom of the window. While the browser is loading the document's text, the green progress bars gradually fill. Once the browser has all the text, it starts loading the graphics; the blue progress bars on the right side then start to fill. (The number in the box between the two progress bars shows how many pictures the Web document contains.)

Now, the simplest way to move around in the Web is to click on a link. The links are the underlined blue text, and some of the pictures. How can you be sure something's a link? Point at it with the mouse pointer; if the pointer changes shape, turning into a large arrow pointing up, you've found a link. Also, in the bottom left of the browser, you'll see the URL that the link points to.

Move around in this document using the scroll bar. You'll notice various categories: Arts & Entertainment, Business & Finance, Humanities, and more. Below each header are various subcategories. Below Health & Medicine, for instance, you'll find Alternative Medicine, Disability, Nutrition, Safe Sex, Veterinary Medicine, and others.

Click on the link and away you go, off to another document somewhere—perhaps on the same hard drive as the one you were just reading, perhaps on another drive on the same computer, perhaps on another computer in the same town, or maybe a computer on the other side of the world. This is international, transcontinental hypertext. Click on a link to see where it goes—follow links around for a while, then I'll show you how to get back.

More Navigation Tools

If all you had were document links, traveling in the Web would be nearly impossible. You could follow links in one direction, but would there be links back? So browsers have several other features that help you find your way around.

Using the History List

A *history list* is a list of the Web documents you've seen in the current session. Internaut places its history list in the **File** menu. Click on **File**, then look at the bottom of the menu—you'll see a list of document titles. Click on one to return directly to that document.

Going Back

Another handy item is the big left-pointing arrow in the toolbar. This takes you back to the document you just saw. Use it again, and it takes you to the one you saw before that, and so on. In effect, it takes you back through the history list one document at a time. The right-pointing arrow goes the other way, *forward* through the hotlist. The big red **Stop** button cancels a transfer; if you clicked on a link, then discovered that the browser is displaying a document that you really don't want, click on the Stop button. You may see an error message. Click on the OK button in the message box, then on the Back button on the browser's toolbar.

Using the Internaut Hotlist: Bookmarks

Most Web browsers let you save a list of Web sites in a *hotlist* of some kind. You can use the hotlist to go directly to a particular Web document. Unlike the history list, the hotlist contains only the documents you want it to contain, and it stores them between sessions. The hotlist is a sort of...well, *bookmark* system.

Surprise, surprise, Internaut's hotlist system *is* its bookmark system. If you find a document you are interested in returning to sometime, select **Bookmarks|Add current document to Bookmark list** or press **Ctrl+A**. That document will be added to the list. For information on how to use the list—how to change the title of the bookmark, delete bookmarks, move them around, and use them, see Chapter 7. (You can open the Bookmarks dialog box from the Web browser using the **Bookmark|Show Bookmarks** command, or by pressing **Ctrl+S**.)

Going Home?

What about going to your *home page*? The term *home page* has two meanings. You'll often hear the term used to refer to a particular Web site's main page. "Dude, check out the Rolling Stones' home page," you might hear someone say. I personally think this is incorrect (it's not a home page, dude, but nonetheless it's at http://www.stones.com/). It would be more correct to call it the Rolling Stones *Web site* or *page* or *document*.

Home page is actually a browser term. It's the page that appears when you first open your Web browser. The home page is a sort of starting point, and most browsers have a command or button that will take you directly back to the home page, wherever you happen to be on the Web. But Internaut's browser doesn't work like this. While most browsers always display the same home page each time you open the browser, in many cases, Internaut's browser opens the page you want to go directly to right now. You open a particular Web document—whether from the bookmarks system, or the gopher, or an e-mail message. Most browsers make you open the home page, *then* open the document you really want.

So there is no real home page command in Internaut. The closest thing to returning to the home page is returning to the first document you opened in this particular Web session. You can do that by selecting it from the history list, or by selecting it the way you did in the first place—by double-clicking on the gopher item you selected, or selecting the bookmark, or whatever.

Multi-Session Browsing

Internaut, true to form, lets you run multiple Web sessions. There are a number of ways to do this. First, you can simply open another Web session using one of the normal means: use the **Ctrl+W** command, double-click on a Web gopher entry, double-click on a Web bookmark entry, or use the **Internet|World Wide Web** command or button. Each time you carry out one of these operations, another Web window opens.

Once you're in the Web browser, however, there are a couple of ways to start new Web sessions:

Action|Clone window   Select this to open a new window, and display the same document. This is a good way to follow two links from a document at the same time. Open the clone, then click on one link, return to the original, and click on another.

Action|New window   Select this to open another blank window. Then enter the URL you want to go to.

You can also simply type a new URL into the text box at the top of the window and press Enter to replace the current document with a new one.

Speeding Things Up—Inline Images

When you first use the Web, you'll love all the pictures. What you won't love is the time it takes to transfer those pictures. After a while you'll realize you don't always need pictures—in most cases, you can get around without them. Why not just view them when you need them, not all the time?

You can speed up transmissions dramatically by turning the images off—use the **Options|Expand Inline Images** command. If there's a check mark next to this command, you'll see the inline images. If there's not, you won't. You can also set the default for this command—on or off—in the Options and Preferences dialog box (see Chapter 7).

Caching and Reloading

Two important features you need to know about are *caching* and *reloading*. First, what's the cache? It's where Internaut stores the information—the text and pictures—displayed in the Web documents you are viewing.

Say you're viewing document A, and click on a link to go to B. Document B is displayed, and A is placed into the cache. (The cache is on your hard disk, in the \PIPEUSA\TEMP directory.)

Grabbing Pictures You can save inline images you find in Web documents by grabbing them from your cache. Go to the \PIPEUSA\TEMP directory. You'll find that some of the .PP files (the larger files) are actually bitmaps—copy them into another directory with the .BMP extension.

What's the point? To spare the browser the hassle (and you the tedium) of repeatedly retrieving the same data from the Web. If you've been to a document once, there's a good chance you'll want to return. For instance, from A you go to B. You read B, then go back to A. Then you go to C, read that, return to A, go to D, read that, return, and so on.

If you had to retrieve a document each time you wanted to view it, you'd spend a lot of time waiting for a document you just had on your computer moments before! All that waiting also slows down the entire Internet, becoming a problem for other Internet users who aren't even on the Web. Web caches reduce these problems to some degree.

The Problem: the Cache. The Solution: Reload

The cache is a great system, speeding up your work and saving Internet resources for everyone. But it also creates problems. Consider this: each time you retrieve a document from the cache, you get the document that is stored on your computer, not the one from the Web. Aren't they the same thing? Not necessarily.

First, you may have turned off inline images. Now you decide you want to view inline images. You return to a document with inline images turned on—but still, the document has no images displayed. Why? Because the document's coming from the cache, not the Web—and the first time you transferred it, you didn't get the pictures. The solution is to use the **Action|Reload current document** command (**Ctrl+R**).

Here's another good reason to reload a document. Suppose you are viewing a document that is constantly updated—an example would be the Dow Jones Industrial Average document at this address:

http://www.secapl.com/secapl/quoteserver/djia.html

Each time you return to the document you see the cached document—with the old data. To get the update you must Reload.

Downloading Files

Some links on the Internet point to files that are intended to be transferred and placed on your hard disk—for instance, you can download programs from many Web pages.

When you click on a link to a file, the Find and Receive Files dialog box appears—the FTP box that we're going to look at in Chapter 15. Simply click on the **Go** button to see the Enter Filename box—click on **OK** and Internaut transfers the file to your download directory.

Customizing the Browser

The Web is based on HTML (HyperText Markup Language), a "coding" system in which text is marked with certain attributes, but each browser makes the decision on how to actually display the document. For instance, a line may be tagged as *Header 1*, but each Web browser can decide what *Header 1* actually looks like.

If you select **Options|Select base font** you'll see a typical Windows Font dialog box. Select a font. This is the normal text font—not the headers or anything else, but what's often known as *body text*. The next Web document you open will use the font you select for the body text.

But Internaut also changes the other types of text—the headers, lists, and so on—according to your choice. For example, increase the size of the base, and the headers will increase in size, too. You can also use the **Options|Change background color** command, which... well, you know.

Clear the Cache There's also an **Action|Clear cache** command. This tells Internaut not to use the cached documents, so when you use the history list or the Back arrow, you'll get a copy of the document from the Web, not the cache.

A Few More Handy Tools

Let's examine a few more handy tools to help you work on the Web.

File|Print Screen This command prints a picture of the information in the browser window. (It doesn't print the entire document.)

File|View source This won't be of use to most people, but it's very handy if you want to see how a Web document was created. You'll see a window containing the original HTML (HyperText Markup Language) file that is used to display the information in your Web browser. You'll see a text window—from here you can save or print the document, or even e-mail it to someone else.

File|Exit   This closes the Web window.

Action|Copy URL to Clipboard   This is a useful command. It copies the current document's URL to the Clipboard. You can then copy it into an e-mail message, for instance, so you can let friends know about neat Web sites you've found.

You can mail a URL directly from the Web browser. Simply select **Action|Mail URL to someone**, and Internaut will open the e-mail Compose window and place the URL into it.

Using Different File Types

You'll find all sorts of different file types while cruising around on the Web. Not just pictures, but sounds and even video. But how do you use them all? Some of the files are displayed automatically; *inline images*—pictures inside a Web document—should always display. But if you click on a link to a picture, that picture is transferred and then, in most cases, displayed in the Picture window. (We looked at this in Chapter 5.)

Many different graphics types can be viewed in here: TIFF, BMP, Targa, GIF, WPG, and more. Use the window's **File|Save as** command to see a list of file types that will work.

But you'll find various file types that won't work in Internaut itself. You'll have to find a program—a *viewer*—that can handle the file format. Then you need to enter information into the browser's viewers list.

First, where do you find these programs? You may have some on your system already—for instance Windows Paintbrush, Multimedia Player, and Sound Recorder come with Windows. You may have loaded others that can handle different file types, but if you need more, take a look out on the Net. Try these Web sites to find viewers:

http://www.ncsa.uiuc.edu/SDG/Software/WinMosaic/viewers.html

http://www.law.cornell.edu/cello/cellocfg.html

Try the following FTP sites for more viewers. (See Chapter 15 for more information on using FTP.)

ftp.cica.indiana.edu

ftp.law.cornell.edu in the **/pub/LII/Cello/** directory (Get the **viewers.zip** file, a bundle of viewers from this site.)

Here are a few freeware and shareware programs you might want to find:

GhostScript and Ghostview   Display PostScript files.

GV057, WinGIF, WinJPEG, and Lview   Programs that display .GIF and .JPEG graphics files, and others.

VIDVUE   For .MPG and .AVI animation files.

Mpegplay, MFW, and MPEGW   Play MPEG video files.

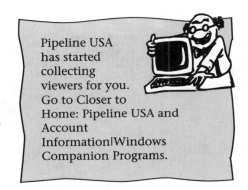

Pipeline USA has started collecting viewers for you. Go to Closer to Home: Pipeline USA and Account Information|Windows Companion Programs.

PC Speaker Driver   A Microsoft driver to play sounds through a computer's speaker.

WHAM   Plays .AU and .AIFF sound files.

Wplany   W-play-any, plays almost any kind of sound file.

Adobe Acrobat Reader   Views and prints .PDF files.

Let Internaut Know—Configuring Your Viewers

Once you find a viewer program you want to add to Internaut, the easiest thing to do is wait until you need it. That is, when you click on a link that transfers a file requiring a viewer, Internaut will help you set up the viewer "on the fly." Here's how it works.

Let's say you just clicked on a link at the Rolling Stones web site (http://www.stones.com/) and a .AU or .WAV sound file is being transferred. It may take a while—those sound files can be very large. While it's being transferred, you'll see a box with a large progress bar. Once it's all transferred, though, you'll see the **What should I do with the document?** dialog box. Internaut tells you that you haven't configured a viewer for the file type. Click on the Add Viewer button and you'll see the **Specify a viewer** dialog box, shown in the following figure.

The **Document type** and **Document extension** will already be filled in for you. Just click in the **Select Viewer** text box and press **Enter**. The **Select a player** dialog box (a typical Windows File Open dialog box) will appear. Find the name of the program you want to use for this viewer. For instance, the WPLANY.EXE program can play .AU and .WAV files. When you've found the program click on it and then click on the **OK** button.

Back in the **Specify a viewer** dialog box, click on the **Update** button and then **OK**. The file you transferred will start playing. When it's finished you'll see the **Save Document to File** dialog box. This lets you save the file on your hard disk, so you can play it again later. Find the directory you want to save the file in and click on **OK** (or click on **Cancel** if you don't want to save it).

What happens the next time that Internaut's browser transfers one of these files? Because you've already configured the viewer, the file will play as soon as transferred.

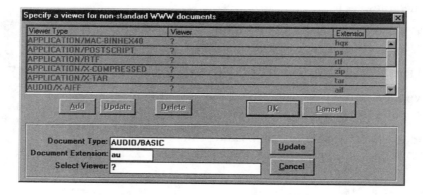

Adding a viewer to your browser.

Finding What You Need

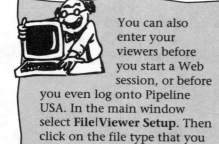

You can also enter your viewers before you start a Web session, or before you even log onto Pipeline USA. In the main window select **File|Viewer Setup**. Then click on the file type that you want to modify and click on the **Update** button.

The Web is a huge place, containing hundreds of thousands of places. How do you find your way around? Visit a few of the Web sites that contain directories or searchable databases. Try these:

➤ **The World Wide Web Initiative** From the W3 Organization, the people planning the future of the Web.

http://info.cern.ch/hypertext/WWW/ TheProject.html

➤ **The Mosaic Communications Internet Directory** A "directory of directories," leading you to other useful listings.

http://home.mcom.com/home/internet-directory.html

140

➤ **Yahoo** A really neat directory that lets you select a category and view a list of related Web sites, or search the entire database.

http://akebono.stanford.edu/yahoo/

➤ **The World Wide Web Worm (WWWW)** A system that digs around on the Web looking for documents. It follows links through the Web and builds an index of Titles and URLs.

http://www.cs.colorado.edu/home/mcbryan/WWWW.html

➤ **Web Crawler** This system crawls around on the Web, creating an index.

http://www.biotech.washington.edu/WebCrawler/Home.html

➤ **The WebCrawler Top 25** A document that lists the 25 most-referenced documents on the Web.

http://www.biotech.washington.edu/WebCrawler/Top25.html

➤ **Best of the Web '94** A list of the "best" Web documents, chosen in an online contest and announced at the International W3 Conference in Geneva.

http://wings.buffalo.edu/contest/

➤ **The Web of Wonder** Another simple directory—select the category, select the subcategory, select the Web document.

http://www.digimark.net/wow/index.html

➤ **NCSA's What's New on the Web** A list of new Web pages. You can view the current month's crop of new stuff, or go back and view previous months.

http://www.ncsa.uiuc.edu/SDG/Software/Mosaic/Docs/whats-new.html

➤ **NCSA's Starting Points** This site is handy for newcomers wanting to get an overview of what's on the Web.

http://www.ncsa.uiuc.edu/SDG/Software/Mosaic/StartingPoints/
NetworkStartingPoints.html

➤ **The WWW Virtual Library** This is at CERN, the home of the Web. Select a category and you'll be shown a list of related Web sites.

http://info.cern.ch/hypertext/DataSources/bySubject/Overview.html

➤ **The CUI W3 Catalog** This directory (the Centre Universitaire d'Informatique W3 Catalog in Geneva) lists over 10,000 Web pages. You type the word you are looking for, and the catalog looks for matches.

http://cui_www.unige.ch/w3catalog

141

➤ **W3 Servers—By Area**   Select the continent, country, and state to see a list or sensitive map showing servers in that area.

http://info.cern.ch/hypertext/DataSources/WWW/Servers.html

➤ **Web Exhibits**   Links to dozens of Web exhibits, from art to the Dead Sea Scrolls.

http://155.187.10.12/fun/exhibits.html

➤ **US Government Web**   A Web site that lets you search for U.S. Government Web documents, such as White House press releases, the National Trade Data Bank, the President's speeches (audio files), and more.

http://sunsite.unc.edu/govdocs.html

➤ **URouLette**   Take a magical mystery tour, courtesy of the **URouLette** site. Click on the roulette wheel, and off you go, who knows where!

http://kuhttp.cc.ukans.edu/cwis/organizations/kucia/uroulette/uroulette.html

➤ **Yahoo's Random Link**   **Yahoo** also has a similar feature, called Random Link.

http://akebono.stanford.edu/~jerry/bin/myimagemap/hothead/Art?31,9

The Least You Need to Know

➤ To start the Web browser, highlight a URL (Universal Resource Locator—a Web address) in the e-mail window and press **Ctrl+W**; or *double-click* on a Web entry in the gopher (the Pathways); or select **Internet|World Wide Web**; or click on the Web button.

➤ Click on links to travel to other documents—the mouse pointer turns into a thick vertical arrow when over a link.

➤ Use the left-arrow button to see the last document. Use the history list at the bottom of the **File** menu to go back further.

➤ The Bookmarks menu lets you add documents to the bookmark list, and go to a Web bookmark.

➤ Use **Options|Expand Inline Images** to turn pictures on and off (it's much faster without them).

➤ If you need to add "viewers" (for video, sound, PostScript, and so on), select **Action|Update viewer list**.

Finding Computer Files— Archie and FTP

There are literally millions of useful computer files waiting for you in cyberspace. There are documents (books, speeches, term papers), sounds (music, sound effects, speech), computer programs (everything you can imagine), and pictures (photographs, sketches, computer creations). There's quite a range of things—much of it shareware, but most of it free. How do you get to all these goodies? Well, you use a system called FTP—File Transfer Protocol.

On a clunky old UNIX Internet connection, FTP is horrible. You have to understand loads of cryptic commands, everything's typed—no pictures, no clicking on files—and you have to find things in huge lists that fly by on your screen too fast to read (unless you know the secret command, that is). It's like trying to find a friend's house for the first time, in thick fog.

Internaut's a *lot* easier than all this. As usual, it provides a variety of ways to start FTP; when you do, it's much easier to work with.

So who's Archie? Well, Archie's another Internet program. FTP helps you transfer files across the Internet. Archie helps you find the files, first. The two programs are integrated in Internaut—use Archie to find a file, then FTP to transfer it.

Archie

Nope, Archie's not an acronym, unlike Veronica and Jughead (see Chapter 6). Take the word *archive* (as in file archive), remove the *v*, and what have you got? *Archie!*

Starting Archie and FTP

Internaut provides several ways to start FTP—though only one to start Archie. You'll find FTP icons in the Pathways. Double-click on one and you'll see a dialog box asking you for a filename. There will already be a filename displayed, but you can change it if you wish. There's also a **Display as picture?** check box. If the file you are downloading is a picture, you can click on this to tell Internaut to download it and then display it in the Picture window (see Chapter 5).

The Enter File Name dialog box.

144

Here's another way to open FTP, though you'll see a different dialog box. If you click on a link in the Web browser to a file that Internaut doesn't recognize (see Chapter 14), the Find and Receive Files dialog box opens. The fields are already filled in—all you have to do is click on the **Go** button.

You can also use the **Internet|Get files ("FTP" and "Archie")** command (or press **Ctrl+A**). This opens the same dialog box, but this time you'll have to enter all the information yourself.

Finding WinZip—with Archie

Let's take a look at how this all works. Why not go looking for WinZip? This is a great Windows program that makes working with PKZIP easier. PKZIP is a program you *must* have. It helps you extract files from .ZIP archive files. Most DOS and Windows software you find will be in compressed .ZIP files, and PKZIP will extract them for you. (In some cases you'll find files in a *self-extracting archive file*; these are .EXE files that, when run, automatically extract files from within themselves— PKZIP can create these special files.)

Let's look for WinZip. Start at the main Internaut window by selecting the **Internet|Get files ("FTP" and "Archie")** command. The Find and Receive Files dialog box opens. We don't know which archive (FTP site) to look in, so place the cursor in the **I have a filename in mind** text box and type the word **winzip**. (Luckily we know the name of the file we are looking for—*winzip*. How? I'm telling you, that's how!)

Then click on the **Advanced** button, to open up the dialog box; these are Archie options. (You'll notice that if there's nothing in the **I have a filename in mind** text box, you won't be able to use the Advanced button.)

> **Anonymous FTP** You'll often hear the term *anonymous FTP*. This is the only form of FTP you can do from Internaut. It refers to public FTP sites, in which users must login using the *anonymous* login name (Internaut does this for you). Some sites are *not* anonymous—that is, they require that you get a login name and password from the site "owner."

The Find and Receive Files dialog box, after clicking on Advanced.

Now, we need to make a few decisions about the type of search we want to do:

Partial match is all right   Select this check box if you entered just part of the filename. For instance, do we know for sure that the file we are looking for is *WINZIP*? Maybe it's *WINZIP55*, to show its version number. Also, we didn't add .EXE to the end of the file. So click on this to tell Internaut that the actual filename might contain more characters.

Case does not matter   This should be checked almost always. On Windows computers *case*—whether names are spelled uppercase or lowercase—doesn't matter. But on the Internet most host computers are UNIX computers—and in UNIX, case matters. *WINZIP* is not the same as *winzip*. But you want to find the file—whether it's *winzip*, *WINZIP*, or *Winzip*. So make sure this is checked.

Maximum hits   This tells Internaut how many matches to find. If you set it to 10, it will only show the first 10 winzips it finds—it might find it on 30 different computers, but you'll only see the first 10. Type another number to increase the number.

Available host machines   These are *archie servers*, host computers that have an index of files at thousands of FTP sites. You can select one if you want, or simply let Internaut select one for you (it will probably use the server at archie.ans.net).

146

Now, when you're ready, click on the **GO** button; Internaut begins the search. The dialog box remains open, though, so you can do another search. If you want to close the dialog box, click on the **Done** button.

Here's a problem with Archie—he's overworked. Many of these Archie sites won't work for you most of the time, because they are simply too busy. So you may have to search, then change the Archie and try again, then try again, and so on. Also, you'll find that it can take some time to get a response from Archie—Internaut displays a message saying *The information is on its way*, and that message may stay there for a minute, or ten minutes, or more.

Internaut only provides a small list of Archie servers, by the way. You can add more, though. In the PIPELINE\SYSTEM\DATA directory you'll find a file called ARCHIE.SRC. Open this in Windows Notepad, then add new servers (in the same format as the originals, of course) to the bottom of the list. I added these:

archie.hensa.ac.uk (United Kingdom)

archie.edvz.uni-linz.ac.at (Austria)

archie.univie.ac.at (Austria)

archie.th-darmstadt.de (Germany)

archie.rediris.es (Spain)

archie.luth.se (Sweden)

archie.switch.ch (Switzerland)

archie.unipi.it (Italy)

archie.uqam.ca (Canada)

archie.ac.il (Israel)

archie.wide.ad.jp (Japan)

archie.kr (Korea)

archie.sogang.ac.kr (Korea)

archie.ncu.edu.tw (Taiwan)

archie.unl.edu (USA (NE))

archie.internic.net (USA (NJ))

When Archie finds something, you'll see a window listing the items—these may be directory names or actual files. You will now use this window like a normal gopher window—see Chapter 5. Double-click on a folder icon to view a directory, or double-click on a file to transfer the file. (Find the WinZip file with the latest version number—get WINZIP55.ZIP or WINZIP55.EXE, not WINZIP50.EXE. The .EXE files are self-extracting archives, remember—double-click on it once you've transferred it to open it.)

Not an FTP Site

You're not at an FTP site after using Archie. Each entry in the list may be on a totally different computer—a different continent even. This is a list of files and directories that match, on different computers.

Going to an FTP Site

Here's another way to get files—go to an FTP site and look around. In Chapter 15, I mentioned a couple of sites that contained *viewers*, programs that display (or play) files of many types—still pictures, video, sounds, PostScript files, Acrobat document files, and more. Let's take a look in one of these sites.

Start at the main Internaut window again, by selecting the **Internet|Get files ("FTP" and "Archie")** command. The Find and Receive Files dialog box opens. This time type the FTP site into the **I have a particular archive in mind** text box. Let's try entering this:

ftp.law.cornell.edu

If you know the actual directory name you want to search, enter that in the **I have a filename in mind** text box, ending it with a /. We do know the directory in this case, so enter this:

/pub/LII/Cello/

(If you *don't* know which directory to search, make sure the **I have a filename in mind** check box is cleared.) Now, click on **Go**; assuming you entered all the information correctly, Internaut will log into the FTP site, and display a window showing you the contents of the directory.

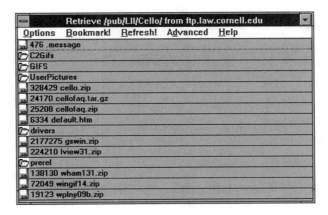

Finding viewers at the ftp.law.cornell.edu FTP site.

Now that you are at an FTP site, you can move around in the normal way, double-clicking on folders to open another window—showing the contents of that directory—or on a file to transfer the file.

You're also able to read text files in the FTP directories, a great advantage over UNIX FTP (you can do it in UNIX, but it's a hassle). These files often tell you what the directory contains; they're a sort of index. Double-click to open one and read it.

If You've Got More Information

If you know the FTP site, the directory, and even the filename, you can go one step further (but you'd better get the filename exactly right!). For instance, let's say you know for sure there's a file called wham131.zip in the **ftp.law.cornell.edu** FTP site's **/pub/LII/ Cello/** directory (there is as I write this; there may not be by the time you read this).

Enter the FTP and directory information as you did before. But this time, add **wham131.zip** to the end of the directory, like this:

/pub/LII/Cello/wham131.zip

This time, you'll notice, there's no / at the end. That would indicate that I'd entered a directory name, not a file.

Now, when you click on **GO**, you'll see the Enter File Name box. I can change the name of the file, if I wish, then click on **OK**; Internaut begins transferring the file to my download directory.

Download Directory
Where's the download directory? Wherever you specified in the Options and Preferences dialog box. See Chapter 7.

The Least You Need to Know

➤ Internaut's FTP tools open automatically when you double-click on a gopher file entry, or click on a Web browser's link to a file.

➤ Use the **Internet|Get files ("FTP" and "Archie")** command (or press **Ctrl+A**) to open the dialog box used for Archie and FTP.

➤ To search for a file, use the **I have a filename in mind** text box only, then click on the **Advanced** button.

➤ You can set the **Maximum hits** to a higher number. Use 20 or 30.

➤ You'll usually want **Partial match is all right**. Turn this off only if you know for sure you've got the exact filename.

➤ To go to an FTP site, enter the host name into the **I have a particular archive in mind** text box. If you know the directory, place that in the **I have a filename in mind** text box. End the directory name with /.

➤ To grab a file directly, enter the FTP site and directory, then add the filename to the end of the directory name.

## Chapter 16

Logging On All Over the World

In This Chapter

➤ Starting a Telnet session

➤ Using Hytelnet to find Telnet sites

➤ Games—MUDs and more

➤ Working in the Telnet window

There are millions of computers connected to the Internet, and some of them have some pretty interesting stuff. Wouldn't it be neat to "reach out" and get onto those computers, take a look at games, databases, and programs on computers on the other side of the world?

Well, you can. At least you can get onto computers whose administrators *want* you to get on, and a surprisingly high number do. A special program called *Telnet* lets you turn your computer into a Telnet *client* to access data and programs on a Telnet *server* somewhere.

Now, a word of warning. Internaut's Telnet program is not as pretty as you may have come to expect. That's not really Internaut's fault. Once you connect to another computer, you're playing by that computer's rules; there's not much Internaut can do to make working with Telnet easy, because it has no way of knowing what sort of system you are connecting to. You'll see what I mean in a moment.

Starting Telnet

You're getting used to this "starting whatever" bit by now. You know, of course, that if you double-click on a Telnet icon in the pathways, a Telnet session starts. And if you click on a link to a Telnet session in the Web browser, the Telnet window opens.

You can also start a session with the **Internet|Connect to another system (Telnet)** command, or by pressing **Ctrl+L**.

For instance, let's say you want to go to the Newton BBS, a telnet system for people who study and teach math and science. Press **Ctrl+L** at the main Internaut window. The familiar Enter Your Choice dialog box pops up. Type **newton.dep.anl.gov**; this is the Telnet "address." If you know you're going to want to come back here, click on the **Add this command to my Bookmarks menu** check box, then click on **OK**.

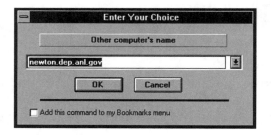

Enter the Telnet host name and click on OK.

The Telnet window will appear; from here on, what you see varies depending on what computer you are connecting to. In some cases, you'll have to log in—in this case all you need do is type **bbs** and press **Enter** at the Login prompt. From then on, follow instructions. The computer you're connected to should tell you what to do.

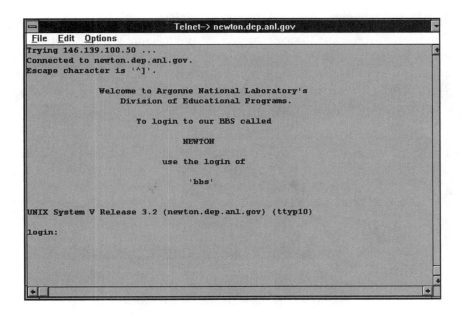

The Telnet window—not pretty, but it works.

Great—But Where Do I Go?

There are many interesting Telnet resources on the Internet, but how do you know where they are? Probably the best way is by using HYTELNET. There used to be a wonderful system at **access.usak.ca**, but last time I looked, it had shut down—it was just too popular. There's another one at **info.umd.edu** (or go through the Pathways to **Internet Guides and Tools|Finding things: many search types|Library and other resources (Hytelnet)**. And you can get Hytelnet information other ways:

World Wide Web   Use your Web browser to go to **http://www.usask.ca/cgi-bin/ hytelnet** (see Chapter 14 for information about entering this URL).

Gopher   Use the **Internet|Gopher anywhere** command to gopher to **liberty.uc.wlu.edu**. Then go into the **Explore Internet Resources** directory, then select **Telnet Login to Sites (Hytelnet)**.

FTP   FTP to **ftp.usask.ca** and look in the **/pub/hytelnet** directory to find software you can load onto your PC.

When using these Hytelnet systems, you can look through various menus of options, then, when you come to one that interests you, actually start a Telnet session with that system. For instance, if you gopher to the Hytelnet site, you'll see several options. You can enter a word you want the system to search for, view a list of library catalogs, view new Hytelnet listings, or view entries categorized in a variety of ways—Electronic Books, Databases and Bibliographies, and so on.

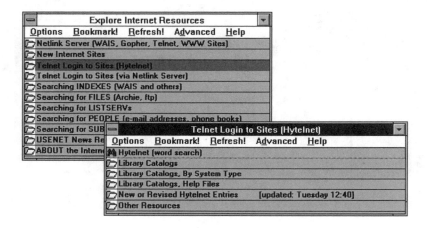

The gopher Hytelnet site.

Sometimes you'll find text files associated with the Telnet entry. Read these; often they tell you the login and password you have to use.

Gopher Telnet?

Sometimes you'll find Telnet connections to gopher systems. Hmm. Not very handy for you (though some Internet users without gopher access might find it useful). Log out, then connect using the **Internet|Gopher anywhere** command.

For instance, while digging around in the Gopher Hytelnet system, I found an entry for the Space Shuttle Earth Observations Projects Photographic Database (**sseop.jsc.nasa.gov**). This database contains information about tens of thousands of photographs taken by the Mercury, Gemini, Apollo, Skylab, Apollo-Soyuz Test Project, and Shuttle Missions, and how to get hold of them. I was able to connect directly from the gopher system. Spend some time in this system and you'll be amazed what you run into.

What Telnet's Really For—Games

Another popular use for Telnet is playing games. You may have seen the term MUD flung around here and there—it means Multiple User Dimensions (or Multiple User Dungeons, or Multiple User Dialogue, take your pick). It's a type of game in which lots of people get together in a *virtual* environment and play a game.

Well, it's not really so virtual—it's more imaginary. These are text-based games, so you'll have to add the real "color" to the environment in your own mind.

Still, MUDs use up many thousands of user and network hours—there's a whole MUD subculture, with different types of MUDs and devotees. Weird stuff like: Tiny and Teeny MUDs (these are 'social' in orientation—players chat, meet friends, make jokes, discuss stuff), LP MUDs, including Diku and AberMUD (Role-playing adventure games—players run around killing monsters, solving puzzles, becoming wizards), chat MUDs or talkers (perhaps a subset of the Tiney and Teeny MUDS—I dunno, can't figure it out—as there's a lot of chatting going on), and many others, such as MOOs, UnterMUDs, TinyMUCKs, cools, TinyMUSEs, tiny muck spinoff chat MUDs, oxmuds, and who knows what else.

A good way to get started with these is by using the **Internet|Gopher anywhere** command to gopher to **actlab.rtf.utexas.edu**. This site has links to many MUDs. You might also try gophering to **gopher.micro.umn.edu**. Then select **Fun & Games|Games|MUDs**, and **Links to MUDS via Telnet**. You'll be able to select from almost 200 MUDs, ranging from ACME Mud to Zork. Or try a gopher site in Germany, at **solaris.rz.tu-clausthal.de**. Select **Student-Gopher|Liste der MUD-SERVER**. (Most MUDs around the world are played in English. There are a few here in German.)

I'm no great MUD fan, but you may like it. Play around in some of these for a while to get the feel of it (it will take a few hours just to get an idea of how to play properly).

While You're There—the Telnet Window

The Telnet window provides menu options that let you configure the system and carry out a few useful functions:

File|Change window title   This changes the text in the title bar. Maybe not so useful!

File|Exit   This closes the Telnet window once you're finished with it. Before you use this command, you should log out from the computer you are connected to, using the correct menu option, or something like **bye** or **exit** or **Ctrl+d**.

Edit|Copy   You can use the mouse to highlight text on the screen, then copy it to the Windows Clipboard. Then you can paste it into a word processor or e-mail window, or whatever.

Edit|Paste   This lets you paste text from the Clipboard to the Telnet session. Handy sometimes when you have to input information.

Options|Change Background Color   This changes the color of the screen—select a color from the list that appears.

Options|Change Foreground Color   This is the text color.

Options|Change Font   Use this command to select the type and size of the font you want to see in the Telnet window.

Options|Emulation   There are different types of terminal connections to Telnet sites. The most common is probably VT100—a DEC computer terminal. The Telnet window can *emulate* these different terminal types; that is, it can *act like* the correct terminal. If you select VT100, you'll usually be okay, but if you connect to a system that *doesn't* work with VT100, you can select from VT52, ANSI, or TTY.

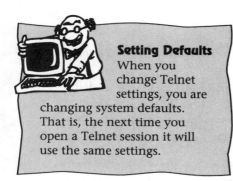

Setting Defaults
When you change Telnet settings, you are changing system defaults. That is, the next time you open a Telnet session it will use the same settings.

Options|Scrollback (session log)   When you are working in the Telnet window, Internaut saves some of the text that you've seen—you can use the scroll bar to *scrollback*, up the window, to see what you did earlier. This menu lets you select **Scrollback buffer size** to tell Internaut how many lines it should save. And you can select **Save Scrollback to file** to provide a filename—Internaut will save what is currently in the scrollback area (the text out of view, above the text you can see) into a text file.

The Least You Need to Know

➤ Open a Telnet session by double-clicking on a Telnet entry in the gopher, clicking on a Telnet link in the Web browser, or by selecting **Internet|Connect to another system (Telnet)**.

➤ You can find a list of Telnet sites by gophering to **liberty.uc.wlu.edu**, and changing to the **Explore Internet Resources** menu, followed by the **Telnet Login to Sites (Hytelnet)** menu.

➤ You can find a list on the Web, too. Go to **http://www.usask.ca/cgi-bin/hytelnet**.

➤ For a list of MUDs and other games, gopher to **gopher.micro.umn.edu**, then select **Fun & Games|Games|MUDs**, and **Links to MUDS via Telnet**. Or try **solaris.rz.tu-clausthal.de** and select **Student-Gopher,** then **Liste der MUD-SERVER.**

➤ Use the Options menu to set colors and terminal emulation. (Usually VT100 should work fine.)

➤ **Options|Scrollback (session log)** lets you define how much information is saved so you can scroll back to view it, and save the scrolled back information to a text file.

## Chapter 17

Internet Private Detective— Tracking Down Users

Once you're up and running on the Internet, you'll want to contact other Internet users—friends, family, colleagues, people you've heard about and want to discuss something with. What if you don't have their e-mail addresses? What if you're not exactly sure where they are? Easy, just look them up in the Internet directory, right? Well, no. There is no Internet directory. This isn't CompuServe or America Online—they can maintain directories fairly easily; anyone they bill is a subscriber, after all.

The Internet's more complicated. There are thousands of different ways to get onto the Internet, all over the world—large corporations, small service providers, government departments, local bulletin board services, FreeNets, and so on. There are ways to track down users, and we'll look at a few in this chapter. But you may have to try several before you find the person you want to reach…and you may *never* find them.

E-mail Problems

First, though, let's look at one reason why you might want to track down an e-mail address: because your e-mail has been returned. You might be sure you've entered the correct address, but just when you think you're finished with an e-mail message, it comes back. You look in your inbox and find a message from <**MAILER-DAEMON @pipeline.com**, with the Subject **Returned mail: User unknown**.

You view the message, and find a horrendous mess of header lines with comments like **Host unknown (Authoritative answer from nameserver)**. (Remember, to view the header, you have to make sure **Options|Show full headers** is turned on.)

Your message has gone out onto the Internet, and nobody knows what to do with it. There may even be occasions when you *have* used a *correct* address—and still the Internet can't deliver it.

There are four reasons why your mail may not be delivered, with some variations:

➤ **Host unknown.** The Internet can't find the host you put in the e-mail address. Remember that e-mail addresses are in the format *user@host*. For some reason the Internet can't get through to the host.

➤ **User unknown.** The Internet can get your mail to the host—but the host claims it doesn't recognize the user, so sends it back.

➤ **Service unavailable.** The address is fine—but the host computer is not accepting mail at the moment. The mail system may be shut down due to hardware or virus problems; or maybe the message was sent at a time when the host simply doesn't accept mail—some systems refuse mail during certain times.

➤ **Can't send.** The host is known, and the host might be inclined to accept the mail, but the Internet can't get through to the host—maybe the network is damaged, maybe the host itself is out of commission due to hardware problems, or maybe it's changed its mail configuration, and the information hasn't been passed on to the right people.

Look carefully at your returned mail—you'll see one of these reasons, or something like it, somewhere in the header (usually, but not always, on the Subject line near the top).

Who Didn't Get It?

If you sent a message to several people, check carefully to see who didn't receive it. For instance, you may have used a mailing list or sent "carbon copies" to other people. The message could have been delivered to all but one person, so look at the header carefully to see who didn't get it. You'll look in the **Transcript of session follows** section. For instance:

```
--Transcript of session follows--
550 apotpeel.com (TCP)... 550 Host unknown
554 <joebloe@apotpeel.com>... 550 Host unknown (Authoritative answer from
name server)
550 ourplace.org (TCP)... 550 Host unknown
554 <fred@ourplace.org>... 550 Host unknown (Authoritative
answer from name server)
```

You can see that this message was sent back from two addresses because, in both cases, the Internet couldn't find the host. The message may have gone through to the other recipients.

So What's the Problem?

Why is your mail coming back? There are a variety of reasons:

➤ **You typed the address incorrectly**. You could have made a mistake while typing the address. Take a look at the address in the returned message to confirm that you got it right. See if you typed a zero instead of an **o**, or a one instead of an **l**, for instance, or simply missed a letter from the address.

➤ **A mailer incorrectly modified the domain**. A mail server somewhere saw the address, misunderstood it, and added its own domain. If the returned message shows the address you entered, and some higher-level domain stuff that you *didn't* put in the address, this is what's happened.

➤ **You've been given an incomplete address**. Some people assume too much when they hand out their addresses—they give you part of it, assuming you know where they are and understand how to complete the highest level of their domain. Also, in many cases a complete address is only needed if the mail is *leaving* your host and going elsewhere. If your host sees an incomplete address, without the higher-level domain, it may assume the address is to someone in the same domain. So if someone is used to giving their address to other local users, they may forget about the higher-level-domain part of the address.

➤ **You used a correct address, but the mailer doesn't know it's correct**. There's not much you can do about this except complain. Some mail servers may not have the latest domain information.

161

➤ **The mail program that sent you a message didn't fill out the From name correctly.** Not all mail programs fill out the From name correctly. They abbreviate it, stripping out the higher levels of the domain name. The From name is for reference only—it's not used to actually deliver the mail. However, if you use the **Addresses|Add sender to address book** command to "grab" the From name, or if you reply directly to this message, you're going to have an incorrectly addressed message. If you know the From address is wrong, you should correct it before you use it, of course. Check the body of the message to see if the sender included a "signature" with his or her full mail address.

Who Ya Gonna Call?

So, what to do about these problems? If it's a system problem, with a mail server not recognizing a message or modifying it incorrectly, there's not much you can do except talk to your service provider. If you can see what the problem is, then correct the address, strip out all the header garbage you don't need, and resend the message. You could use your mail program's Forward command to do all this.

Bookmarks
Why not create a bookmark folder called Search, then add these various tools as bookmarks? See Chapter 7.

You might also have to try contacting the person some other way (the telephone, remember?) and get the correct address. Sometimes, though, you may be stuck with a bad address and no other way to find the person. That's when things might get tough. So here we are, needing an e-mail address and not knowing where to look. Well, maybe we do know where to look. The following sections explain a few things you can try.

Talk to the Postmaster

If you're sure a user is at a particular host, you could ask the host's postmaster. Write an e-mail message to **postmaster@*hostname***. Provide as much information about the person as you can, and maybe the postmaster will be able to send you the correct mail address.

Ask Someone Else

Think about who else the person might know—other people the person has worked with or communicated with. Then e-mail them and ask if they know where he or she is. (Is that one too obvious?)

finger Them

UNIX has a command called **finger** that lets you ask a host about someone (if you know his or her name). To get to the finger command, follow the pathways to **Internet Guides and Tools|Finger**. You'll see a dialog box into which you can type the finger information. You can enter the information in this format: ***name@host***.

Let's say I know there's someone called Peter Kent at a host called usa.net. But I don't know his username at that host. So I want to ask that host for the username.

I could enter **kent@usa.net**, or **peter@usa.net**. I'll get a list of names back—a list of all the Kents with accounts, and a list of all names that include Peter. I can look through the list, and, I hope, find the person I'm looking for.

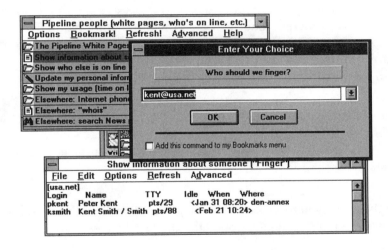

Bingo! finger found two matches.

The finger command doesn't always work. Some hosts simply don't allow it—many Internet system administrators believe that it provides too much information, and poses a security risk. And in some cases, systems only let you finger someone if you know their username—they won't let you get a list of all the people named Kent, for instance. It all depends how the system administrator set it up.

Search for Newsgroup Users

In Chapter 11 you learned about newsgroups, "areas" in which public messages can be posted and read, on thousands of different subjects. There's a system that lets you search a database of people who have posted messages to newsgroups. It's not perfect—it doesn't include *everyone* who's posted—but it's worth a try.

Follow the Pathways to **The Internet: Guides and Tools|Finding things: many search types|Find people: search News postings**. A dialog box appears, into which you'll enter the name you are looking for. When you click on **OK**, the search begins. With a little luck you'll eventually get a list of names, amongst which will be the one you want.

There are a few problems with this method. You have to know an exact match from the From: line. You can't use a partial name, for instance, and you can enter only one name, with no spaces. And many people use aliases (in the sense of "fake names") when they post messages in the newsgroups.

Using KIS

You can use the Knowbot Information Service (KIS) to search a variety of directories at once. A *knowbot* is a program that can search the Internet for requested information. Follow the pathways to **The Internet: Guides and Tools|Finding things: many search types|Knowbot information service|Knowbot information service**. You'll Telnet (see Chapter 16) into the information service, and see something like this:

```
Trying 134.82.20.31 ...
Connected to regulus.cs.bucknell.edu.
Escape character is '^]'.
Knowbot Information Service (V1.0). Copyright CNRI 1990. All Rights Reserved.
Try ? or man for help.
>
```

Type the name you're looking for, and press **Enter**. If you're lucky, you'll eventually find the person you're looking for—something like this:

```
Name:           Kent Bergen
Phone:          +46 8 777 77 77
E-Mail:         kent@bergsoft.se
Address:        Riksradio
                Z-101115 10 Stockholm
                Sweden
Source:         RIPE
Last Updated:   05/20/92
```

If you're *really* lucky, you may get the e-mail address and a phone number; in some cases, though, you may not get the e-mail address, but still get the phone number. Did this system find me? Nope.

If you'd like to use KIS, spend a few moments reading the user manual—type **help** or **?** and press **Enter** at the > prompt. Then, after reading what you are shown, type **man** and press **Enter** to see some more. You can, for instance, specify an organization name, use a first and last name, and so on. To search the RIPE directory for the name **Kent** you would do this:

>**service ripe**

>**kent**

If you wanted to search MCI Mail, the first line of this would be **service mcimail**. (To see a list of the service names, type **services** and press **Enter**.)

As with some of the other directory services, KIS also lets you search using e-mail. Send a message to **netaddress@nri.reston.va.us** or **netaddress@sol>bucknell>edu**, and type the command in the body of the message (the same command you'd use if you were using KIS directly). You might want to try this rather than sit and wait for KIS to do its work.

> **It's Slow!**
> KIS has a lot to do when it carries out a search. It has no directories of its own, so it is sending requests out across the Internet for information. That means a search can be very slow. Be patient. I've also found that even when you're not searching (just entering commands or reading the online manual), it can be pretty sluggish.

Using Netfind

There's another system you might want to try: Netfind. Follow the pathways to **The Internet: Guides and Tools|Finding things: many search types|Find people: Internet phone books|Internet-wide e-mail address searches**. You'll find a series of Netfind servers. When you double-click on one of these you'll go to a Telnet session.

If this is all running correctly (and last time I looked, it wasn't), you'll be logged into a Netfind session. You'll find yourself viewing something like this:

```
Top level choices:
        1. Help
        2. Search
        3. Seed database lookup
        4. Options
        5. Quit (exit server)
>
```

You'll probably want to read the Help file to get a good idea of the different forms of search that you can use. Then, when you are ready to search, you can use option 2. If you'd like to search a list of host names, you can use option 3. (You enter a portion of the hostname, and Netfind searches for matches within various different hostnames.) Let's search for my name. I'll enter my last name, and the city in which I live:

```
> 2
Enter person and keys (blank to exit) > kent lakewood
Please select at most 3 of the following domains to search:
     0. amc.org (amc cancer research center, lakewood, colorado)
     1. burner.com (the back burner bbs, lakewood, colorado)
     2. cobe.com (cobe laboratories, inc, lakewood, colorado)
     3. ecog.edu (eastern co-operative oncology group, lakewood, colorado)
     4. lakewood.com (lakewood microsystems, lakewood, new jersey)
```

Unfortunately, it didn't find me. Notice that it searched for Lakewood in both the hostname and the host description. The next step is to pick up to three of these to search again. You'll be prompted to enter up to three numbers. If those domains have "nameservers," you'll be able to see more information—perhaps information on the person you are looking for. But there's a good chance that the one you select *won't* have more information.

This search didn't do me any good. I searched for various things, such as my domain (I searched for **lab** and **press** to try to track down **lab-press.com**, to no avail). Still, maybe you'll have better luck.

Using Whois

Here's another form of directory search, the Whois search. To search Whois, follow the pathways to: **The Internet: Guides and Tools|Finding things: many search types|WHOIS Searches**. Type a name. The name you enter can be a first name, last name, or login name. If you are not sure of the complete name, end it with a period: **whois ken.** will find Ken, Kent, Kentworth, and so on. And you don't need to worry about capitalization. You can only use one name at a time—you can't enter a person's first and last names.

Click on **OK**, and a search begins. Within a minute or two, with luck, you'll get your results. Using this method, I was able to find myself—plus two other people with the same name!

If you enter an unusual name, the system might find just one person, so it will display all the information it has about that person. More likely, though, it'll find several or many, so it will display a one-line entry for each. You'll see listings like this:

```
Bloe, Joe (BJ31)    joebloe@apotpeel.com        (303) 555-1869
```

The **BJ31** in parentheses is the person's *handle*. You can now use the whois command with the handle to get full information—precede the handle with !. For instance, searching the same server for **!bj31**, in this case, will find the person's full information, which may include his e-mail address, USPO address, telephone number, and the date the record was last updated.

Here's a way to do a more focused search with Whois. Follow the Pathways to **The Internet: Guides and Tools|Finding things: many search types|Find people: Internet phone books|WHOIS Searches**. You'll find dozens of different servers—use the **NextPage** command to move through the list.

Double-click on one of the entries, then type a name and press **Enter**. You'll see another gopher menu, with two options: **Mull over what might happen** and **Commit to search**. The first of these is simply a text file that tells you that the search might not work. Read it once, but ignore it in subsequent searches. Double-click on the **Commit to search** to begin the search. You'll probably find that most of these searches won't work—you won't get through, or it won't find what you want. Try a few anyway—you might find what you are looking for.

Again, you can search for someone's handle—but remember, you must precede the handle with !. (In some cases that won't work—you may have to precede it with \! or not precede it with anything.)

Most of these servers search only a limited area. That's great if you know the person you are looking for is at the Dana-Farber Cancer Institute or Gettysburg College, of course, but not so handy if you are trying to search the world at large. If you don't know where the person is, you're better off with the first Whois method.

Using X.500

Some time ago a group called the International Standards Organization came up with a standard called *X.500*, a method for letting computers search directories. It uses a "hierarchical" system to track down system users—the computer (or you) will provide the country, organization, and person; X.500 follows this path down the directory to the exact person in whom you are interested.

If you want to search this system, follow the pathways to **The Internet: Guides and Tools|Finding things: many search types|Find people: Internet phone books|X.500 Gateway**. You can then select a country or region, followed by an organization—a university or company, for instance. It can take a little time, but you can end up with a list of departments or people at that organization—double-click on a person to find information about him, or on a department to go a level lower—or a search option.

Also, you'll find a Search option that lets you search the entire country for a particular Internet user, rather than going through organizations.

More Directories

Follow this path to find even more directories: **The Internet: Guides and Tools|Finding things: many search types|Find people: Internet phone books|Phone books at other institutions**. This leads to all sorts of other listings. Select a continent, for instance, to see a list of various phone books—select Africa, and you'll see Rhodes University and the University of Natal (Africa's not too well-represented on the Internet right now). Try Asia Pacific, and you'll get institutions in Japan, Australia, New Zealand, and India.

You can also select the **Search All the Directory Servers** option, and Internaut will search all at once for you (*perhaps*—it wasn't working when I tried).

Coming Soon: Finding Pipeliners

Pipeline USA is adding a few tools to help you track down just Pipeline USA subscribers. These tools are not in the pathways yet, but will probably be under **Closer to Home: Pipeline USA and Account Information**. Once you get here you'll find two useful tools:

➤ **The Pipeline White Pages**   Helps you find other users.

➤ **Show who else is on line now**   Tells you who's online right now.

The Directory

If you want to get into the Pipeline USA directory, select **The Pipeline White Pages**. You'll be in another gopher menu, with various options: you can select **Directory of Pipeline Subscribers (long)**. This is a giant directory of names—all of them—in alphabetical order by username. It's very big, and very slow (there are over 10,000 subscribers right now, probably many more by the time you read this).

You can pick a particular alphabetical grouping, though: **A–C, D–F**, and so on. These will take you to a list of names, sorted by last name. If you find the person you are interested in, double-click on the entry to see more information.

Easier still is the **Search directory for someone**. Enter the name you're looking for—it must be a last name or a username, not a first name—and click on **OK**. If anyone with that name is a subscriber, and has chosen to be listed in the directory, you'll see their information. Remember, though, that not everyone is in the directory. If you double-click on the **Add or update my listing** entry you'll see the Update My User

Information dialog box. There's a **List me in the Pipeline directory** check box that lets users remove themselves from the directory.

Who's Online?

Is he? (Okay, no Abbott and Costello routine.) When you use the **Show who else is online now** tool, you'll get a list of all the people who are currently connected to the Pipeline. You can double-click on a name to see information about that person. Why do you care? Well, maybe you want to talk with a particular person, and want to see if he's connected right now. *Talk*, by the way, in Internetspeak, means *type*—see Chapter 18 for information about using the Talk program. Or maybe you are just cruising around, looking for *anybody* to talk to. (As one Internet user told me, "I virtually live on the Internet, and spend most of my mornings talking with people.")

How successful are all these search techniques? The Pipeline directories are good—as long as someone *wants* to be included, you'll be able to find them. As for the other methods? They're so-so. With some, for instance, I can find myself; with others, I can't. Use a few of them—you may be lucky.

The Least You Need to Know

➤ Check the header of the returned message carefully—it should tell you why it was returned, and who didn't receive it.

➤ The easiest way to get someone's e-mail address is to talk to them. Pick up the phone. Or get it from someone who knows them.

➤ If you know the person is at the host that returned the e-mail, send e-mail to the postmaster and ask about them. Address the message to **postmaster@*hostname***.

➤ The **finger** command's a useful way to track someone if you know the hostname.

➤ If you know the user uses the newsgroups, search the newsgroup-user database.

➤ Whois is a good system that lets you search the Internet in general or a specific institution.

➤ X.500 lets you see lists of users in institutions all over the world.

➤ You will soon be able to view or search the Pipeline directory, or see a list of who's online.

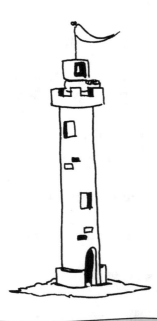

## Chapter 18

Tower of Babble—Internet Relay Chat and Talk

In This Chapter

➤ Entering Internet Relay Chat

➤ Finding channels

➤ Joining and creating channels

➤ Finding more information

➤ Starting a Talk session

➤ Working in the Talk window

➤ Connecting to non-Pipeline users

Do you have too many hours in your day? You do everything you need to do by lunch, and you're at loose ends for the rest of the day? Have you exhausted all the time-wasting techniques you learned in college, and are looking for something new?

Welcome to chatting on the Internet, a step above newsgroups and e-mail. Yeah, those techniques are okay—you send a trivial message and get trivia in return. But what if you want instant trash—instant feedback on your analysis of yesterday's *Melrose Place* or *90210*, for instance? You need to be able to actually talk to someone.

Well, okay, not actually *talk*, but *type* to someone, at least. You type; they type back. You type again; they type back again. It's *almost* like having phone a conversation, only without the throat clearing, intonation, chuckles, laughter, and background noise. It's slower, too. Well, I suppose it's a poor imitation of conversation, really, but hey, some people like it. Here's why:

➤ It's a lot cheaper to talk to Moscow over the Internet than by phone.

➤ You may be able to contact someone for whom you have an Internet address but no phone number.

➤ Your boss thinks you are typing a memo—you're actually discussing last night's blind date with your buddy.

➤ The office administrator tracks personal phone calls, but wouldn't know what the Internet was if he fell into it.

➤ Large groups of people can put together a conference call online more easily and cheaply than with Ma Bell.

➤ If you're contacting someone in another country, it may be easier to read broken English than listen to it.

What Ya Want to Do?

There are two basic forms of these "conversation" programs on the Internet. There's the type that allows two people to "talk" to each other. Even if you've never been on the Internet, you may have used programs that can do this—many networks have programs that let two network users swap "real-time" messages.

The other form of conversation program is more like a conference call—groups of people chatting together in a giant "conference room." Well, maybe it's more like a party, really, with people in lots of rooms. People walk in and out of the rooms, spending a little time here, a lot of time there—depending on how much time they have to waste, or how important the conversation is.

Internet Relay Chat—an Electronic Cocktail Party

Okay, time to spread our wings and get out and about on the Internet and meet some people. And what better way than to use Internet Relay Chat?

This is a giant system for chatting to different groups of people. You don't select a single person and talk only to that person; instead, you join a group discussion with whoever happens to be there.

Chat sessions are almost like parties or meetings, when groups of people get together and talk amongst themselves, in small groups. If you spend a couple of hours in a chat session, you might spend 20 minutes in one group, 10 in another, 15 talking privately with someone, and so on....

There are a number of chat systems on the Internet, but the best-known system is Internet Relay Chat. It connects dozens of countries, tens of thousands of users. When you log on and pick a channel, you could be talking to users in Istanbul, Adelaide, or London. If you're lucky, you may even speak the same language.

Starting IRC

Start IRC by selecting **Internet|Chat (IRC)**. The Internet Relay Chat System Console opens, and you are connected to an IRC *server*. (You'll probably want to maximize the window and the document window inside it—double-click on the title bars.)

The first thing you may want to do is change your "nickname." That's the name that will identify you in the session—by default it's set to your username, but you can change it if you wish. Select **Commands|Change Nickname**, enter a new one, and click on **OK**.

Finding a Channel

The next thing to figure out is how to find a chat channel—the server has dozens, maybe hundreds, active at any time. Select **Commands|List channels**. In the dialog box that appears, type a search word and click on **OK**. This searches for the word in the channel names, and in the topics—a sort of subject assigned to many channels. You'll see a list appear in the main "work" area of the window. For instance, if you enter the word **sport**, you may find SportCar, passport, sports, and so on. This list will probably appear quite slowly, though, so be patient. You'll know you're at the end when you see the line **Total *nn* channels**.

If you're looking for proof that the Internet is a corrupting influence—that it attracts people who just want to goof off in the most offensive way possible, that it's a huge drain on the economy as thousands of highly paid programmers and engineers draw salaries while wasting time online—what better place to look than IRC? You'll find an immense amount of rubbish in IRC. That's not to say you won't find intellectual stimulation or spend a worthwhile hour or two communicating with colleagues about your profession, but you are more likely to talk about aliens, sex, *Star Wars*, or studpoker.

Anyway, where was I? Ah, yes—look at the list, and you'll find three pieces of information: the channel name (#SportCar, for instance), the number of people in the group, and, perhaps, the channel topic.

Let's Get Moving

So, you found a channel you want to join. Simply select **Commands|Join a channel**. Type the channel name, without the preceding # sign (channels are listed with a # prefix). For instance, type **cricket**, not #cricket.

Then click on **OK**, and you'll join the channel. A new window will open, in which you'll see the text of the conversation.

You can then just sit back and observe what's going on—though each time someone joins a channel everyone sees a message giving that person's nickname.

If you want to get involved, type your message into the **Type your message here:** text box. Take a look at the **Send to:** drop-down list box. This shows you where the message is going (which channel). If you have several open channels, you can select one from the **Sent to:** drop-down list box, or simply click on its window.

After typing a comment, press **Enter**—nobody sees what you type until you press **Enter** (unlike the Talk program, in which every character you type is transmitted). To type a command rather than a comment—we'll look at a few more in a moment—start the line with a forward slash (/).

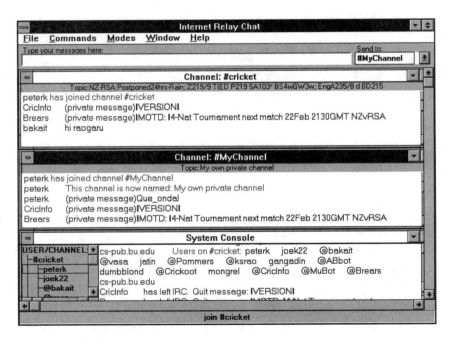

Two channels (#cricket and #MyChannel); some people really like this stuff.

174

You can actually join several channels, if you wish; each will have its own window, so take a look at the **Window** menu to figure out how to manage them all—use the **Cascade** and **Tile** options to move them all to where you can get to them, and the numbers at the bottom of the menu to go directly to a particular window. Of course this is for "power" IRC users; how anybody without multiple personalities is able to handle half a dozen or more IRC channels is beyond me!

In the channel window you'll see the session, in all its glory. Stuff like this:

```
Kimba      y=e**ipi
poem       Peppr wwould never ignore You
zooey      *sigh*
sierra     imm: just finished dinner.. chilling our for 0.5 hours
Bob34      howya doin Sarge?
Peppr      Right Herb...I wouldnt'
zooey      *sigh*
Albundy    proposes to ZOOEY. Hehehhe
immigrant  zooey- im in the middle of franney and zooey  right now :)
Sulu has joined channel #30plus
Kimba      Peppr's ignoring folk
Kimba      Peppr's ignofing flok
mfp        Kimba is back....yahoo
mfp        Sulululululululululululul
Albundy    Sulu!!!!!!!!!! my love.
Prism      bye, all.
me3 has joined channel #30plus
zooey      immigrant  aren't you that yallie i was talking to
me3        hi all
poem       zooey is 29
Kimba      SULU!!!!
Peppr      ARGH!!!!
mickk has left channel #30plus
Kimba      mfp!!!!!!!!!!!!!!!!!!
Salgak     hmm.... zooey is definitiely 29 and sighs a lot
Sulu       Albundy!!
Sarge      Bob: Still having terminal probs... Sent a msg to help!
```

Well, okay, maybe your channel's more intellectual. Anyway, notice that it gets a little confusing as to who's talking to whom (or why, for that matter). People often type a name followed by a colon to indicate that their comments are directed at that person. For instance, the user named Sarge on the last line is talking to Bob. Bob was talking to Sarge about 23 lines earlier.

Do It Yourself

If you can't find a channel that quite suits you, create your own. Simply select the **Command|Join a channel** command, and type a channel name that doesn't exist (don't leave any spaces in the name). Now you can change the channel topic—the text that appears next to the name in a listing—by selecting **Commands|Topic**.

Of course a channel's no good if you're in it alone—so invite someone in! Select **Commands|Invite**, enter the IRC user's nickname, enter a comment **??what is this??**, and click on **OK**.

The user will see some kind of invitation. If they're another Internaut user, they'll see the same dialog box that appears when they're invited to a Talk session. To join, all they have to do is click on **Accept**, and a channel window opens. And if they overstay their welcome? Well, get rid of them with the **Commands|Kick** command.

Who's Who

Take a look at the System Console window—that's the window that appeared before you opened a channel, the one with the gray bar down the left side. Now, in that bar you'll see channel names and nicknames. Each channel you've joined is listed. Double-click on a channel to open or close its *nickname list*—the list of all the people in the channel.

Want to find out who a person is? Double-click on his name in this gray area, and you'll see information about him in the System Console, including, probably, the person's real name and host.

Had Enough Yet?

It's hard to imagine, but eventually you'll get tired of this stuff. To get out of the current channel, use the **Commands|Leave channel ("part")** command. To log out of IRC altogether, use the **File|Exit all** command. If you are the last one out of the channel, you'll automatically turn out the lights—the channel will expire. Die. End. Wither away.

I'd Like a Word with You!

Now let's take a look at the simple **Talk** program that Internaut will soon provide. First, find someone to talk to. If you know another Pipeline user, arrange for that person to be online at the same time as you. If you don't have friends (or at least friends who want to talk to you), go and find someone who's online (see Chapter 17).

Now, when you are ready, select **Services|Talk (chat with someone)**. Type the username of the person you want to talk to—you're connecting to someone else at The Pipeline, so you won't need the @hostname stuff (I'll talk about connecting to non-Pipeline people in a moment). If you've talked with the person before, the name is probably in the drop-down list box.

Click on **OK**, and Internaut sends an "invitation" to the other person. That person will see a couple of buttons in a dialog box—he can click on **Accept** or **Refuse**. If he refuses, you'll see a message back from him saying, "Sorry, I can't talk right now." This is a polite message sent by Internaut, actually; it might not reflect the recipient's sentiment. Anyway, you can type a one-line response to this message, which goes back to the other person—who can also type a response. You can continue like this for some time if you want, though you may as well go into a Talk session proper. This little to and fro will end as soon as one of you clicks on the message box's **OK** button without entering a one-line response.

Let's say, though, that one user clicks on the **Accept** button. You'll find yourself in a two-panel window. Type in the top panel, and the other user will see your typing in their Talk window. When they type, you'll see the text in your bottom panel.

Every character you type is transmitted to the other person—including typos. They'll even see you correct your typos!

No Friends? No Colleagues?
If absolutely nobody wants anything to do with you, you can always have a talk session with yourself (or your multiple personalities). Simply enter your own username to connect to yourself. You'll end up with two Talk windows on your screen.

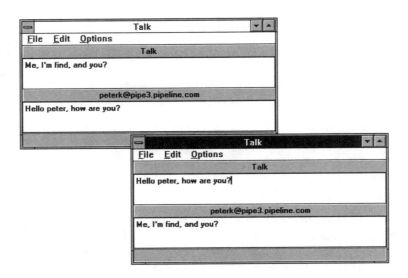

Talk—it's clunky, but some people like it.

Background Noise

That's pretty much all there is to talking. But you do have a few menu options to help you along. The two most important are on the **File** menu. You can use **Add someone** to add another person to the session—you'll have to enter their username—a sort of conference call. Or use **Close** to get out of the session.

Then there are the normal **Edit** menu options. Cut, Copy, and Paste let you remove or copy text to the Clipboard, then place it in another application. Or try this trick to make someone think you can type really fast: copy pre-typed text from your word processor and paste it into the Talk window.

You can also **Clear screens**, to remove all the junk and start fresh—though it only clears *your* Talk window, not the other person's. And you can quickly place those silly little smiley things by selecting **Edit|:-) smile**, **Edit|:-(frown** or **Edit|;-) wink**. (Turn the book so the left margin of the page is up, the right margin is down, and you'll see that these are little faces: ;-) is a wink, for instance.)

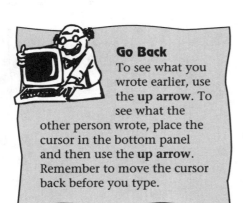

Go Back
To see what you wrote earlier, use the **up arrow**. To see what the other person wrote, place the cursor in the bottom panel and then use the **up arrow**. Remember to move the cursor back before you type.

You can also use **Options|Colors** and **Options|Font** to change the background and text colors, and choose a different font. (For a real challenge, select the WingDings font.)

Talking with the Rest of the World

Well, that was easy enough. Talking with other Pipeline users is a breeze, once you get them to answer. But what about talking with someone in London, Paris, or Moscow?

Well, there are a few pitfalls. Other Internet talk programs work differently :-(. The other person may be running a program that turns off the "paging" that informs a user of an incoming talk request. Some programs turn off these messages to make sure that they don't mess up the program's output.

Also, make sure the other talk programs you are using are compatible—not all are. And you need to be calling a system that allows talk sessions. Not all do.

Even if the other person has a compatible program, and it's ready to accept calls, you may still have problems. First, that person may be working on his workstation but you get a message saying he's not logged in. For instance, when I tried connecting to a friend in Dallas who was working on a Sun system, that was the case—it wasn't until he opened a "console window" that we were able to connect. This won't happen if the other person is using a dial-in line. If your friend has an Internet connection through a network at a company, school, or government department, however, he may have to ask the network administrator how to make sure he's fully logged on to the Internet.

Another problem is the address—you may find that the e-mail address won't work. If not, you may have to ask your service provider or system administrator which address to use. For instance, here's a sample address: **robinhood@sherwood.com**. Now, this address may work fine for e-mail, but when you try to use Talk you may find it's no good. Again, you may get a message saying that robinhood is not logged on, even though he is. Try to find out if there's more to his address. If he's using a workstation connected to a network, you may find his address is actually **robinhood@techws07.sherwood.com**. He doesn't need the techws07 for his e-mail, but he needs it for a Talk connection.

Finally, what if you can connect to another person, but he can't call you? Well, tell him to try the address in the page message, the message he sees when Talk "rings" him. The actual address shown may be different from your e-mail address.

The Least You Need to Know

➤ Select **Internet|Chat (IRC)** to enter the IRC server.

➤ IRC is like a cocktail party with lots of party rooms called *channels*.

➤ Using IRC takes time and effort to learn the commands and get used to what's going on. Practice, practice, practice.

➤ Talk lets you type messages to other users—they see what you type, you see what they type.

➤ Click on the **Talk** button and enter a username.

➤ Connecting to a user outside the Pipeline system is more complicated, thanks to system incompatibilities and address problems—but it *can* be done.

➤ Talk lets you add people to a session to create a "conference call."

## Chapter 19

Finger, WAIS, and News— More Internet Tools

In This Chapter

➤ Using **finger** to find information, from earthquakes to sports

➤ WAIS search for any subject

➤ Searching for news

There are a few more tools to look at before we leave Internaut; tools like finger, WAIS, and News. These are handy little programs that most Internet users never find, but which you may want to experiment with nonetheless.

finger for Information

In Chapter 17, I explained how you can use the **finger** program to find information about a user, a way to track down Internet e-mail addresses in some cases.

Well, here's another use: to receive information. If someone creates a .plan file and places it in their home directory, when someone fingers them, the information in the plan is sent with the information about the user. This provides a simple way to distribute information, from earthquake reports (**quake@seismo.unr.edu**), to news from NASA (**nasanews@space.mit.edu**).

You'll find finger in the Internet Guides and Tools pathway menu. Type the finger address into the dialog box (for instance, try **nasanews@space.mit.edu**), and click on **OK**.

In a short while you'll see information in a text window. You can scroll through this to read the entire message, save it to a file, copy it to the Clipboard, e-mail it to someone else, use the **Edit|Find** command to search it, and so on.

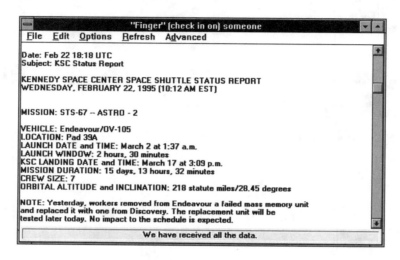

The latest from NASA (nasanews@space.mit.edu).

Here are a few more finger sites you may want to try out:

Auroral Activity (you know, the world's aura, the aurora)

aurora@xi.uleth.ca

Computer Science FTP Sites

msc@eembox.ncku.edu.tw

Earthquakes, North America

quake@gldfs.cr.usgs.gov

Earthquakes, world-wide

quake@gldfs.cr.usgs.gov

Florida, N.W. beaches, weather forecast

beach@awis.auburn.edu

182

Newsgroup periodic postings, list of

nichol@stavanger.spg.slb.com

NFL info

nfl@spam.wicat.com

nflines@spam.wicat.com

NASA news

nasanews@space.mit.edu

Soda machine

drink@csh.rit.edu

Solar activity

solar@xi.uleth.ca

daily@xi.uleth.ca

Today in History

copi@oddjob.uchicago.edu

Typhoons & hurricanes

forecast@typhoon.atmos.colostate.edu

WAIS

WAIS, the *Wide Area Information Server*, is a system that helps you search for documents containing information you want. WAIS provides a list of subjects, lets you select one, then provides a list of databases. You can select the ones you want to search, enter the word you want to search for, and WAIS carries out the search for you.

Follow the pathways to **The Internet: Guides and Tools|Finding things: many search types|WAIS: many databases (by subject)**. Double-click on a subject that interests you. If another subject listing—it will show subcategories—appears, select another. You'll come to a list of databases. Double-click on the one you want to search, and enter your search term. Click on **OK** and hang around a while. Eventually, with luck, you'll get some kind of response: it could be anything from a blank text window to a large document. You can save this information in a text file, copy it to the Clipboard, and so on— all the usual stuff.

You can only search one database at a time, so you may have to try several to find what you're looking for. Also, you'll sometimes get a message back telling you that the database couldn't find what you're looking for, but providing the database catalog (a list of the articles in the database). This may or may not be useful; it may simply be a list of article authors, for instance, without article titles.

Search for News

Pipeline USA will soon be adding another service—a way to get your daily news fix.

Select **Internet|Search current news** from the main Internaut window. You'll see a little dialog box into which you can type a word related to the subject you are interested in. You can also adjust the **Maximum hits to show**—if 5 appears in this incrementer, Internaut will stop looking when it gets to five items. (Increase the number by clicking on the little up triangle.) This is actually a form of WAIS search. Click on **OK** and in a few moments you'll see a list of matches. Double-click on each one to read it.

The Least You Need to Know

➤ The **finger** command is a great way to grab information on many subjects—see the sample list.

➤ Use WAIS (**The Internet: Guides and Tools|Finding things: many search types|WAIS: many databases**) to search databases for documents.

➤ Select **Internet|Search current news** to search for a news subject. (This is a feature Pipeline USA is adding soon.)

Part 4
Beyond Internaut

It's true. Internaut isn't the only *way to connect a Windows machine to the Internet, even if it is one of the easiest. There are suites of Internet programs, shareware and freeware, and online services such as America Online and CompuServe. Each has its advantages... and disadvantages.*

In Part 4, we'll take a quick look at the different ways to set up an Internet connection, and at a range of different programs you'll find to help you work out on the Internet. You may never want to leave Internaut, but if you do, these chapters will give you an idea of what's available.

Also, check out the "Speak Like a Geek" glossary; it'll help you understand many of the buzzwords and much of the jargon you'll hear out on the Net.

## Chapter 20

Making the Connection

In This Chapter

➤ The four types of Internet connections

➤ Using NetCruiser

➤ Using the online services

➤ Using Internet suites

➤ Shareware and freeware

➤ Windows (95/96?), OS/2, and the Macintosh

Installing and running the Internaut software is relatively easy—about the same as installing and running most Windows programs. That's not always the case with other Internet connections. In fact, when James Gleick and Uday Ivatury got together and decided to create Internaut, they wanted to make sure it was easy to install and run, because they knew how hard it was to get onto the Internet.

Internaut uses a special system called PinkSlip™ to communicate with the PSI and Pipeline USA host computers. This is an unusual system—only Internaut uses it. Out in the rest of the Internet world, things are different. So let's take a quick look at how most people connect to the Internet.

The Types of Connections

There are four basic ways to connect to the Internet, plus a few variations:

➤ Permanent connections

➤ Dial-in direct connections

➤ Dial-in terminal connections

➤ Mail connections

You won't necessarily hear these terms elsewhere. In fact, different service providers use slightly different terms, and the terminology can get blurred. It gets confusing, but the following definitions should clarify things a little.

Permanent Connections

A *permanent connection* means your computer is connected directly to a TCP/IP network that is part of the Internet. Actually, the usual case is that your organization has a large computer connected to the network, and you have a terminal connected to that computer. (You may even have a computer that is acting as a terminal—that is, all the work is done by the other computer, and your computer is simply passing text to and from your screen.) This sort of connection is often known as a *dedicated connection*, sometimes as a *permanent direct* connection.

TCP/IP

TCP/IP means Transmission Control Protocol/Internet Protocol. A *protocol* defines how computers should talk to each other. It's like a language—if a group of different people all agree to speak French (or English, or Spanish), they can all understand each other. Communication protocols provide a set of rules that define how different modems, computers, and programs can communicate.

Such connections are often used by large organizations—universities, groups of schools, and corporations, for instance. The service provider places a *router* at the organization's office and leases a telephone line that connects the router to the service provider's computer (known as a *host* computer). The details vary—the service provider might provide the router, or might tell the organization which router to buy—but once this is done, the organization can connect its computers and terminals to the router. Because they have a *leased line*, they are always connected to the Internet. There's no need to make a telephone call to reach the service provider's computer. Rather, the user will simply *log on* to the Internet from his terminal. Once on the Internet, he can transfer files between his organization's computer and other computers on the Internet.

This sort of service is very expensive; thousands of dollars to set up, and thousands of dollars to run.

Dial-in Direct Connections

A *dial-in direct connection* is often referred to as a *SLIP* (Serial Line Internet Protocol), *CSLIP* (Compressed SLIP), or *PPP* (Point-to-Point Protocol) connection. These are also TCP/IP connections (like the permanent connection), but they are designed for use over telephone lines instead of a dedicated network. This type of service is the next best thing to the permanent connection. While a permanent connection is out of the price range of individuals (and most small companies), it can be quite cheap to get a SLIP account. Prices have dropped considerably in the last year—you can get a dial-in direct account for a $30 to $40 setup fee (sometimes no setup fee at all), and connect rates that are the same as for dial-in *terminal* accounts, which we'll look at in a moment.

This is a "dial-in" service; you need a modem in your computer, and you have to dial a telephone number given you by the service provider. Once you connect to the service provider's computer and logged on, other than speed, you can't tell any difference between a SLIP account and a dedicated account—you can transfer files to and from your computer exactly as if it were a host computer—in fact, it will be identified on the network as a host.

File Transfers

There is one important way you'll see the difference between dial-in direct and permanent connections: file transfers between your computer and others, as well as "telnet" sessions, will be much slower than between your service provider's computer and others on the Internet.

Also, depending on the software you are using, you may be able to run *multiple sessions* at the same time. That is, just like the service provider's computer permits dozens of people to work on the Internet at the same time, you'll be able to do several different things on the Internet at the same time, in different program windows—you'll be able to transfer files from computer A in one window, search a database on computer B in another window, and work in your own file directories in another window.

Don't confuse this service with a *dial-up* connection—that type of service also requires you to dial a telephone number, but the service it offers is slightly more limited than that of SLIP (as we'll see in a moment).

Dial-in Terminal Connections

With this type of connection you'll have to dial into the service provider's computer. It's confusing that this connection is often called a *dial-up connection,* because you have to dial a call before connecting to a SLIP account as well. (To differentiate, some service providers call this an *interactive* service, which seems only slightly less ambiguous, or a *shell* account.) I've called it *dial-in terminal connection* because you have to dial the call to your service provider—and once connected, your computer will act as a terminal.

This arrangement is unlike a permanent or dial-in direct connection; your computer won't appear as a host on the network—it'll simply be a terminal of the service provider's computer. All the programs you run will be running on the service provider's computer. That means you can transfer files across the Internet to and from your *service provider's* computer, not to and from yours. So you have to use a separate procedure to move files between your computer and that of the service provider—normally you'll use a transfer procedure such as Zmodem or xmodem.

In one way, the permanent connection and dial-in terminal connection are very similar—in both cases, your computer is nothing but a terminal of the host computer. (With a dial-in *direct* connection, your computer *becomes,* temporarily, a host computer.)

But there's an important difference. In the case of the dial-in terminal connection, you don't really *want* your data stored on the host computer, and have to mess around to get it back. In the case of a permanent connection, you either have your data stored on your organization's large computer (you are using a terminal, for instance, and you can probably print directly from the host computer) or you have the networking tools that let you transfer data readily between the host and the computer sitting on your desk.

Mail Connections

This form of account is *not* the preferred form! While millions of people are still working with this type of account, most new users prefer to get a dial-in direct account. A dial-in direct account lets you work with neat graphical programs; a dial-in terminal account, on the other hand, forces you to work with some clunky command-line system, perhaps augmented by a text menu of options. No pictures, no color, no sounds, no video. Working with a dial-in terminal account is like stepping back into the early 1980s.

There are several different mail connections to the Internet. In fact, you may already have one. If, for instance, you have a CompuServe or America Online account, you have an Internet mail connection. You can send mail to the Internet, and have friends and colleagues on the Internet send mail to you. On CompuServe you would simply precede the Internet mail address with INTERNET:.

But when people talk about having an Internet connection, it's not usually e-mail they're talking about—they want access to newsgroups, the World Wide Web, Telnet, WAIS, Gopher, and all the other wonderful tools. So we'll forget about e-mail connections.

So Where Does That Leave Us?

Now that you know the basic ways to connect to the Internet, here are two important things to remember:

1. If you want to run the fancy Windows Internet software, you need either a permanent connection or a dial-in direct connection. Otherwise you'll need to get a connection through one of the online services (a form of dial-in terminal connections). Forget other forms of dial-in terminal connections and e-mail connections.

2. Internaut provides a sort of hybrid system—a cross between a dial-in terminal connection and a dial-in direct connection. No, it doesn't use TCP/IP—it uses the special PinkSlip™ system—but it does provide many of the benefits. While your computer won't appear on the Internet as a host computer, you *will* have multitasking (you can run several programs at once) and you'll have easy-to-use Windows programs for getting around on the Internet.

If You Want to Try Something Else...

If you want to go beyond Internaut and Pipeline USA, you have two options. You can get a permanent connection—at work, for instance—from your Windows computer to the Internet. But most people don't have that option, as their company, school, or government department doesn't provide that sort of connection; and even if you have a permanent connection, it may not be from Windows. Your computer may be acting as a terminal of a UNIX computer with a permanent connection, without the network software needed to connect Windows.

So the other option is to get a dial-in direct connection. But here you will run into a problem: How do you hook your Windows computer up to a TCP/IP connection? There are a number of ways, but only a few of them are guaranteed to be easy.

NETCOM and NetCruiser

We'll start with an easy method: NetCruiser. This is a Windows program provided by NETCOM, a large service provider. The theory is the same as Internaut and Pipeline USA. You buy a NETCOM account, and they give you the software. You run the installation program, and connect to NETCOM. Installing and running the software is easy, because it's already set up with all the information it needs to connect to NETCOM—after all, that's the only service provider it will ever connect to. It's a very nice program, and, as we went to print, NETCOM announced that they'd improved it greatly.

Under the old NetCruiser system, all you could run were the NetCruiser tools—the Web browser that came with it, e-mail, newsgroups, Gopher, Telnet, FTP, and finger. But NETCOM have now made their TCP/IP stack "Winsock-compliant." That means you can run *any* Windows TCP/IP program once you install NetCruiser, not just the NetCruiser applications. You can go onto the Internet and download all sorts of shareware programs—Netscape, InternetWorks, Mosaic, WS_FTP, WinWAIS, and lots more. If the program's written to run on a Winsock TCP/IP connection, then you can run it through your NetCruiser connection.

The Online Services

Here's another easy way to connect to the Internet—through an online service—CompuServe, GEnie, America Online, and PRODIGY. All four of these services are currently in a race to connect to the Internet. For instance, at the time of writing CompuServe has e-mail, newsgroups, and FTP; America Online has e-mail, newsgroups, and a simple hybrid Gopher and WAIS system; and PRODIGY has just released a Web browser.

The advantage of these systems? In general, they're easy to install and use. The disadvantages? They tend to be a bit pricey, though prices are plummeting (CompuServe just cut its prices in half). They also don't have full Internet access—they've added the easiest tools (e-mail came first, then newsgroups, and so on), but they still lack a lot. Still, 1995 will see these services add more Internet services; by the time you read this, all of them may have blossomed. In general, they still won't match the flexibility of a dial-in direct account (they are more like dial-in terminal accounts with very nice interfaces) because they won't multi-task. You'll be able to transfer a file with FTP, but you won't be able to go into a newsgroup and read while you are waiting. (That may come, but not until the online services change the form of data-communication they use.) And will these services provide as much access as a true Internet account? Will they give you finger and ping, WAIS, Telnet...? We'll have to wait and see.

Non-Provider-Specific Systems

Most of the rest of the software you'll run into is not service-provider-specific. That is, it's designed to be used by any TCP/IP connection, from any service provider. That causes a major problem; all service providers' systems are different. You have to do two things to get TCP/IP software to work: you have to enter the configuration data—IP (Internet Protocol) addresses, for instance—and you have to create a *login script*, a set of commands that tells the program what to do when it connects to the service provider. Entering all this information is not easy—one mistake, perhaps one wayward character in a script, and nothing works.

There are three ways around this little problem. First, the software may already have the information you need. Most of the commercial TCP/IP software comes with at least a few service providers already set up. If you have an account with one of these providers, simply select it from a list, and everything's done for you. The problems? You may not have an account with one of the service providers in the list, the information for the service provider you pick may not have been entered correctly, and the service provider you pick may have changed things since the information was entered, so it no longer works.

Well, let's look at the second way around the problem. Your service provider may have already created the necessary configuration and login-script files you need. Copy them to your hard disk, change one or two things, and everything works fine. This is perhaps the best solution (certainly better than the one we're about to look at!). But not all service providers are this nice or this sensible. Some providers don't *provide* much at all, let alone service! Others are very good—they will walk you through the procedure and make sure it all works. Ask around for a good service provider before you pick one.

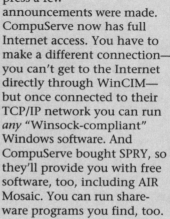

Stop the Presses!
As we went to press a few announcements were made. CompuServe now has full Internet access. You have to make a different connection—you can't get to the Internet directly through WinCIM—but once connected to their TCP/IP network you can run *any* "Winsock-compliant" Windows software. And CompuServe bought SPRY, so they'll provide you with free software, too, including AIR Mosaic. You can run shareware programs you find, too.

America Online demonstrated their Web browser at the San Jose Internet World, so by the time you read this it will be available, integrated into the rest of the America Online software. The Web browser is very good, based on the InterNetWorks browser (though it doesn't look the same).

The last solution is to enter the configuration information and login script yourself. This is *not* a great solution for everyone, especially if you view your computer as a necessary evil rather than something you enjoy tinkering with! Writing a login script is usually quite tricky, and even entering the configuration data properly can be a real problem.

Shareware Versus Commercial

Another decision to make is whether you use shareware and freeware, or whether you use commercial software. There are now a number of commercial suites of Internet programs—they generally come with the TCP/IP stack you'll need to set up a dial-in direct account, though they vary in ease of installation. You'll hear of programs such as **Internet Chameleon**, **Internet-in-a-Box**, and **SuperHighway Access**. Each provides a suite of tools; none provide *all* Internet tools. (Once you install the TCP/IP stack, however, you can then add shareware or freeware programs to your suite.)

If you decide you prefer to use shareware and freeware—you'll find loads of excellent software you can download directly from the Internet—the first step is to set up your stack. The most popular stack is called Trumpet Winsock—it may be shareware, but it's as good as—or better than—any of the commercial stacks (see Chapter 25 for more information). It's actually a *de facto* standard—Internet software providers usually make sure their products work with Trumpet Winsock.

If you're lucky, your service provider will already have a Trumpet Winsock set up that you can use—many do. Once you set up the stack, you can install WS_FTP—the very best Windows FTP program around—and then go hunting for shareware and freeware tools. (Note that just because these programs are shareware and freeware, it *doesn't* mean they're inferior to commercial tools. The commercial tools are, in many cases, quite clunky. The *best* Web, FTP, and WAIS programs, for instance, are shareware and freeware.)

So Where's Windows and When?

One very important development on the horizon (well, maybe just over the horizon), is *Windows 95*, the next version of Microsoft Windows. This has missed various release dates, but *may* be released around August of 1995. By the time it's released it may have to be renamed *Windows 95 3/4*, or *Windows almost 96*. (I wouldn't be surprised if its final release name is *Windows 96*, but at the time of writing it seems probable that Microsoft will meet the August release date.)

Anyway, whatever you want to call it, this new operating system will have a very important feature for Internet users—built in TCP/IP support, including a dialer. In other words, Windows 95 users will be able to connect their computers to a TCP/IP network, or a dial-in direct connection, without buying extra TCP/IP software.

Unfortunately, Microsoft hasn't done a good job of making this stuff easy to use. For instance, although Windows 95 has support for PPP connections (not SLIP), it doesn't let you write a login script. A login script tells the program what to expect when it dials into your service provider, and what information to send—your username, password, a PPP command perhaps, and so on. As Windows 95 doesn't *have* a login script, you have to login "by hand" each time—a terminal window appears, you type the commands, and then, hopefully, the PPP connection is set up (though I had trouble getting mine to work).

A Microsoft product manager told me that login scripting would eventually be added to Windows 95—though probably not by the scheduled August release date.

Microsoft is also starting its own online service, called the Microsoft Network. The August release won't have full Internet access—it will have newsgroups and e-mail, but that's it. Soon after release though, Microsoft will add other Internet tools, including a Web browser. These will probably be part of an add-on package.

Don't Forget OS/2 and Apple!

IBM is actually one step ahead of Microsoft, by adding Internet tools to OS/2. OS/2 Warp has FTP, Telnet, Gopher, e-mail, newsgroups, and a Web browser. It's also very easy to connect to IBM's own Internet service, *Advantis*. And the price is well under $100. The only problem is that you've got to install OS/2 to get to the Internet tools—which is, according to a variety of anecdotal reports, not always easy. OS/2 proponents will love the new tools, but I doubt that many Windows users will switch just to get easier Internet access.

And let's not forget Apple. They're bundling MacTCP with System 7.5, their latest operating system. You'll still need additional software, however—such as MacPPP or InterSLIP—to get a dial-in direct connection up and running.

The TCP/IP connection is still the sticking point for many users. Once you've got your TCP/IP connection up and running, installing your Internet tools is very easy. Installing a Web browser such as Mosaic or Netscape, for instance, takes no more than 10 minutes—but the TCP/IP connection might take a few hours (or days?), and many users give up in frustration. Windows 95, OS/2 3.0, and System 7.5 should make this problem disappear for many users (though Windows 95 and System 7.5 still need a little work to make them easier).

The Perfect System

You want the perfect Internet Windows system? You're going to have to do some work. First set up a TCP/IP connection of some sort—use Trumpet Winsock or a commercial

TCP/IP stack (see the following chapter for more information). Then pick and choose among the freeware, shareware, and commercial tools. Get Netscape and InternetWorks as your browsers (get both—they're both excellent, and each has particular strengths); get WS_FTP for FTP, and WS_Archie for Archie; get WinGopher for gophering. For e-mail you should at least try Eudora, but I haven't found a perfect one yet—they all seem a bit buggy.

For WAIS, try both EINet winWAIS and WAIS for Windows. Get WSIRC for Internet Relay Chat, and Com*t* for Telnet—it lets you run any serial-communications program for your Telnet sessions.

There's more—much more. The point is, it takes some time and effort to put together the very best system money and time can buy. I've got all these programs, and many more, on my system—but then, I'm paid to do this, and people keep sending me free software!

So that's the great strength of Internaut: it's an easy-to-install system with a good range of integrated tools that you can get running in a few minutes, not weeks!

The Least You Need to Know

➤ In general, there are four types of Internet connection: permanent, dial-in direct, dial-in terminal, and e-mail.

➤ Internaut provides a sort of hybrid connection. It's not a true TCP/IP dial-in direct connection, but it has many of the advantages. For instance, it allows multi-tasking.

➤ NetCruiser is another service-provider-specific system that gives you quick and easy installation.

➤ All the online services are planning Internet services. Most have limited service right now, but will add more soon.

➤ Installing a shareware or commercial TCP/IP stack is often difficult—get your service provider to help.

➤ Microsoft Windows 95 will soon provide a built-in TCP/IP stack. OS/2 Warp and the Macintosh System 7.5 already do (though you still need to add MacPPP, InterSLIP or similar to System 7.5 to use a dial-in direct account).

➤ Creating the perfect Internet system takes a lot of work. That's the advantage of Internaut—it's very quick to install, and provides a good suite of Internet tools.

FREE Software? Shareware and Freeware

Internet users have been spoiled. They've come to *expect* free software. Because so many people have written shareware, freeware, and public-domain programs for the Internet—individuals, colleges, government departments—you'll find lots of excellent software you can download. And it's often free, though there's sometimes a small registration fee.

Now, if you've used shareware before, you might not want to try Internet freebies. Shareware is often of poor quality; not always—there's excellent shareware in many fields—but it's certainly possible to run across some garbage. The great:garbage ratio is quite low. But on the Internet, the great:garbage ratio is much higher—a lot of excellent Internet tools, and much less garbage.

In fact, many of these tools are *far* better than their commercial counterparts. Of the two best Web browsers, one is currently free, and the other is shareware ($39). The very best FTP program for Windows is free—WS_FTP. And in some cases there are no real commercial counterparts. There's a shareware Internet Relay Chat program, but the only other one is Internaut's IRC program (and that won't work on anything but a PSI/Pipeline connection, of course).

Making the Connection

To create your TCP/IP connection, install Trumpet Winsock, a $20 shareware program. (See Chapters 24 and 25 for detailed instructions for installing this program.) Unfortunately, setting up Trumpet Winsock is not always easy—but you may find your service provider has already created a configuration file and login script. (If you have one of the commercial suites of programs, you can use its TCP/IP stack, and then add shareware and freeware.)

Once your TCP/IP connection is up and running, you can install all sorts of free and low-cost programs.

You can find this in **ftp.ncsa.uiuc.edu** in the **PC/Mosaic/sockets** directory, or **biochemistry.bioc.cwru.edu** site in the **/pub/trumpwsk** directory.

WS_FTP

The first program you should get is WS_FTP, because you can then grab other programs easily from FTP sites. Compared to WS_FTP, UNIX FTP is like eating soup with a fork. Not particularly satisfying. WS_FTP is what FTP should be. You've got all the commands at your fingertips, and a library of ftp sites to select from—no more mistyping ftp host-names. You can transfer files, of course, but also view text files (handy for reading directory indexes), select a target directory on your own hard drive, and add new directories, change filenames, delete files, and so on.

You can find this in **ftp.usma.edu**, in the **/pub/msdos/winsock.files** directory.

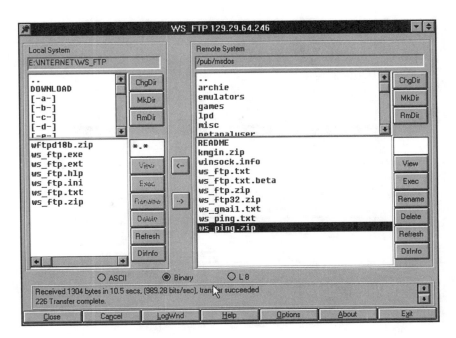

WS_FTP's Session Profile dialog box stores your FTP site information.

WS_Archie

It's all well and good being able to run out and grab files from all over the world, but what if you know the file you want, but not where it is? You need Archie, right? And if FTP is the clunkiest application on the Internet, Archie can't be far behind.

Which is why you need WS_Archie. Not only does WS_Archie automate Archie searches, it also automates getting the files you want, by interacting with WS_FTP, ordering it to go and get the file you select.

Type the text you want to search for, click on **Search**, and off it goes. When Archie finally responds, you'll see something like the following figure. If you've found what you need, click on the file, select **File|Retrieve**, and Archie launches WS_FTP, which downloads the file and then closes.

You can find this program in the **ftp.demon.co.uk** FTP site in the **/pub/ibmpc/ winsock/apps** directory, or at **oak.oakland.edu** in **/pub/msdos/winsock**.

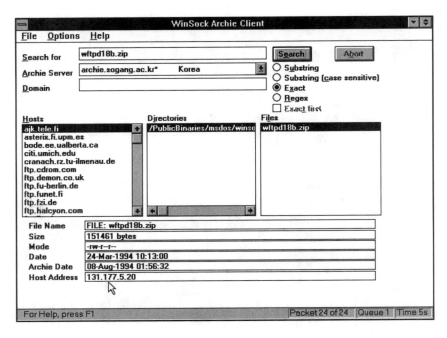

Archie meets Windows.

Web Browsers

You've probably heard a lot about Mosaic, the best-known Web browser, but Mosaic is no longer the best. Currently the two best browsers are Netscape and InternetWorks. The first has a small registration fee; the second is, at the time of writing, free. There is also a Microsoft Word for Windows add-on (Internet Assistant) that converts your word processor to a Web browser! (You must have 6.0a or later.)

For Netscape, try **ftp.mcom.com**, in the **/Netscape** directory, or the **http:// home.mcom.com/info/how-to-get-it.html** Web document. This is a very busy site, though, so you can use a "mirror" site, such as these: **ftp.digital.com** in **/pub/net/ infosys/Netscape**; **ftp.barrnet.net** in **/netscape**; and **ftp.uu.net** in **/networking/ info-service/www/netscape**.

For InternetWorks, go to **http://www.booklink.com**, or **ftp.booklink.com**. For MS Internet Assistant for Word, try **ftp.microsoft.com** in the **/deskapps/word/winword- public/ia/** directory.

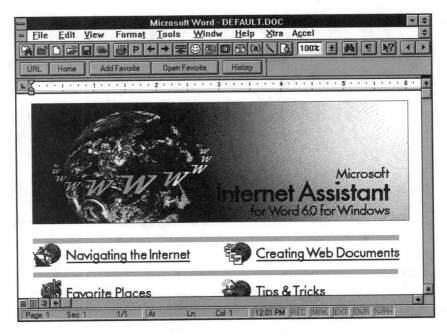

Word processor as Web browser—MS Internet Assistant for Word.

HGopher

HGopher is a British contribution to gopherspace, and a pretty good one, too. (I may be British, but I'm not biased—really!) It's not the simplest gopher to use, but it has all sorts of goodies built in—like the ability to transfer three items at once, for instance. You'll find this program in the **lister.cc.ic.ac.uk** FTP site, in the **/pub/wingopher** directory.

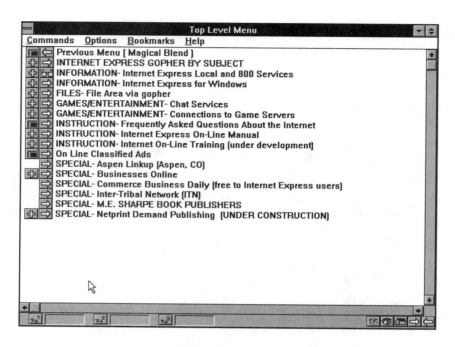

HGopher takes time to learn, but is a really fancy Windows gopher tool.

WSGopher

WSGopher is also a very good gopher—perhaps the best. It has a really good Bookmark system—and what's even better is that it's already set up with dozens of different entries to useful gopher sites. Bookmarks can be assigned to various categories—Libraries, Music, Business, Weather, and so on. Click on a toolbar button to open a dialog box, select a category, then double-click on a bookmark to go there or download the item referenced by the bookmark. (Strange thing is, from the Bookmark menu you can create categories and bookmarks—and edit them—but I never did find a menu option to open the dialog box where you actually *use* the bookmarks; I had to use the toolbar button.)

WSGopher actually has the feel of a commercial program more than a shareware or freeware program. It has lots of configuration options, makes selecting a viewer quite easy, has a nice little utility to delete downloaded files from its download directory, and has an excellent online help system.

WSGopher is in the **sunsite.unc.edu** site's **/pub/micro/pc-stuff/ms-windows/ winsock/apps** directory.

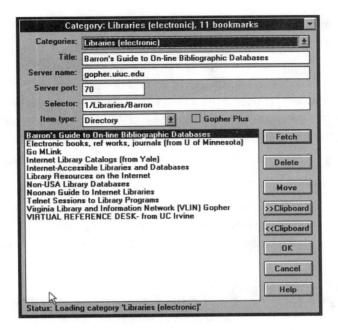

WSGopher has an excellent Bookmark system.

Telnet—Comt

If you have a good telecommunications program—HyperACCESS, ProComm, or whatever—you may want to use it for your Telnet sessions. Most Telnet programs are not very good, not nearly as good as a commercial serial-telecommunications program. So you may want to find Com*t*.

Com*t* is a little utility that fools your computer's communications ports into working with your network or dial-in direct connection. You will "connect" your communications program to a communications port that isn't being used—COM4, for instance—then start your WINSOCK.DLL connection and "dial" your communications program through that port, using the hostname or IP address as the phone number. Com*t* intercepts the program's communications, and sends it onto the WINSOCK.DLL, which connects you to the Telnet site. It's just like dialing into a bulletin board, only without the dialing (if you see what I mean).

Com*t* can be found at **ftp.std.com**, in **/customers/software/rfdmail**.

WinTalk

Remember Internaut's Talk program? Well, there's a shareware program that's very similar: *WinTalk*. WinTalk has a little smiley face icon that sits on your "desktop." When you want to talk with someone, click on the icon then click on Talk in the menu that pops up. Select the person from a drop-down list box and then click on **OK**. A window opens up with two parts: one part is where your typing appears, the other is where the other person's typing appears.

WinTalk is in the **ftp.elf.com** FTP site's **/pub/wintalk** directory.

WSIRC

WSIRC stands for Windows Sockets Internet Relay Chat. If you're an IRC junkie, there's no need to go cold turkey just because you set up a dial-in direct Windows system. Use WSIRC to get your fix.

The version I looked at was an early one, and a little unstable. By the time you read this, however, perhaps it will be a bit easier to use. It provides three windows, one large one in which most of your "work" is done, a small one at the bottom where you type, and a vertical strip along the right side where certain information is displayed—such as lists of the IRC channels. The help file is useful, too; it has a list of IRC commands and servers (the program doesn't automate entering commands—you still have to type them in).

Look in the **cs-ftp.bu.edu** site's **/irc/clients/pc/windows** directory.

Finger

Finger's a handy little tool. You can use it to make sure an e-mail address you have is correct, or to get information from someone's .plan file. There are a couple of Windows finger applications you should check out, **Finger 3.1** and **WS Finger**. Both are simple to use, but there's a problem with the current version of WS Finger: the window it uses is so narrow, it sometimes truncates lines of text.

You can find these programs at the **sunsite.unc.edu** FTP site in the **/pub/micro/pc-stuff/ms-windows/winsock/apps** directory (Finger 3.1), and in the **ftp.halcyon.com** site's **/local/seasigi/slip/windows/apps** directory (WS Finger).

```
┌─────────────────── Finger - typhoon.atmos.colostate.edu ───────────▼ ♦┐
│ Host                                                                   │
│Login name: forecast                      In real life: Forecast status│
│Directory: /users/forecast                                             │
│Never logged in.                                                       │
│No unread mail                                                         │
│Plan:                                                                  │
│**********************************************************************  │
│STATUS OF GRAY'S ATLANTIC        1944- | Nov 24 | Jun 7 | Aug 5 |Observed│
│SEASONAL HURRICANE FORECAST       1993 |  1993  |  1994 |  1994 |       │
│FOR 1994                          Mean | Fcst.  | Fcst. | Fcst. |       │
│======================================================================= │
│Named Storms                       9.3 |  10    |   9   |   7   |    1  │
│Named Storm Days                  46.1 |  60    |  35   |  30   |   2.0 │
│Hurricanes                         5.7 |   6    |   5   |   4   |    0  │
│Hurricane Days                    23.0 |  25    |  15   |  12   |    0  │
│Major Hurricanes (Category 3-4-5)  2.2 |   2    |   1   |   1   |    0  │
│Major Hurricane Days               4.5 |   7    |   1   |   1   |    0  │
│Hurricane Destruction Potential   68.1 |  85    |  40   |  35   |    0  │
│**********************************************************************  │
│                                                                        │
│                                                                        │
│            ▷                                                           │
│                                                                        │
└────────────────────────────────────────────────────────────────────────┘
```

Getting the typhoon forecast with Finger 3.1.

WS Ping

Ping is a useful command for a few reasons, even if you don't understand all the network gobbledygook it provides. You can use it to make sure your network connection is working. You can use it to make sure the host you are trying to reach actually exists, and is reachable. And you can use it to convert a hostname to an IP number—you ping the hostname and get an IP number back. Try WS Ping, an easy to use and flexible Ping program. You'll find it in the **ftp.usma.edu** site's **/pub/msdos/winsock.files/** directory.

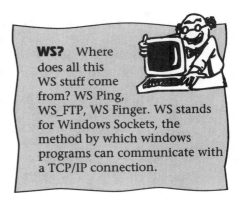

WS? Where does all this WS stuff come from? WS Ping, WS_FTP, WS Finger. WS stands for Windows Sockets, the method by which windows programs can communicate with a TCP/IP connection.

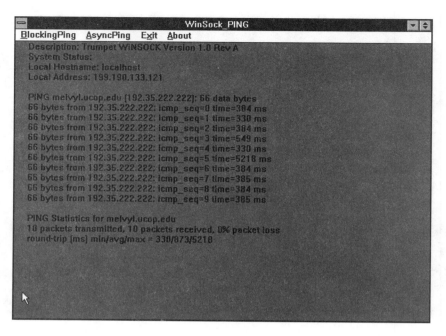

WS Ping checks your Internet connections for you.

It's Him Again—Trumpet for Windows

The Aussie Peter Tattam has been pretty busy. Not only did he bring us Trumpet Winsock, but Trumpet for Windows, too (plus a few other Internet programs). Trumpet for Windows is a very nice little e-mail and news program that's easy to install and use. You can find this in **ftp.utas.edu.au**, in the **/pc/trumpet/wintrump** directory.

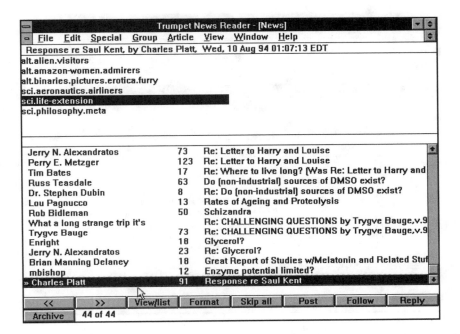

Trumpet for Windows.

Eudora

Eudora is a commercial e-mail program available from QUALCOMM Incorporated. But they also release a freeware version—obviously it won't have all the features that the commercial program has, but it's pretty good, nonetheless. Make sure you download the user manual, or you'll have trouble figuring out some of the features. Installation's pretty easy. Eudora is available in the **ftp.qualcomm.com** site, in the **/quest/windows/eudora** directory.

The Macmillan Site Where can you get *all* this software? At the Macmillan Publishing Internet site, of course! You can FTP to ftp.mcp.com, or travel through the Web to http://www.mcp.com.

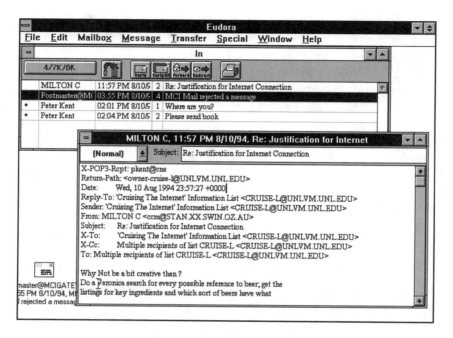

Eudora places lists and messages in their own windows.

The Least You Need to Know

➤ Trumpet Winsock is the most popular shareware TCP/IP stack, though it's a little complicated to set up.

➤ WS_FTP and WS_Archie are excellent FTP and Archie programs, better than commercial.

➤ The best Web browsers are cheap or free—Netscape and InternetWorks. Also see MS Internet Assistant if you have Word for Windows.

➤ Probably the best Windows gophers are HGopher and WSGopher.

➤ Com*t* lets you run any serial-communications program as a Telnet program.

➤ WinTalk and WSIRC let you talk and chat on the Internet.

➤ Finger 3.1, WS Finger, and WS Ping are pretty good finger and ping applications.

➤ For e-mail and newsgroups, see Trumpet for Windows. Another excellent e-mail program is Eudora.

You'll Have to Pay—Commercial Suites

Commercial Internet software is spreading like mold on that gray thing that's been in my fridge for six months. Every few days someone announces some new and fancy tool for doing Internet stuff from Windows.

There's no way to look at all the options, so we'll just look at the four most popular suites of Internet applications. Remember, though, that a program you pay for isn't necessarily the best; in many cases, better freeware or shareware tools are available. What you *will* get, however, is technical support and a package of all the most important tools you need. And setting up the TCP/IP stack that comes with the commercial tools is usually easier than setting up Trumpet Winsock, the most popular shareware stack.

NetCruiser

NetCruiser is the only other Internet suite that matches Internaut for ease of installation. It's also a little "prettier" than Internaut, but it doesn't have as many Internet tools.

NetCruiser provides tools for working with e-mail, newsgroups, the World Wide Web, FTP, Telnet, Gopher, and finger. These tools all have nice big toolbar buttons that are fairly understandable. Click on a picture of a house to return "home," on a picture of a spider's web to start the World Wide Web browser, and so on.

The NetCruiser main screen—the starting point.

NetCruiser is a very nice system. It's easy to use, fairly quick, and seems to be stable, too.

Just as I was finishing this book, NETCOM announced that they'd added "winsock compliance." Under the old NetCruiser system, all you could run were the NetCruiser tools—the Web browser that came with it, e-mail, newsgroups, Gopher, Telnet, FTP, and finger. But now that their TCP/IP stack is "winsock-compliant," you can run *any* Windows TCP/IP program once you install NetCruiser, not just the NetCruiser applications. You can go onto the Internet and download all sorts of shareware programs—Netscape, InternetWorks, Mosaic, WS_FTP, WinWAIS, and lots more. If the program's written to run on a winsock TCP/IP connection, then you can run it through your NetCruiser connection.

For more information about NetCruiser, call 800-353-6600 or 408-345-2600, or e-mail **info@netcom.com**.

Internet Chameleon

The NetManage claim is that you can install Internet Chameleon and get it running in five minutes. That's a little optimistic. Maybe the box should say "five-minute installation *if* you are connecting to a service with a pre-configured setup, and everything goes well." It took me several hours to get it running—including a couple of calls to technical support—mainly because the documentation was weak when it came to writing logon scripts. Also, there are a few bugs. I had the system freeze once or twice, and several times it crashed Windows and sent me straight back to the DOS prompt. Still, if you want a full solution—and don't want to run around on the net looking for all the different components—you may want to consider this product. (And let's face it, how many Windows programs *don't* kick you out now and again?)

So What's It Got?

Here's what you get with Internet Chameleon:

➤ **Custom**   This is the program you use to make the connection to your service provider—to load, in effect, WINSOCK.DLL. Just open the application, click on **Connect**, and away you go.

➤ **Finger**   Automates the finger command.

➤ **FTP & FTP Server**   An FTP application to make transferring files easier. The FTP Server lets you make files on your system available to others via FTP.

➤ **Archie**   Search for files with Archie.

➤ **Gopher**   A File-Manager-type Gopher menu system.

➤ **Mail & Mail Utilities**   E-mail made easy.

➤ **NEWTNews**   Simplifies your access to newsgroups.

➤ **Ping**   Test the connection to other hosts using ping.

➤ **Telnet**   Log in to other computers on the Internet.

➤ **TFTP**   A Trivial File Transfer Protocol program. TFTP is used to transfer files between systems without any directory or file listings, but you probably won't use this much—use FTP unless you run into a system that doesn't support FTP (rare).

➤ **Whois**   Use the Internet Whois system to track down other Internet users.

➤ **WebSurfer**   Internet Chameleon recently got a Web browser.

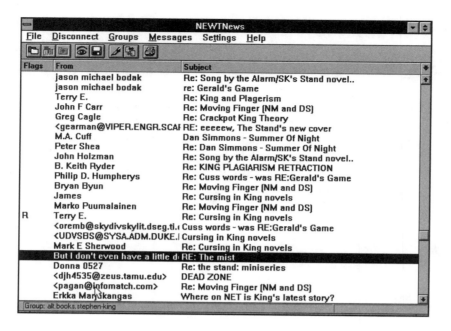

If you've ever used the rn or trn newsreader programs, you'll appreciate NEWTNews.

One major complaint I have about Internet Chameleon is the poor documentation. Remember to check the online help—it's more detailed than the book. But the two contradict each other in places, so you'll have to play around to figure out which is correct. There are a few basic usability problems with the programs; they could have been better thought out. And the programs tend to be a bit buggy—I found that the Web browser often doesn't display inline pictures correctly, and that the e-mail program—although it can use the MIME method of transferring files—often seems to stall while sending or receiving files.

Once you've got Internet Chameleon up and running, however, you can always add other—shareware and freeware—programs. The Chameleon TCP/IP stack will let you run any TCP/IP program.

For more information, call 408-257-7171, or e-mail **info@netmanage.com**.

Internet in a Box

Perhaps the greatest strength of Internet in a Box is that its programmers spent some time and effort figuring out how to make connecting to a service provider easy. For instance, you don't *write* a script, you enter information into a dialog box, telling the program

what to look for, and what to do when it sees it. Once you know what your login procedure looks like, you can create the script in less than five minutes, with ease.

The Internet in a Box programs, by the way, are also sold in various combinations as
the *AIR Series—AIR Connect, AIR NFS*, and so on. *Internet in a Box* is regarded as the con-
sumer product, the AIR Series as the corporate product.

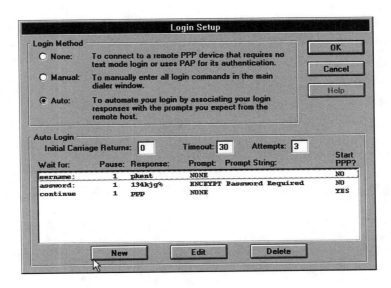

Finally, creating a login script is simple.

Internet in a Box runs on PPP connections, so it's pretty fast. It comes with these
programs:

➤ **AIR Mosaic (World Wide Web)**

➤ **AIR Mail (email)**

➤ **AIR News (newsgroups)**

➤ **AIR Gopher**

➤ **Network File Manager (FTP)**

➤ **AIR Telnet**

➤ **Image View (graphics viewer)**

➤ **UUCODE (UUENCODE and UUDECODE)**

It's really a very good product, certainly better designed than Internet Chameleon.
All the applications are well designed, with easily understandable toolbars, menus, and

procedures. Where it fails is that it's only a partial solution. (That's where nearly *all* the "kits" fail, not just Internet in a Box.) There's no WAIS, ping, finger, or Archie. The loss of Archie, in particular, seems important. There's no Internet Relay Chat, no Talk. Perhaps these elements will be added in the future; for now, you'll have to do without them if you buy this product.

Internet in a Box is available in many bookstores and software stores. For more information, call 800-777-9638 or 206-447-0300, or e-mail **info@spry.com**. CompuServe recently bought SPRY, and has started providing the Web browser to its subscribers.

SuperHighway Access

SuperHighway Access is another suite of Internet tools. It does have an unusual feature: it combines different tools in a program called WinTapestry. You access these tools through a sort of "card file." Click on a tab—**Entertainment**, **Food**, **Best of the Web**, **Legal**, **Religion**, or whatever—and a list of folders and items appears.

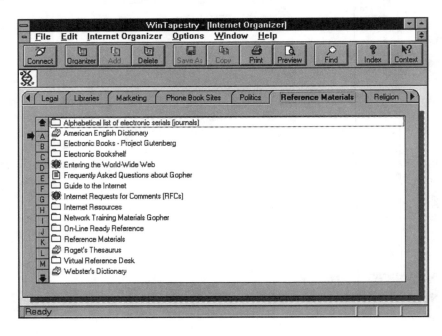

The WinTapestry Internet Organizer, a kind of "card file" of Internet sites.

Some of the items are Web sites, but others may be gopher sites, Telnet sessions, FTP sites, files of various kinds, and so on. Click on one of the Web icons, and another window opens—this is where you do your actual browsing. You can add bookmarks, of course—you'll get a chance to select the category (there are about 30, and you can create your own), and the document is added to the card file.

The program is supposed to organize your work around your interests, rather than the various tools. In some ways it's similar to Internaut—WinTapestry, functionally speaking, might be compared to the Internaut bookmark system, which also lets you group different types of Internet resources.

The SuperHighway setup program is fairly good—the publisher checked dozens of service providers in North America for configuration and login-script information, so there's a good chance setup will be quick.

For more information about SuperHighway Access, call 414-241-4555 or e-mail **info@frontiertech.com**.

The Least You Need to Know

➤ There are *loads* of commercial Internet software, and more programs arrive all the time.

➤ Commercial software tools are not always better than shareware or freeware.

➤ The advantages to commercial suites are technical support, an all-in-one package, and a simpler TCP/IP-stack setup.

➤ NetCruiser is very easy to install, but has only the basic tools (though you can add shareware and freeware).

➤ Internet Chameleon has the most tools—more than any other commercial suite—but it's poorly designed and buggy.

➤ Internet in a Box has a very easy setup program and well-designed tools.

➤ SuperHighway Access provides WinTapestry, an integrated system from which you can run various Internet tools.

Picking a Provider

If the last few chapters have intrigued you and you want to try all the other neat Windows software, you'll have to find another service provider—or at least change the type of account you have. Pipeline USA lets you run the Internaut software and nothing else. Pipeline USA is owned by PSINet, and they can also provide you with another type of account, if you want—what they call their InterRamp account. This uses the Internet Chameleon software. For more information, call 1-800-827-7482, or e-mail **interramp-info@psi.com**.

There are hundreds of service providers around the country, though, so you might want to spend some time finding the best deal for you. This chapter will help you track down a service provider and figure out if they can provide the service you need.

How Do I Know What's Out There?

About 18 months before I wrote this book, the Denver area had just one or two service providers. Now there are almost two dozen. The same has happened all over the country. But how do you find these service providers?

Start by looking in your city's local computer publication for ads. Ask at your local computer store (preferably a small store, not a big superstore where the staff has as much computing knowledge as your average prairie dog). Check with the local computer-book store, if there is one in your area, or the manager of the computer department at a regular book store. Ask everyone you know who uses a computer.

You can also use your Pipeline USA account to send a message to **info-deli-server@netcom.com** (see Chapter 8 for information on working with Internet e-mail). In the body of the message, type **Send PDIAL**. The recipient automatically returns a message that includes a large list of service providers in the United States, some of which have international access.

You might want to get a copy of the publication *Internet Access Providers* (Mecklermedia, $30). It's an international directory of service providers, regional networks, and bulletin boards, all with Internet access. (You can order it through your local bookstore; you can also call 800-632-5537 or 203-226-6967, or send e-mail to **info@mecklermedia.com**.)

Home-Town Operations

Look for all service providers with service in your area, not just the ones that are head-quartered near you. Even if a provider is in, say, Maine, they might be able to provide local telephone number support all over the country by buying phone service in lots of different cities. You might find that the service closest to you is *not* the cheapest deal; a service based in another city might have a local phone number in your city, with lower rates.

One-Eight-Hundreds

Some services provide a 1-800 number you can call, regardless of where in the United States you happen to be. (Others have 800 numbers that work only within their home states.) You won't pay for the phone call connecting you to their computer, but you *will* pay a higher per-minute rate while connected than you normally would. For instance, if a service provider normally charges $1/hour for evening use, you might pay $6/hour if you are using their 1-800 number.

Still, there are two benefits to using a service provider with a 1-800 number: if you travel a lot, you can continue to use the Internet when you're out of town, and if you're far from a local-number connection, you can get onto the network without paying for long-distance calls. The extra $5 or so per hour might still be less than the long-distance charges.

Data Networks

Depending on where you're located, you might be able to use a data network to connect. It's like this: a number of companies have leased telephone lines and numbers all over the country. A service provider can sign up with one of these companies, so the data network is linked to the service provider's computer.

For example, a service provider named The World has telephone numbers only in the Boston area. But users in, say, Phoenix or Dallas who want to use The World's services can sign up with CompuServe Packet Network or PC-Pursuit (Sprint Data Services). These two companies have local numbers all over the country, so a user can dial the CompuServe or Sprint number, log onto the network's computer, then log onto The World's computer.

Of course there's a charge, perhaps $5 or $6 per hour. (Some services are as low as $1/hour during evenings and weekends.) If you find a service provider with low rates but no local number, ask them if they have a data network through which you can connect, then figure out the total cost.

You don't need a CompuServe Information Service account to use Compu-Serve's Packet Network.

Service? What Service?

The standard of service you get can vary widely. Some service providers are very helpful and have responsive technical support, good documentation, and even setup programs to lead you through installing a dial-in direct connection. Others will set up an account for you on their end, but leave the rest for you to figure out. Also, some services are currently overused, in which case you'll run into busy signals when trying to connect, and might find that the system seems to "hang" now and again. If you know other Internet users, ask for a recommendation. Otherwise, you just have to pick a service and see what it's like.

Comparison Shopping

Once you find a few promising service providers with local numbers, data networks, or 800 numbers, call or write them to get their rates. Before you buy, compare. Making the best deal can save you hundreds of dollars in setup fees, and hundreds of dollars a year in *connect fees* (the money you are charged for actually using the service).

Explaining What You Want

When you first contact a service provider, make sure you're both talking about the same thing. If you don't understand the account types they're talking about (and there are plenty of variations, with many service providers creating their own product names), make sure they clarify what they are offering.

You might hear a service provider use one of these names for the types of service we've been discussing:

Permanent might be called direct, permanent direct, or dedicated service. **Dial-in terminal** might be called interactive or dial-up service. **Dial-in direct** might be called SLIP, CSLIP, PPP, or TCP/IP service. **Mail** might be called UUCP, e-mail, or messaging service.

Of course, if you are reviewing information sent in the mail, you'll have to dig through it carefully to figure out the different options.

Once you are both talking about the same thing, you can use the following list of questions to compare the rates of different service providers.

➤ *How much is the connect or startup cost for dial-in direct service?* To get started, you might have to pay a setup charge, which is a one-time fee and runs between $20 and $45.

➤ *Do you provide free software for dial-in direct accounts?* It's possible to get dial-in direct accounts quite cheaply, but you might have to provide your own software. Other service providers might charge more but give you the software. Some service providers provide shareware that you can install—though it's not always easy to do so.

➤ *Is there a fixed fee?* The amount you pay per hour can vary tremendously. Some service providers don't charge by the hour; they charge a single monthly fee and provide unlimited time on the Internet ($15 a month for unlimited use, for instance). Also, some service providers charge different fees for different modem speeds. Make sure you get the price for the speed of the modem you are using.

➤ *If there's a fixed fee, is it for limited access?* If the service provider is charging a fixed fee, make sure you know what hours you will be allowed onto the system. Some providers might have a low fixed fee account, but will only let you on in the evenings.

➤ *How much do you charge per hour during weekdays?* Many providers charge an hourly rate, such as $2 an hour for online time between, say, 8:00 a.m. and 8:00 p.m. during the week. You might have to make a few notes along with the numbers. For example, some providers charge a minimum that gets you a few free hours ($10/month with 10 free hours) and then charge a set fee for subsequent hours (say, $2/hour for the fifth and subsequent hours). In addition, some providers might have two or more payment plans for the same service, so you might need more than one column for each provider when you're comparing services. And remember to check rates for your modem speed.

➤ *How much per hour in the evening?* What hours do you consider "evening?" Rates are sometimes lower from 8:00 p.m. to midnight.

➤ *How much per hour at night?* What hours do you consider "night?" Rates are often lower still between midnight and 8:00 a.m., perhaps around $1/hour.

➤ *How much per hour during weekends?* Check to see if there's a lower rate during weekends. Some service providers use the same schedule for all seven days, the only variation being the time of service and not the day.

➤ *Is there a minimum number of hours I must use each month?* The service provider will probably charge a minimum monthly fee. This might be combined with an hourly rate.

➤ *Can I pay for a maximum number of hours, after which all hours are free?* If a service provider charges by the hour, they might have a maximum. For example, once you've paid $80 in hourly fees, everything is free for the rest of the month.

➤ *Do you have a local number?* Ideally, you want a service provider with a telephone number in your area code, so you don't have to pay long-distance charges.

➤ *Is there a surcharge on that local number?* Some service providers charge you extra to use their local number—perhaps as much as $9 an hour! Ideally, you want a *free* local number.

➤ *Do you have 1-800 access? Is it national, or state only? What is the surcharge?* Some service providers have 1-800 numbers you can use.

If a service provider says it has a **POP** (Point of Presence) in your area, it means they have a local telephone number in your area. You won't have to pay for long-distance calls to connect to the Internet.

You pay a surcharge (maybe $5–$12/hour), but if you live in the boonies with no Internet number in your area code, it might be cheaper to use the 1-800 number than to pay long-distance charges. The 1-800 number is also convenient for people who want to be able to use the Internet while away from home.

➤ *Do you have data-network access? What is the surcharge?* Some service providers have data networks they work with. The surcharge will vary from $1/hour to about $6/hour, depending on the time of day that you use Internet.

➤ *What modem speeds do you support?* The slower the connection, the more time everything will take, and the more expensive your online work will be—in terms of both the money you pay the service provider, and the value of your time. If all your service provider can manage is 2400 bps (bits per second), it's probably too slow. They should have at least 14400 bps (many will soon be operating at 28800 bps). Of course, the data-transmission speed you want to use is limited by the speed of your computer's modem. If all you've got is a 300 bps modem, it doesn't matter if the service provider does have 14400 bps modems; *your* connection will be at 300 bps.

Many people use the term *baud* instead of bps. The two terms are pretty much interchangeable, although they're not exactly the same—and purists will tell you that bps is the more correct of the two when referring to your modem's speed. Baud is named for J. M. E. Baudot, who invented the Baudot telegraph code, and refers to the modulation and demodulation rate of the modem (the rate at which the modem converts between the computer's digital signal and the phone line's analog signal).

➤ *How much is disk space per megabyte per month?* Your service provider will probably charge you if you store too much stuff (messages and files) on his computer's hard disk. This doesn't have to be a problem, though. A provider might let you use up to 1 MB (megabyte) for free, then charge from 50 cents to two or three dollars a month for each additional MB. As you're planning to get a dial-in direct account, 1MB is plenty of room—files and messages are transferred to *your* computer, so you won't store much on theirs.

➤ *How much is domain service?* When you get a dial-in direct account you can establish your own *domain name* or use the service provider's. Establishing your own domain name might be free, or it might cost $10 or $20. For instance, if you subscribe to Internet Express, your e-mail address would be **name@myplace.com**. If you get your own domain, it might be **name@myplace.com** or **name@bedrock.com**, or whatever you choose.

➤ *Are there any other charges?* There are as many ways to charge you as there are service providers. Check the fine print.

The Least You Need to Know

➤ Don't look at just the service providers close to you; some non-local ones might have local numbers.

➤ If you are a long way from a service provider's coverage area, look for one with a 1-800 number or data network access.

➤ Remember to check the service provider's modem speed. Some still use slow modems.

➤ Compare costs carefully—rates vary widely.

Setting Up TCP/IP— Gathering the Information

In This Chapter

➤ Collecting information for dial-in direct

➤ Testing your dial-in direct account

➤ Gathering information for the login script

In Chapter 20 I talked about the "perfect" system. There is no perfect off-the-shelf system. If you want the very best, you're going to have to put it together yourself, by finding the best shareware and perhaps picking up bits and pieces from the commercial suites. But first you need your dial-in direct connection to the Internet, a connection using what's known as a TCP/IP "stack."

In the next chapter you'll learn how to install Trumpet Winsock, the best shareware TCP/IP stack. But before you can do that, you need to do a little data collection. Setting up a TCP/IP connection is a little tricky, and requires that you are prepared before you get started.

You may not want to get started. Before we go on, let me just explain the easiest ways to set up a TCP/IP connection from Microsoft Windows. First there's NETCOM's NetCruiser and CompuServe. These two services just announced (as we were about to go to print), that they have full "Winsock compliance." That means if you install their TCP/IP stacks you'll be able to run *any* other Windows TCP/IP programs that are also Winsock compliant. You can use all the programs we looked at in Chapter 21, for instance. Installing these systems is pretty easy. Because the software is already configured to run with the system you are connecting to, there's no configuration for you to do.

Then there are a few commercial programs that try to simplify the process of connecting a TCP/IP stack. There's Internet Chameleon, SuperHighway Access, and Internet in a Box. These products try to simplify the process by providing preconfigured setup files for a variety of service providers around the country. Of course they may not have *your* service provider, or they may an out-of-date configuration for your provider. So setting up one of these programs can take between 10 minutes and a few hours. If you decide to try one, ask your service provider if they have configuration and login-script files ready for you to use. (PSI's InterRamp service, which I mentioned in Chapter 23, uses Chameleon, and comes with the configuration and login stuff already done for you.)

In this chapter, I'm going to help you gather information for setting up a TCP/IP connection. You won't have to do this if you use a service provider that provides the configuration and login files for you, or software that is designed to run with only one service provider (such as CompuServe or NETCOM's NetCruiser). But if you have to set up a TCP/IP connection yourself from scratch, you'll have a little homework to do. There are all sorts of tricky little numbers and names you need to know, so this chapter is all about what you need and where to get it. Then, in the next chapter, I'll explain how to use this information to set up Trumpet Winsock.

Call Your Service Provider

Okay, e-mail them, then, I don't care. Whatever's easiest. (There's a bias against calling people in much of Internet-land, but there are times when you just can't beat the phone.) Whatever you do, you must somehow gather the information discussed in this chapter. If you find that your service provider is not very helpful, consider finding another provider before attempting to connect your dial-in direct account. You can write the data as you collect it in the table at the end of this chapter. But first, take a look at the information you're going to need.

Basic Connection Information

First, let's find the information about the connection you are going to make, and how it connects at the service provider's end.

What's the telephone number? Critical information, this. No number; no connection.

What type of connection is this? (SLIP, CSLIP, PPP)   There are several different kinds of TCP/IP dial-in direct connections. Make sure you know exactly which type your service provider is using, as you'll have to let your TCP/IP software know. Some service providers may let you use any of these. For instance, when I log in, I can use SLIP, CSLIP, or PPP. CSLIP may be slightly faster than SLIP, though perhaps not much. CSLIP simply compresses the *header* information, which is information sent by your programs telling the service provider what each batch of data is and what to do with it. PPP is supposed to be much faster and more reliable. But if your modem has error-correction capability, you may find little difference. (Some engineers claim PPP has little effect, except for improving communications on noisy lines.)

SLIP, CSLIP, and PPP

That's Serial Line Interface Protocol, Compressed Serial Line Interface Protocol, and Point to Point Protocol. These are all types of TCP/IP (Transmission Control Protocol/Internet Protocol) connections that can run over the phone line. Less than one Internet user in a thousand can tell you what these acronyms mean, so feel free to forget them.

What is your username or account name?   This is the name you use to log into the service provider's system. You usually take this from your name. For instance, at one service provider, I had a login of pkent, at another peterk. In most cases, though, you'll be able to tell the service provider what name you want to use (assuming nobody else is already using it). Your service provider may give you two account names, one for the dial-in direct account, and one for another, associated, account (often called a *shell account*).

You can dial into the shell account with an ordinary dial-in terminal connection. This is handy, because you can then dial in and check your e-mail even if you're having trouble with your SLIP software, or if you are calling from a machine without the fancy software, such as a laptop. Some service providers may make you pay extra for the shell account. Other service providers will simply give you one account name and password, and the ability to log in with both a dial-in direct and a dial-in terminal connection (not simultaneously, of course).

What is your password?   You may get to choose your password, or the service provider may give you one. Either way, change it when you log in. Again, you may have *two* passwords, one for your dial-in direct account, and one for your shell account. Make sure you have the right one. Typically, passwords are eight characters or more, and are case-sensitive—thus 324iel4 is not the same as 324IEL4. And different service providers may have different rules about how to create passwords; some won't allow real words.

What is the TCP/IP startup command?   When you first make your connection to the host computer, it probably doesn't know if you are going to be using a dial-in direct or dial-in terminal connection. It may give you the option of making either kind of connection. At some point during the login session, you have to tell the host computer that you want to change to a TCP/IP dial-in direct mode. Generally, you have to type *slip* or *ppp* or something similar, and then press **Enter**. (To use CSLIP, you'll probably still type **slip**. Your service provider's computer will figure out if you are using SLIP or CSLIP when it receives data from you.) Check with your service provider on what you must type.

When do you use the startup command?   You also need to know at which prompt you use the startup command, though this is usually pretty straightforward. You enter your username and password, and then the system displays a prompt asking you what you want to do. (You'll see an example later in this chapter.) This is the point at which you must enter the command. However, if you don't have a ready-made login script, you need to know this information so you can write your own. (I'll discuss scripts later in this chapter.)

What is your Internet Protocol (IP) address?   Once connected to the Internet, your computer will act as a host, so it needs a host address. This is a four-part number, each part separated by a period. For example, my IP address is 199.190.133.121.

What is your hostname?   Once connected to the Internet, you'll also need a hostname. This is normally the same as your login name. If your login name is jbloe, you will use jbloe as your hostname also.

What is your domain name?   You also need to know the domain name of the service provider's system. This is the part that appears after the @ sign in your e-mail address. For example, if your e-mail address is jbloe@cscns.com, the domain name is cscns.com. Many service providers will let you create your own domain name, in which case you should enter it here (sometimes there's a small charge, sometimes they'll do this for free).

Having your own domain name can be handy—once you have one, you can change service providers and take the domain name with you. You will have to register the name to the new provider when you do so, and there may be a charge for that. Changing service providers doesn't mean you have to change your e-mail address. (If you didn't get your own domain name when you first signed up for the dial-in direct account, you may still be able to do so. Check with your service provider.)

What is the domain name server (DNS) address? This DNS address is the address of the host computer that your service provider uses to figure out network addresses. If you send e-mail, the Internet has to figure out where to send it. It does this by contacting a DNS (domain name server) and asking it for information. Your service provider should give you at least one DNS address, but maybe several. Again, this is a four-part number (the DNS I'm using is 192.156.196.1).

What's the subnet mask? Your service provider may give you a subnet mask number, but he probably won't. This is simply one of those strange network-thingy numbers that only network nerds understand, so don't worry too much about it.

What is the gateway address? Your service provider may have a gateway address, the address through which they actually connect directly to the Internet. Then again, they may not. This is *not* the mail gateway, by the way—we'll look at that later.

More Connection Stuff

There's more. We already have the information you need to get your account up and running, but once connected, you may need more information to carry out certain operations. Ask your service provider for these items (you may find the addresses are all the same, perhaps even all the same as the name server address):

What is the Mail POP (Post Office Protocol) server name or address? You use this server to get your mail from your service provider. Although while connected, your computer will become a "host" on the Internet, while it's not connected your mail is being stored somewhere in the POP server. When you connect, your mail program can then grab your messages from the server. There are different POP versions—most systems run POP3 these days. You should get the address and the port number.

What is the SMTP (Simple Mail Transfer Protocol) server name? You can use SMTP to send and receive mail. You'll probably use SMTP to send mail; you can't use it to receive mail. An SMTP mail program can receive mail directly. That is, the mail doesn't need to go through the POP server. If you're not connected when mail arrives, the service provider's system will probably store the mail and try to resend it every 15 minutes or so. When you reconnect, the mail will go into your SMTP mail program. The advantage of this is that you can set up your own e-mail accounts, using your domain name. For instance, you can have separate accounts for each person in your company, or each member of your family, your dog, or whatever. Not all programs do this, however, so you may or may not need this address. You might as well get it anyway. Get the address and port number.

What is the mail gateway name or address? A mail gateway receives your mail on its way out. That is, when you write and send a message, the first place it goes to is the mail gateway. The gateway takes a look at the address and then sends the message on.

What is your Internet mailbox username? You need a username to log into your mailbox. This is usually the same as your account username.

What is your Internet mailbox password? You also need a password for your mailbox. Again, this is usually the same as your account password.

What is the NNTP (Network News Transfer Protocol) news server name or address? You can use NNTP to transfer newsgroup messages and to store local newsgroups. You need this address to connect your newsgroup program so it can find the newsgroup messages. Get the address and the port number.

What is the gopher host name or address? If you want to connect your gopher client up to your service provider's gopher server, you need the host name or address. Also, make sure you get the port number.

Is it a Gopher+ server? Gopher+ is a new gophering standard, in which gopher servers can provide more information about items in a gopher list. In most cases, you won't need to tell your gopher client program whether a server is a gopher+ server or not, but in some cases you may.

What is the World Wide Web home-page URL? URL means Universal Resource Locator, and it's a sort of WWW address. If you want to connect to your service provider's "home page" on the web, you'll need the URL. It will look something like this: **http://usa.net/HomePage.html**. You learn more about URLs in Chapter 14.

Your Modem

You also need information about your modem and its connection to the service provider's system. Here's what you need:

COM port You must know the communications port that you connect your modem to. It's probably COM1 or COM2. If you're not sure, check your computer's documentation.

Baud rate   The baud rate is a measurement of how quickly a modem transfers data. It's *almost* synonymous with bits per second (bps), though not quite—and I have no intention of getting into the argument of whether or not they are the same thing. Just be aware that you'll see both terms used to describe the same thing, the data-transmission speed. At the time of writing, many Internet service providers are switching to 28,800 bps. Some may soon go with faster modems. You need at least 14,400 bps. You'll be transferring data directly back to your computer, and you need all the speed you can get.

Telephone number   You already have the phone number you must dial to connect to the service provider. You also need to know any other numbers you need to dial to get through, such as **9** to get an outside line and ***70** to turn off call waiting. With most modems you can also use commas (,) to add a short pause between these numbers. For example, *70,,555-4567.

Modem type or initialization string   For now, you probably just need to know the modem type. Some communications programs will give you options, such as Hayes, Telebit, and MultiTech. If yours isn't one of these, you'll select Hayes, as it's the industry standard that most modems try to emulate these days. However, modem initialization strings are a constant source of problems. If you have trouble with your modem not connecting, you may have to enter a custom initialization string. You can find the information from your modem's user manual, and, we hope, your service provider will be able to help.

Which COM Port?   Here's a quick way to find out where your modem is. Open **Windows Terminal**. Select the **Settings|Communications** command. Click on COM1 and then on OK. If a message says that you have the wrong port, try again with **COM2**. Continue until you find a COM port that doesn't give you the error message. Then select the **Settings|Phone Number** command and enter a number to dial. Close the dialog box, and select the **Phone|Dial** command. If the modem dials, you have the right port. If not, go back and try another port.

No 14,400?   Many communications programs, including some TCP/IP programs, don't show a 14,400 option. If not, you can select the next higher speed, such as 19,200.

231

Hardware handshake   Ask your service provider whether your modem should use hardware handshaking. *Handshaking* is the means by which two computers tell each other when they are able and unable to accept further data, and there are two ways to do this: software handshaking and hardware handshaking. You are unlikely to be using software handshaking, but may be using hardware handshaking.

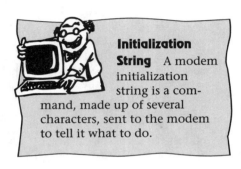

Initialization String   A modem initialization string is a command, made up of several characters, sent to the modem to tell it what to do.

Parity   What parity setting should your modem use. This is probably set to None.

Stop bits   What stop-bits setting should your modem use. This is probably set to 1.

Data bits   What data-bits settings should your modem use. This is probably set to 8.

Communications port speed   Some TCP/IP software requires that you enter the speed of the communications port. Not the speed of the modem, but the speed the data is transferred from your computer through the COM port. You may not run into such a program; we're not going to look at one in this book (though earlier versions of some of the programs we will look at used to ask for this information). If you do, though, you may be able to find the port speed using a computer diagnostics program. (Windows comes with Microsoft Diagnostics. Close Windows, change to the WINDOWS directory, type **MSD**, and press **Enter**.)

These diagnostics programs are not always good at showing the port speed (MSD is kind of flaky). The program should show the UART chip type, though, if it's an 8250, it will be slow. If it's a 16450, it should be much faster. If it's a 16550, it may be 19,200 bits per second or as much as 57,600 bps. Try entering 19,200 into any program that asks for this speed; it will probably be correct. Then experiment to find the highest speed you can use.

An Exercise for the Eager: Testing the Login

It's a good idea to test logging into your system using an ordinary telecommunications program, such as Windows Terminal, CrossTalk, or HyperACCESS. You can dial into the number given you by your service provider and try to use the dial-in direct logon procedure. You won't be able to get all the way, because these communications programs are not TCP/IP programs, but you will be able to check that you have the correct username, password, and startup command.

Record the session; virtually all such programs these days let you record every word that passes over the lines during the session. In Windows Terminal, you'll use the **Transfers|Receive Text File** command to select a file in which Terminal can store the session.

Here's a sample session I recorded when testing my connection to Colorado Springs' Internet Express:

```
ATDT758-2656
CONNECT 14400/ARQ/V32/LAPM/V42BIS


====> Connected 10:41am Wednesday, June 22, 1994
Checking authorization, Please wait...
CHECK OUT THE NEW BBS MENU SYSTEM & TELECONFERENCE:
     Select Z from the top menu (in Power Tools)
     Communicating with fellow users has never
     been easier.


Welcome to the CNS Network
       If you are a new user, please login in as
                    userid    "new"
                    password  "newuser"


Username: pkent
Password:
(I entered my password, but it's not "echoed" back, so it doesn't appear)
Permission granted


                         Community News Service (CNS,Inc.)
                              in affiliation with
                            ==TELEPHONE EXPRESS==
                         If you need assistance,
                      please call CNS at 719-592-1240


Type "c" followed by <RETURN> to continue slip


Switching to SLIP.
Annex address is 165.212.9.10.  Your address is 199.190.133.121.
_E4_@-_b¥_
            ç__y x_____Ü_Ä_
(this is where I hung up, ending the session)
NO CARRIER
```

From this session, we can see that the service provider's system is asking for a Username: and Password:. I entered both, and both worked. There's the line, Type "c" followed by <RETURN> to continue. I'd type c if I wanted to access my dial-in terminal account, but to get to my SLIP account, I have to type slip and press Enter to get into SLIP mode. The service provider's system then tells me my IP address. Check this number against your IP number, and make sure they are the same. In this case, the address was not the same as the one given to me by the service provider. If you find such a problem, call the service provider and ask why you are getting a different number.

Once in slip mode, I just see garbage—that's okay, I've gotten as far as I need, so now I can disconnect using the telecommunications program's hang-up command. This test has helped me make sure the account was set up correctly (after I got the mismatched numbers problem cleared up, that is), but it gave me something else—the information I need to write a login script.

Creating a Login Script

Many programs require a login script for you to connect to your service provider's system. That is, you write a short text file telling the program what the host system will do, and what the program should tell the host.

If you are lucky, your service provider has already written a script for the program you plan to use. For instance, if you are using Internet Chameleon, you'll find that there are already setups—including the scripts—created for ANS, NetCom, PSI, Alternet, Cerfnet, and, currently, four other services. If you want to use Trumpet Winsock, you may find your service provider has already created a setup that you can download from them using a dial-in terminal account.

However, you may have to create your own login script. So testing the connection using a telecommunications program not only ensures you are using the correct username and password, but it also provides information you can use when writing a login script: the sequence of events that occur when connecting to your dial-in direct account. (You'll see how to create a Trumpet Winsock script in Chapter 25.)

Be Nice!

If your service provider doesn't have the script and configuration files you need, why not "donate" them once you've created them and are sure they work. The service provider could put them in his library and let others use them. (But if you put your password in the script, remember to remove it!)

Your Info Here

Gathering the info you need for a TCP/IP account is a messy business, as you've just spent the last 10 pages discovering. I've included the following table to help you compile all the information you need. Later, when you are setting up your TCP/IP software, you can refer to this table to find the data you need.

Hey, We're Not Idiots!

You will probably find that your service provider gives you incomplete information, and when you ask for more details treats you like an idiot (slipping into "techno-babyspeak"). That's the nature of technical support people (I've spoken with hundreds). Don't be intimidated. The more information you have, the smoother things will go.

Essential Account Information

Telephone number to call

Type of connection (SLIP, CSLIP, PPP)

Username (e.g., pkent)

Password

"Shell account" Username (e.g., pwkent)

"Shell account" Password

Startup command (e.g., slip)

System prompt at which you enter the startup command

Internet Protocol (IP) address (e.g., 199.190.133.121)

Hostname (e.g., pkent)

Domain name (e.g., cscns.com or kent.com)

Domain name server (DNS) addresses (e.g., 192.156.196.1)

Subnet mask (e.g., 255.255.255.254)

Gateway address (e.g., 192.156.196.1)

More Stuff

Mail POP server name or address and port number

SMTP server name or address and port number

Mail Gateway name or address

Mailbox username

Mailbox password

NNTP news server name or address and port number

Gopher address and port number

Gopher+ (yes or no)

WWW home page (e.g., http://usa.net/HomePage.html)

Modem Information

COM port (e.g., COM1)

Baud rate (e.g., 14,400)

Modem type/initialization string (e.g., Hayes)

Telephone number prefix (e.g., 9,*7)

Hardware handshake (yes or no)

Parity

Stop bits

Data bits

Communications port speed (e.g., 19,200 bps)

The Least You Need to Know

➤ Make sure you get all the information in this chapter's table before trying to set up a dial-in direct account.

➤ Test the login procedure using Windows Terminal or another telecommunications program. Make sure you have the right username, password, IP address, and TCP/IP startup command, and know where to enter the command.

➤ Record the login procedure in case you need to use the information later to write a login script for your TCP/IP program.

Pulling Up Your Winsocks

I'll warn you now—this chapter's the toughest in this book. Installing Internaut was a breeze—the procedure in this chapter is more like a gale. So grab a bottle of aspirin and a pot of coffee, take a deep breath, and read on.

If you've read Chapter 21, you know that you need to install a file called WINSOCK.DLL in order to run Windows on the Internet. WINSOCK.DLL is a *dynamic link library*, a system from which programs can "borrow" when they want to carry out some common task.

WINSOCK.DLL provides a way for Windows programs to communicate across a TCP/IP link. That makes it much easier for software writers to create new Internet programs. Instead of writing a program that contains the necessary tools to transmit data over a TCP/IP link, all a programmer needs to do is write a program that can talk to WINSOCK.DLL. For example, the programmer who created WS_FTP, an excellent FTP program for Windows, just needs to concentrate on the FTP features. (See Chapter 15 for information about this program.) He doesn't really care about transmitting information directly to and from the Internet; he just cares about sending it to and from WINSOCK.DLL, and WINSOCK.DLL takes care of the rest.

That means a lot of Windows software can't talk directly to the Net. They have to have WINSOCK.DLL first. And although various programmers have created a WINSOCK.DLL, there's a set of standards—the *Windows Sockets* standards—that define what the file should do. A program that can work with one version of WINSOCK.DLL should be able to work with any of them.

Decisions, Decisions—Which Do I Use?

Which to use? Easy question:

➤ If you are using a commercial Internet package, such as Internet Chameleon or WinGopher, use the WINSOCK.DLL that came with the product.

➤ If you have Windows 95, you may want to use the WINSOCK.DLL that comes with the operating system. However, in the first release of Windows 95 you'll probably find that the dialer doesn't let you create a login script, making it awkward to use, so you may want to skip this option.

➤ If you have Windows for Workgroups 3.11 and are setting up a permanent (not dial-in direct) connection, get ahold of the latest TCP/IP software. It's not included with the installation disks, but you can get it from Microsoft.

➤ If you want to install shareware, freeware, or public domain Windows software, use the Trumpet Winsock. This is a shareware program ($20). You'll find this all over the place. You can get it from the **ftp.ncsa.uiuc.edu** FTP site, for instance, in the **PC/Mosaic/sockets/** directory. The latest version should be in the **biochemistry.bioc.cwru.edu** FTP site, in the directory **/pub/trumpwsk**.

General Winsock Installation Wisdom

First, before you do anything, *talk to your service provider*. Some service providers have already set up the necessary files—just download the files, make a few small changes, and away you go. If your service provider has done this, you can save a lot of time by grabbing those files. However, you may find that your service provider's documentation is still rather vague. Try to get Winsock up and running, but if you have problems, come back to this chapter and see if I can help.

If your service provider doesn't have a Winsock setup available for users, ask yourself this: "If I try to go it alone, will I get any help from the service provider?" This is not something that's easy to do on your own. One service provider told me, "We'll connect the SLIP account on our end, but if you have problems with your SLIP software, that's your problem. We can't help."

It's Not So Hard! Maybe I'm making this all sound too complicated. You might get your connection running in a few minutes and wonder what I'm talking about. I hope this chapter will help you avoid the problems I've run into!

They then went ahead and made several mistakes in setting up my account, making it impossible for me to connect the SLIP account. If you want to connect a SLIP or PPP account, you must have a cooperative service provider. If you think you can rely on your service provider to help, go ahead and find the compressed file containing all the Trumpet Winsock bits and pieces. At the time of writing, the most recent version was 2.0B.

Assuming You Chose Trumpet Winsock...

The rest of this chapter concerns installing Trumpet Winsock, the most popular WINSOCK.DLL widely available on the Internet. This is a shareware product; the registration fee is $20. You can use this program to connect in either of two ways: to a dial-in direct account (using SLIP, CSLIP, or PPP), or to a network with an Ethernet *packet driver* already installed and a permanent connection to the Internet.

Packet Driver A packet driver is a program that sends "packets" of data out through your network card and across the network. Ethernet is a common form of Local Area Network.

If you are planning to install on a network, you'll have to look elsewhere for help. There are many different configurations, and how you install Trumpet Winsock will depend on how you are running your network. If you are the network's system administrator, you'll probably be able to figure it out from the Trumpet Winsock documentation relatively easily. If you are not, talk with the administrator and find out if he can help. An ordinary user shouldn't be messing with this sort of thing, anyway. If you know nothing about network software, don't touch it.

Let's run through installing Trumpet Winsock step by step.

1. Start by creating a directory from which you will run Winsock. Call this something like **C:\WINSOCK** or **C:\TRUMPET**.

2. Copy the Winsock files to the directory. You'll probably have these files:

BUGS.LST   A text file containing information about Winsock versions and bugs.

BYE.CMD   A text file containing the commands sent to your modem to end a session.

DISCLAIM.TXT   A text file containing a disclaimer and copyright notice.

HOSTS   A sample text file containing a list of host names. Some TCP/IP programs may refer to this list, but most don't, so you can forget about it for now.

INSTALL.DOC   A text file containing the Winsock user manual.

INSTALL.TXT   A Word for Windows file containing the Winsock user manual.

I'm going to assume you understand a few basics, such as how to create directories and copy files, and how to edit an AUTOEXEC.BAT file. If you don't, you may find Winsock a little more of a problem than you imagine. Pick up *The Complete Idiot's Guide to DOS* for a quick education on the subject.

LOGIN.CMD   A text file containing the commands sent to your modem to begin a session.

PROTOCOL   A text file containing a list of Internet protocols. Not used for dial-in direct connections.

README.MSG   A short text file providing the software author's e-mail address.

SERVICES   A text file containing a list of Internet services. Not used for dial-in direct connections.

TCPMAN.EXE   The program that you run to set up and use the WINSOCK.DLL program.

WINSOCK.DLL   The Windows dynamic link library that is the "guts" of TCP/IP driver.

Later, after running setup, you'll find a **TRUMPWSK.INI** file in this directory. This is a text file containing the initialization information used when starting a Winsock session. It's created the first time you enter setup information.

3. Use Windows Notepad or Windows Sysedit to change the PATH statement in your AUTOEXEC.BAT file to include the name of the directory you put the Winsock files into. For example, if you put them in **C:\TRUMPET**, make sure the path statement contains **C:\TRUMPET** (such as, PATH C:\DOS;C:\WINDOWS;C:\TRUMPET). (You can find the AUTOEXEC.BAT file in your root directory.)

4. Reboot your computer and then restart Windows.

5. Start the **TCPMAN.EXE** program. You can create an icon, if you want, and start the program by double-clicking on the icon. Or select **Run** from the Program Manager or File Manager **File** menu, then type **TCPMAN** and click on **OK**. The program will start. (If it doesn't, you didn't put the path information into AUTOEXEC.BAT correctly.) The Trumpet Winsock Network Configuration dialog box should appear (see the following figure).

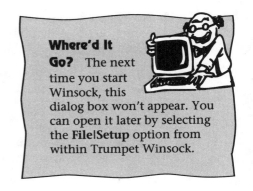

Where'd It Go? The next time you start Winsock, this dialog box won't appear. You can open it later by selecting the **File|Setup** option from within Trumpet Winsock.

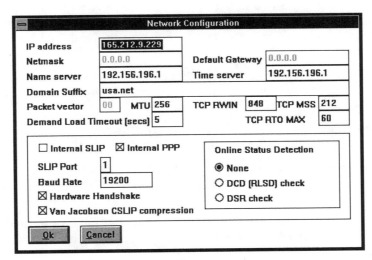

The Trumpet Winsock Network Configuration dialog box, after you have entered all the data.

6. Go find the data you collected in Chapter 24. You're going to need this data to set up Trumpet Winsock.

7. Click on the **Internal SLIP** or **Internal PPP** check box, depending on the type of connection you are going to make. This disables certain options you don't need, and enables others that you do need. (If you were connecting to a network with a permanent connection, you would leave these check boxes cleared.)

8. Type your Internet Protocol address into the **IP address** text box. This is the address by which your computer will be identified on the Internet once connected. (In some rare cases, you may have to type **bootp** instead of a number. Only do so if instructed by your service provider.)

9. Now enter your service provider's domain nameserver IP address into the **Name server** text box. If you have more than one nameserver IP address, you can enter them one after the other, leaving a single space between each one.

10. The **Time server** option is, at the time of writing, unused, though future versions may use it. If so, your service provider will give you the time server address.

11. Enter the domain name given to you by your service provider. For instance, if you connect to Internet Express, and your e-mail address is jbloe@usa.net, you'll type **usa.net** in the **Domain Suffix** text box. You may be given several domain names to put in here; separate them with spaces.

12. TCP MSS means *Transmission Control Protocol Maximum Segment Size*, some kind of network thing (measured in bytes) you don't need to worry about too much. If you are using a SLIP account, enter 512; if you are using a CSLIP account, use 212. If your service provider suggests certain values for this and the next two items, use those instead.

13. TCP RWIN means *Transmission Control Protocol Receive Window*, another esoteric network term. Make this value about three to four times the TCP MSS value; say, 1536 for SLIP and 765 for CSLIP.

14. MTU is the *Maximum Transmission Unit*. (Yes, another one.) This is usually the TCP MSS value plus about 40; 552 for SLIP and 294 for CSLIP.

15. The **Demand Load Timeout** is the number of seconds that the Trumpet Winsock program remains loaded after an application has finished with it. You can leave this set to 5 seconds.

16. Enter the port number of your COM port that your modem connects to in the **SLIP port** text box. Enter **1** for COM1, **2** for COM2, and so on.

17. In the **Baud Rate** text box, enter the modem speed you want to use. If you have a 14,400 bps modem, try entering 19,200.

18. If your service provider's system supports a *hardware handshake*, also known as *hardware flow control* (a method for two modems to keep synchronized during transmissions), check the **Hardware Handshake** check box. Also, if your modem does not use hardware handshake as the default, you need to turn it on in the login script. See your modem's documentation for information for the correct command.

19. If you have a CSLIP connection, check the **Van Jacobsen CSLIP Compression** check box.

20. If your modem can use DCD (Data Carrier Detect) or DSR (Data Set Ready), click on the appropriate **Online Status** option button. These are methods that modems use to tell a program their on-line status. You may need to turn on the feature if it is not the modem's default. In the script, you would have to use the modem command for turning it on. (Generally, AT&C1 for DCD and AT&S1 for DSR.)

21. Click on the **OK** button. You'll see a message telling you to restart Trumpet Winsock.

22. Click on the **OK** button in the message box, then select **File|Exit** to close Trumpet Winsock.

23. Reopen **Trumpet Winsock.**

Whew! You made it. But no, the TCP/IP hell week isn't over yet. It's time to set up your login script. Read on.

Script Writing 101

It's time to write (or, at least edit) the script that Trumpet Winsock will follow when connecting. First, go find the sample login session you created in Chapter 24. Then select **Dialler|Edit Scripts** in Trumpet Winsock. A typical File Open dialog box appears. Double-click on the **login.cmd** file, and the login script appears in a Notepad window. Here's the script you'll probably see:

```
# initialize modem
#
output atz\13
input 10 OK\n
#
# set modem to indicate DCD
#
output at&c1
input 10 OK\n
#
# send phone number
#
output atdt242284\13
#
# my other number
#
#output atdt241644\13
#
# now we are connected.
#
input 30 CONNECT
#
```

```
#  wait till it's safe to send because some modem's hang up
#  if you transmit during the connection phase
#
wait 30 dcd
#
# now prod the terminal server
#
output \13
#
#  wait for the username prompt
#
input 30 username:
username Enter your username
output \u\13
#
# and the password
#
input 30 password:
password Enter your password
output \p\13
#
# we are now logged in
#
input 30 >
#
# see who on for informational reasons.
#
output who\13
input 30 >
#
# jump into slip mode
#
output slip\13
#
# wait for the address string
#
input 30 Your address is
#
# parse address
#
```

```
address 30
input 30 \n
#
# we are now connected, logged in and in slip mode.
#
display \n
display Connected.  Your IP address is \i.\n
#
#  ping a well known host locally...  our slip server won't work
#  for a while
#
exec pingw 131.217.10.1
#
# now we are finished.
```

All the lines that begin with **#** are simply comment lines: they don't do anything. Let's break the script down, piece by piece.

output atz\13   First, at the top, you have the initial message sent to the modem. The line means "send the ATZ command." This command resets the modem, clearing out any settings that it may have picked up from an earlier communications session. (\13 means "send a carriage return," the same as pressing **Enter** or **Return**.)

input 10 OK\n   This means "wait 10 seconds to see if the modem sends the OK signal back." OK means that it's ready to receive more commands.

output at&c1   This is a message being sent to the modem; at&c1 turns on the Data Carrier Detect feature of your modem, if available. DCD sends a signal to the program when connecting to or disconnecting from another modem. In some cases, you may have to modify this line, if your modem can't seem to connect to the service provider's. If so, talk with the service provider's technical support about what you should use.

input 10 OK\n   Again, the script waits for up to ten seconds for the modem to respond.

output atdt242284\13   This line sends the telephone number to the modem; the modem dials the number. Replace the number (after the **t** and before the \) with the number you need to dial to connect to your service provider. If you need to add a number to get an outside line, precede the phone number with that number and a comma or two for a pause, for example, **9,,5551212**. If you are dialing long-distance, include all the necessary numbers (such as **18005551212**). If you have call waiting on the line you are using, use the correct code to turn it off, along with a comma or two to create a pause (usually ***70** as in **9,,*70,,5551212**).

 # my other number and **#output atdt241644\13**   This is a sample script, and below where you change your telephone number is space for an additional number, in case the first is busy. If you have two numbers, place the second number in this space. Remember to remove the # sign from the start of the line.

input 30 CONNECT   The script now waits up to 30 seconds for the message from the modem informing the program that it has connected to the other modem. That message is, for most modems, CONNECT, so it's unlikely that you will have to change this line.

wait 30 dcd   This tells the script to wait for 30 seconds, to make sure you fully connect before continuing. When you've established a connection for the first time you may want to experiment with this number, to reduce it and speed up your connection time. The **dcd** at the end of the line means "wait for a Data Carrier Detect signal from the modem." You can remove this if you want.

output \13   This is a sample script, and the way in which your service provider's system works will probably differ from this sample system. In this sample, after connecting, a user has to press **Enter** to send a carriage return to get the host's "attention." This line sends the carriage return. Your system may not require this.

input 30 username: This line tells the script to wait for up to 30 seconds for the **username** prompt. Your system may not have such a prompt, though. The prompt may be **login:**, for example. If so, replace the word **username** with **login:**.

Make sure you enter the text that is being waited for exactly like it appears on the screen. If your service provider's system displays the word *username*, don't enter **Username** or **USERNAME**. The case of each letter must be correct. If there's a colon at the end of the word, include that. Make sure you don't add any spaces after the word.

username Enter your username   This line tells Trumpet Winsock to display a dialog box at this point. The dialog box will say, "Enter your username." (You can change that to login, if you want.) You will have to type your name and then press **Enter**. If you would rather have the script enter your username automatically for you, remove this line.

output \u\13   This tells the script to send the username you typed into the dialog box. If you removed the previous line, though, you should replace the **\u** with your username, leaving a space between **output** and your username. For example, **output pkent\13**.

input 30 password: This time we're waiting for the password. Same warning applies; make sure you get the case of the prompt correct (Password or password or PASSWORD). Include a colon if necessary; don't add extra spaces.

password Enter your password   Again, this tells the program to display a dialog box into which you can type your password. If you don't want to type it—if you want to automatically send your password—remove this line.

output \p\13   This tells the script to send the password you just typed in. If you deleted the previous line, you must use your actual password, replacing the **\p**. For example, **output password\13**.

input 30 >   This tells the program to wait for the > prompt. There's a good chance that your system won't display a > prompt. (In a moment, I'll show you what my script does after the password.)

> You wouldn't want to break the first rule of security—*Don't write down your password!*—would you? Well, maybe you would, if your computer is not accessible to other users.

output who\13   This line sends the word **who**, to run the UNIX **who** command (which shows you who is logged on).

input 30 >   Again, we're waiting for the > prompt.

output slip\13   Now we send the word **slip**, the command that puts the system into slip mode.

input 30 Your address is   We're waiting here for the words **Your address is**. That's the line where the service provider tells you your IP address.

address 30   This means "take a look at the IP address that's about to be sent, and store the address."

input 30 \n   This says, "wait for the IP address."

display \n   This says, "display a carriage return and line feed on the screen." That is, move all the previous text up a line.

display Connected. Your IP address is \i.\n   This says "display the words **Connected. Your IP address is**," followed by the IP address that has just been stored, followed by a carriage return and line feed. The term **\i** is the IP address that has been stored. **\n** is a carriage return and line feed.

exec pingw 131.217.10.1   This executes the **pingw** program, which automatically pings another site for verification that you are up and running. You should remove this, it's really not essential.

My Sample Script

I modified the script we just looked at so it would work on my system. Here's what I ended up with. You can compare it with my sample login session I showed you in Chapter 24.

```
output ATZ&H1\13
input 10 OK\n
output atdt7582656\13
input 45 CONNECT
input 30 sername:
output kent\13
input 30 ssword:
output not-my-real-password\13
input 30 continue
output slip\13
input 30 Your address is
address 30
input 30 \n
display \n
display Connected.  Your IP address is \i.\n
```

This is similar to the sample script we just looked at. Notice these differences, though:

output ATZ&H1\13   I changed this line and used the commands advised by my service provider. This tells my modem to use hardware flow control.

input 30 sername: Notice that I have **sername** instead of **username**. This is common practice in the writing of such scripts, just in case the case of the word is changed (from Username to username or vice versa).

output kent\13   Notice that I'm not using the dialog box to ask for my username, I'm entering it automatically.

input 30 ssword: Again, I've knocked off the first letter (okay, the first two, so I didn't upset anyone) of the prompt the program is looking for.

output not-my-real-password\13   Okay, so I'm breaking a security rule by putting my password in here instead of making Trumpet Winsock prompt me for it. I live in a concrete bunker with one door and no windows and I never leave home, so I figure I'm safe.

input 30 continue   As you can see from my session in Chapter 8, my service provider's system will prompt me to "Type "c" followed by <RETURN> to continue." Instead, I have to type **slip** and continue to get into slip mode.

Now, Let's See If It Works...

Save your login script. Then select **Dialler|Login** and the script begins. You can follow through, and if you run into any problems, you can figure out more or less where in the script the problem lies. If you reach the **Script completed   SLIP ENABLED** lines, you've succeeded. You are logged in with your SLIP account running (see the following figure). However, if your script just hangs up, you'll need to log out. First, press **Esc**. Then select **Dialler|Bye**. This runs the BYE.CMD script, which tells your modem to hang up.

Go examine your script and see where it hung. If you can't find anything obvious, check all your Trumpet Winsock configuration settings, too. Try a different baud rate, perhaps. Make sure you entered the correct IP addresses. Check the script for spelling errors.

If you still can't get it working, talk with your service provider. Maybe you need a particular modem setup. You may need to change the Packet Vectors in the Network Configuration dialog box. You may need to use the **bootp** command somewhere in the script. Your service provider should be able to tell you exactly how to set up your script and configuration. If you register the program, you can contact the program's publisher for technical support.

> **Won't Log Off?**
> I had trouble getting Trumpet Winsock to hang up the phone line. I added this line to my BYE.CMD script, and it fixed the problem:
> **sleep2**

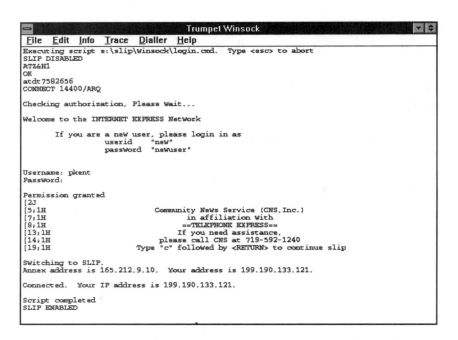

Logging into my SLIP account with Trumpet Winsock.

Getting Out of Cyberspace

To close Trumpet Winsock, first make sure you close all your other TCP/IP programs: your FTP program, your e-mail program, and so on. Then use this method to close:

➤ Use the **Dialler|Bye** command to run the BYE.CMD script, which hangs up the modem.

If you have the **Automatic login and logout on demand** option set (see later in this chapter) you can also use these options:

➤ Double-click on Trumpet Winsock's **Control** menu.

➤ Press **Alt-F4**.

➤ Select **File|Exit**.

If you have any TCP/IP programs running, you'll see a warning message. Also, you'll find that in some circumstances Trumpet Winsock can't close. You'll have to press **Esc** first, then use one of the above methods to close.

Some More Details Before We Leave

There are a few more things to know about Trumpet Winsock. Let's look at some of the other menu options.

Edit|Copy Highlight text in the Trumpet Winsock window, and then select this option to copy it to the Clipboard. This can be very useful when using the Trace menu commands, if you understand what the text means.

Edit|Clear Clears all the text from the window.

Special Info and **Special|Kill Socket** and **Trace|all sorts of weird stuff** These are options that you can use to diagnose network connection problems. If you understand what all the terms on the menu mean, you'll know how to use them. If you don't, leave them alone—they can crash the system in some cases.

Dialler|Bye Runs the BYE.CMD script, which hangs up the modem.

Dialler|Other You can create other types of scripts that run from this option. For instance, if you have two SLIP accounts, you could run one with the **Dialler|Login** menu option and the other from **Dialler|Other**.

Dialler|Manual Login Lets you log into your account manually, by typing commands into the window. Press **Esc** to end this mode.

> **Why Didn't It Hang Up?** If you don't have the **Automatic login and logout on demand** option set, and you close the window without using **Dialler|Bye** first, Trumpet Winsock will close but will not hang up the connection. Your Internet TCP/IP programs won't be able to run without Trumpet Winsock, even though you are connected to the service provider. Reopen Trumpet Winsock, press **Esc** a couple of times, select **Dialler|Bye**, and then close the window.

Dialler|Options This is handy. Select **Automatic login on startup only** to run the LOGIN.CMD script each time you start the Trumpet Winsock application. Select **Automatic login and logout on demand** to automatically run the script when you start the application, and to close Trumpet Winsock automatically after the **SLIP inactivity timeout (minutes)** value. For instance, let's say this value is 5. That means that if you go for five minutes without a TCP/IP program running, Trumpet Winsock will close automatically. It does not mean that if you have a TCP/IP program open and don't use it for five minutes Trumpet Winsock will close. This will happen only if there are no such programs open. Also, when you have **Automatic login and logout on demand** selected, closing the Trumpet Winsock window will automatically run the BYE.CMD script, hanging up the phone. (If you want to use this feature but not the inactivity timeout, put **0** in the **SLIP inactivity timeout** text box.)

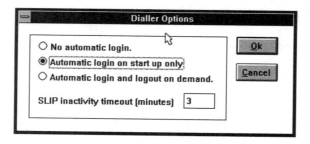

The Dialler Options dialog box lets you automatically start and close Trumpet Winsock.

Help|About   Displays the Trumpet Winsock version number.

Be Ethical—Register the Program!

Trumpet Winsock can open up a totally new Internet world, letting you bring the 1990s to a system still stuck in the 1970s. If you use Trumpet Winsock for 30 days or more, please register it. You receive a registration number that will remove the UNREGISTERED VERSION signs that appear here and there. You'll also get technical support, and Trumpet Software International says that it will give registered users preference for requests for bug fixes and enhancements.

Working on the Internet with a dial-in terminal account is like writing a book with a typewriter. Working on the Internet once you've got Trumpet Winsock installed is like writing a book with a word processor. Pay the registration fee. (See the end of the INSTALL.TXT or INSTALL.DOC file that came with Trumpet Winsock.)

The Least You Need to Know

➤ Don't be intimidated. Installing Trumpet Winsock can be relatively easy if you follow these instructions.

➤ You need a login script to automate your connection to your service provider. It's reasonably easy to create one.

➤ This program is shareware; remember to register it (it only costs $20).

➤ Once Trumpet Winsock is up and running, you can easily install your other Windows Internet software.

Speak Like a Geek—the Pipeline Glossary

alias   A name substituted for a more complicated name. For instance, a simple alias may be used instead of a more complicated mailing address or for a mailing list.

alpha test   A program test based on the premise that "we've got a few features ready, let's put them together and see what happens when we give the program to a few people." See also *beta test*.

America Online   An online information system.

anonymous ftp   A system by which members of the Internet "public" can access files at certain *FTP* sites without needing a login name—they simply log in as *anonymous*.

Archie   An index system that helps you find files in over 1,000 FTP sites.

archive file   A file that contains other files, generally *compressed files*. Used to store files that are not used often, or files that may be *downloaded* by Internet users.

ARPANET   Where it all began—the Advanced Research Projects Agency (of the U.S. Department of Defense) computer network that was the forerunner of the Internet.

article   A message in an Internet *newsgroup*.

ASCII   The American Standard Code for Information Interchange, a standard way for computers to use bits and bytes to represent characters. An ASCII file contains simple text without any special formatting codes.

backbone   A network through which other networks are connected.

bandwidth   Widely used to mean the amount of information that can be sent through a particular communications channel.

baud rate   A measurement of how quickly a *modem* transfers data. Although, strictly speaking, this is not the same as *bps* (bits per second), the two terms are often used interchangeably.

BBS   See *bulletin board system.*

BCNU   Be Seein' You.

beta test   A program test based on the premise, "This program's virtually finished, we just need a little help getting the rough edges off—let's give it to a few more people." See also *alpha test.*

BIND   Berkeley Internet Name Domain, a UNIX implementation of the *DNS* standard.

BITNET   The "Because It's Time" network (really!). A large network connected to the Internet. Before the Internet became affordable to learning institutions, BITNET was the network of choice for communicating.

bits per second   A measure of the speed of data transmission—the number of bits of data that can be transmitted each second.

BOOTP   The Bootstrap Protocol, a method used on some networks to connect and start *nodes.*

bounce   The action of e-mail being returned because of some kind of error.

bps   See *bits per second.*

BTW   By The Way.

bulletin board system   A computer system to which other computers can connect so their users can read and leave messages, or retrieve and leave files.

chat   A system by which two users can "talk" with each other by typing; what you see, the other person sees almost instantly—and vice versa. (This is unlike *e-mail*, in which you send your words, and wait for the recipient to read and respond.)

chat   Similar to *talk* programs, except that chat systems let large numbers of users chat together. Where a talk program is like a phone call, a chat system is like a party, sometimes with different "rooms" known as channels or groups.

CIX   The Commercial Internet Exchange, an organization of commercial Internet service providers.

client   A program or computer that is "serviced" by another program or computer (the *server*). For instance, a *Gopher* client program requests information from the indexes of a Gopher server program.

compressed files   Computer files that have been reduced in size by a compression program. Such programs are available for all computer systems. For instance, PKZIP in DOS, tar and compress in UNIX, and StuffIt for the Macintosh.

CompuServe   A computer information service owned by H&R Block. CompuServe is part of the Internet network (though few CompuServe users realize this).

cracker   Someone who tries to enter a computer system without permission. This is the correct term, though the term hacker is often mistakenly used in its place.

CSLIP   Compressed SLIP. See *SLIP*.

cyberspace   The "area" in which computer users travel when "navigating" around on a network.

daemon   A UNIX *server*, a program running all the time in the "background" (that is, unseen by users), providing special services when required.

DARPANET   The Defense Advanced Research Projects Agency network, created by combining ARPANET and MILNET. The forerunner of the Internet.

DCE   Data Circuit-terminating Equipment.

DDN   The Defense Data Network, a U.S. military network that is part of the Internet. *MILNET* is part of the DDN.

dedicated line   A telephone line that is *leased* from the telephone company, and used for one purpose only. In Internetland, dedicated lines connect organizations to service providers' computers, providing dedicated service.

dedicated service   See *permanent connection*.

DFS   A variation of *AFS*.

dial-in direct connection   An Internet connection that is accessed by dialing into a computer through a telephone line. Once connected, your computer acts as if it were an Internet host. You can run client software (such as *Gopher* and *WWW* clients), and can copy files directly to your computer. This type of service is often called *SLIP*, *CSLIP*, or *PPP*. See also *dial-in terminal*.

dial-in service   A networking service used by dialing into a computer through a telephone line.

dial-in terminal connection   An Internet connection accessed by dialing into a computer through a telephone line. Once connected, your computer acts as if it were a terminal connected to the service provider's computer. This type of service is often called *Interactive* or *dial-up*. See also *dial-in direct*.

dial-up service   A common Internet term for a *dial-in terminal connection*.

dig   Domain information gopher, a program that provides information about hosts on the Internet.

direct connection   See *permanent connection*.

DNS   See *Domain Name System*.

domain name   A name given to a host computer on the Internet.

Domain Name System   A system by which one Internet host can find another so it can send *e-mail*, connect *FTP* sessions, and so on. The hierarchical system of Internet host names (**hostname.hostname.hostname**) uses the Domain Name System. The DNS, in effect, translates words into numbers that can be understood by the Internet's computers. For instance, if you use the domain name *firefly.prairienet.org*, DNS translates it into 192.17.3.3.

dot address   A term for an IP address, which is in the form *n.n.n.n*, where each *n* is a number (each number is a byte).

download   The process of transferring information from one computer to another. You *download* a file from another computer to yours. See also *upload*.

DTE   Data Terminal Equipment.

e-mail or **email**   Short for *electronic mail*, this is a system that lets people send and receive messages with their computers. The system might be on a large network (such as the Internet), on a bulletin board, (such as CompuServe), or over a company's own office network.

EARN   The European network associated with *Bitnet*.

EFF   See *Electronic Frontier Foundation*.

EFLA   Extended Four-Letter Acronym. Acronyms are essential to the well-being of the Internet. See also *TLA*.

Electronic Frontier Foundation (EFF)   An organization interested in social, legal, and political issues related to the use of computers. The EFF is particularly interested in fighting government restrictions on the use of computer technology.

Elm   An *e-mail* program.

emoticon   The techie name for a *smiley*.

encryption   The modifying of data so that unauthorized recipients cannot use or understand it.

etext   Electronic text; a book or other document in electronic form, usually simple *ASCII* text.

Ethernet   A system by which computers may be connected to one another, and exchange information and messages.

FAQ   Frequently Asked Questions. A menu option named "FAQ" or "Frequently Asked Questions" will lead you to a document that answers common questions. You may also find text files named FAQ.

Fidonet   A network connected to the Internet.

file transfer   The copying of files from one computer to another over a network or telephone line. See *FTP*.

File Transfer Protocol   See *FTP*.

finger   A *UNIX* program used to find information about a user on a host computer.

flame   An abusive newsgroup message.

flamer   Someone who writes a *flame*.

forum   The term used by CompuServe for its individual bulletin boards. In Internet-speak, the term is *newsgroups*.

fragment   Part of a packet. Packets can be broken down into small pieces (fragments), transmitted, then reassembled. See *packet switching*.

Free-Net   A community computer network, often based on the local library, which provides Internet access to citizens, from the library or sometimes from their home computers. Free-Nets also have many local services, such as information about local events, local message areas, connections to local gover nment departments, and so on.

freeware   Software provided free by its originator. Not the same as *public domain software*, for which the author retains copyright. See also *shareware*. Freeware can be freely used, though it still belongs to someone. The owner often defines certain conditions on its use—it may be used for non-commercial purposes, for instance.

FTP   File Transfer Protocol. A *protocol* defining how files are transferred from one computer to another. FTP is also the name of a program used to move files. And FTP can be used as a verb (often in lowercase) to describe the procedure of using FTP. As in, "ftp to **ftp.demon.co.uk**," or "I ftp'ed to their system and grabbed the file."

257

FTPmail   A system maintained by Digital Equipment Corporation (DEC) that lets people use e-mail to carry out FTP sessions.

gateway   A system by which two incompatible networks or applications can communicate with each other.

geek   Someone who knows a lot about computers, but very little about communicating with other people. Geeks spend more time in front of their computers than talking with real people. Geek may have started as a derogatory term, but some geeks even call themselves geeks—thus the term *geekhouse*.

geekhouse   A place where computer geeks hang out, or even live together. Some of the geekhouses in San Diego even have their own WWW servers.

GEnie   A computer information service owned by General Electric.

GML   Generalized Markup Language, a way in which a simple text document can be marked using various codes, so a special reader can format the document. This allows different programs to display the document in different ways, and, perhaps more importantly, the document to be used on different computer types.

Gopher   A system using Gopher *clients* and *servers* to provide a menu system used for navigating around the Internet.

gopherspace   Anywhere and everywhere you can get to using Gopher is known as *gopherspace*.

Gore, Al   A vice president who believes the "Information Superhighway" is critical to the U.S.'s future. Reportedly wants all the United States' high schools connected to the Internet in the next few years.

GUI   Graphical User Interface. A user interface is what you use to communicate with your computer, and there are two basic types—a command line like the UNIX shell (with which you type all your commands) and a graphical user interface. The GUI provides tools such as menus, icons, scroll bars, borders, toolbars, and so on, all designed to make working with the program easier. The GUI, in effect, provides graphical "prompts" to remind you how to do things and lets you do them more quickly using a mouse.

hacker   Someone who enjoys spending most of his life with his head stuck inside a computer, either literally or metaphorically. See *geek*, *cracker*.

hop   A network-routing term. Data being transferred over a network travels through a series of hops.

host   A computer connected directly to the Internet. A service provider's computer is a host, as are computers with *permanent connections*. Computers with *dial-in terminal* connections are not—they are terminals connected to the service provider's host. Computers with *dial-in direct* connections can be thought of as "sort-of-hosts." They act like hosts while connected.

host address   See *IP address.*

host number   See *IP address.*

hostname   The name given to a *host.*

HTML   HyperText Markup Language. A collection of codes that are entered into a document to denote certain WWW components, such as links between documents.

HTTP   HyperText Transfer Protocol. The system used by the World Wide Web to allow documents around the world to be linked into a giant *hypermedia* system.

hypermedia   Similar to *hypertext,* though the term hypermedia implies that there's more "stuff" in the hypertext documents—pictures, sounds, video, and so on.

hypertext   A text document containing "links" between pages, chapters, or topics. Users can "navigate" through such a document, usually by clicking on colored or underlined text. In a *hypertext system,* documents contain links that allow readers to move between areas of the document, following subjects of interest in a variety of different paths. The *World Wide Web* is a hypertext system.

HYTELNET   A directory of *Telnet* sites. A great way to find out what you can do on hundreds of computers around the world.

IAB   See *Internet Architecture Board.*

IETF   See *Internet Engineering Task Force.*

IMHO   In My Humble Opinion.

Integrated Services Digital Network (ISDN)   A digital telecommunications system that everyone's been waiting for, but that the telephone companies seem unable to get installed in a decent time. ISDN allows voice and data to be transmitted on the same line in a digital—rather than the normal analog—format.

Interactive service   See *dial-in terminal connection.*

internet   The term *internet* spelled with a small "i" refers to a group of networks connected to one another. "The Internet" is not the only internet.

Internet address   See *IP address.*

Internet Architecture Board   The "council of elders," elected by *ISOC,* who get together and figure out how the different components of Internet will all connect together.

Internet Engineering Task Force   A group of engineers that makes technical recommendations concerning the Internet to the *IAB*.

Internet Protocol   The standard *protocol* used by systems communicating across the Internet. Other protocols are used, but the Internet Protocol is the most important one.

Internet Relay Chat (IRC)   See *IRC*.

Internet Society   The society that runs Internet. It elects the Internet Architecture Board, which decides on technical issues related to how Internet works.

InterNIC   The Internet Network Information Center. This *NIC*, run by the National Science Foundation, provides various administrative services for the Internet.

IP   See *Internet Protocol*.

IP address   A 32-bit address that defines the location of a host on the Internet. Such addresses are normally shown as four bytes, each one separated by a period (e.g., 192.156.196.1). See also *dot address*.

IRC   Internet Relay Chat, a popular *chat* program. Internet users around the world can chat with other users in their choice of IRC channels.

ISDN   See *Integrated Services Digital Network*.

ISO/OSI Protocols   The International Organization for Standardization Open Systems Interconnect Protocols, a system of *protocols* that may someday replace the *Internet Protocol*.

ISOC   See *Internet Society*.

job   A *UNIX* term referring to a program you started.

Jughead   Jonzy's Universal Gopher Hierarchy Excavation And Display tool, a new gopher search tool, similar to *Veronica*. The main difference between Veronica and Jughead is that Jughead searches a specific gopher server, while Veronica searches all of gopherspace.

Kermit   A file transfer system from Columbia University.

KIS   See *Knowbot Information Service*.

Knowbot   A program that can search the Internet for requested information. Knowbots are in an experimental stage.

Knowbot Information Service   An experimental system that helps you search various directories for a person's information (such as an e-mail address).

LAN   See *Local Area Network*.

leased line   See *dedicated line*.

LISTSERV lists   Mailing lists—using *mail reflectors*—that act as *newsgroups*. Messages sent to a LISTSERV address are sent to everyone who has subscribed to the list. Responses are sent back to the LISTSERV address.

Local Area Network (LAN)   A computer network that covers only a small area, often a single office or building.

logging off   The opposite of *logging on*, telling the computer that you've finished work and no longer need to use its services. The procedure usually involves typing a simple command, such **exit** or **bye**.

logging on   Computer jargon for getting permission from a computer to use its services. A "logon" procedure usually involves typing in a *username* (also known as an *account name* or *userID*) and a *password*. This procedure makes sure that only authorized people can use the computer. Also known as *logging in*.

login   The procedure of *logging on*.

lurker   Someone involved in *lurking*.

lurking   Reading *newsgroup* or *LISTSERV* messages without responding to them. Nobody knows you are there.

mail gateway   A computer connecting different e-mail systems, so the systems can transfer messages.

mail reflector   A mail address that accepts e-mail messages and then sends them on to a predefined list of other e-mail addresses. Such systems are a convenient way to distribute messages to a group of people.

mail server   Used to mean two things. A program that distributes computer files or information in response to e-mail requests. Or a program that handles incoming e-mail for a *host* (as in POP3 mail server).

mailing list   A list of e-mail addresses to which a single message can be sent by entering just one name as the To address. Also refers to discussion groups based on the mailing list. Each message sent to the group is sent out to everyone on the list. (*LISTSERV* groups are mailing-list groups.)

Martian   A data packet that accidentally ends up on the wrong network, or which has a bad address. See *packet switching*.

MB   Abbreviation for *megabyte*.

MCI Mail   An *e-mail* system owned by MCI.

megabyte   A measure of the quantity of data. A megabyte is a lot when you are talking about files containing simple text messages, not much when you are talking about files containing color photographs.

MILNET   A U.S. Department of Defense network connected to the Internet.

MIME   Multipurpose Internet Mail Extensions, a system that lets you send computer files as e-mail.

mirror site   An FTP site that is a "mirror image" of another FTP site. Every week or two the contents of the other FTP site are copied to the mirror site; if you can't get into the original site, you can go to one of the mirror sites.

modem   A device that converts digital signals from your computer into analog signals for transmission through a phone line (*mod*ulation), and converts the phone line's analog signals into digital signals your computer can use (*dem*odulation).

MUD   A type of game popular on the Internet. MUD means Multiple User Dimensions, Multiple User Dungeons, or Multiple User Dialogue. MUDs are text games—each player has a character. Characters communicate with each other by the users typing messages.

navigator   A program that helps you find your way around ("navigate") a complicated BBS. Several navigator programs are available for CompuServe, for instance. Navigators can save you money by letting you prepare for many operations—such as writing mail—offline, then go *online* quickly to perform the operations automatically. Internet navigators are currently in a developmental stage, and not in wide use.

NCSA   National Center for Supercomputing Applications, the people who make the Mosaic World Wide Web browser.

netiquette   Internet etiquette, the correct form of behavior to be used while working on the Internet and USENET. Can be summed up as "Don't waste computer resources, and don't be rude."

Netnews   See *USENET*.

Network File System (NFS)   A system from Sun Microsystems that allows computers to access files over a network as if the files were on local hard disks. Using one, you to can work with files on a remote host as if you were working on your own host.

Network Information Center   A system providing support and information for a network.

Network News Transfer Protocol (NNTP)   A system used for the distribution of USENET newsgroup messages.

Network Time Protocol (NTP)   A system used to synchronize network clocks.

newbie   A new user. The term may be used to refer to a new Internet user, or a user who is new to a particular area of the Internet. Since everyone and their dog is getting onto the Internet, these loathsome creatures have brought the general tone of the Internet down a notch or two, upsetting long-term Internet users who thought the Internet was their own personal secret. As the commercial online services (such as Delphi, America Online, and CompuServe) expand their Internet access, the Net is being swamped by literally millions of newbies.

news server   A computer that collects *newsgroup* data and makes it available to *newsreaders*.

newsgroup   The Internet equivalent of a BBS or discussion group (or "forum" in CompuServe-speak) in which people leave messages for others to read. See also *LISTSERV*.

newsreader   A program that helps you find your way through a *newsgroup's* messages.

NFS   See *Network File System*.

NIC   See *Network Information Center*.

NNTP   See *Network News Transfer Protocol*.

NTP   See *Network Time Protocol*.

NOC   Network Operations Center, a group that administers a network.

node   A computer "device" connected to a computer network. That device might be an actual computer, or something else—a printer or *router*, for instance.

NREN   The National Research and Education Network.

NSF   National Science Foundation, a U.S. government agency. The NSF runs the *NSFNET*.

NSFNET   The "National Science Foundation" network, a large network connected to the Internet.

nslookup   A program that provides detailed information about a host on the Internet.

online   Connected. You are online if you are working on your computer while it is connected to another computer. Your printer is online if it is connected to your computer and ready to accept data. (Online is often written *on-line*, though the non-hyphenated version seems to be gaining acceptance these days.)

packet   A collection of data. See *packet switching*.

Packet InterNet Groper   A program that tests whether a particular host computer is accessible to you.

packet-switching A system that breaks transmitted data into small *packets* and transmits each packet (or package) independently. Each packet is individually addressed, and may even travel over a route different from that of other packets. The packets are combined by the receiving computer.

permanent connection A connection to the Internet using a leased line. The computer with a permanent connection acts as a *host* on the Internet. This type of service is often called *direct*, *permanent direct*, or *dedicated service*, and is very expensive to set up and run.

permanent direct See *permanent connection*.

PINE An e-mail program.

PING See *Packet InterNet Groper*.

ping A simple program that sends a message to another host and waits for a response, in order to analyze the connection between the two hosts.

point of presence Jargon meaning a method of connecting to a service locally (without dialing long-distance). If a service provider has a POP in, say, Podunk, Ohio, people in that city can connect to the service provider by making a local call.

Point-to-Point Protocol A method for connecting computers to Internet via telephone lines, similar to SLIP (though, at present, less common).

POP See *Post Office Protocol* and *Point Of Presence*.

port Generally, "port" refers to the hardware through which computer data is transmitted—the plugs on the back of your computer are ports. On the Internet, "port" often refers to a particular application. For instance, you might telnet to a particular port on a particular host. The port is actually an application.

Post Office Protocol (POP) A system for letting hosts get e-mail from a server. This is typically used when a dial-in direct host—which may only have one user and may only be connected to the Internet periodically—gets its e-mail from a service provider. The latest version of POP is POP3.

posting A message (*article*) sent to a *newsgroup* or the act of sending such a message.

postmaster The person at a *host* who is responsible for managing the mail system. If you need information about a user at a particular host, you can send e-mail to **postmaster@hostname**.

PPP See *Point-to-Point Protocol*.

process A *UNIX* term referring to some kind of operation being carried out, either as a result of a program you started or some kind of automatic process—such as the program that runs the UNIX shell.

PRODIGY   A computer information service.

protocol   A set of rules that defines how computers transmit information to each other, allowing different types of computer and software to communicate with each other.

public domain software   Software that is not owned by anyone. You can freely use and distribute such software without paying its creator, and even modify it if the source code is available. See also *freeware* and *shareware*.

Qwkmail   A system by which e-mail and newsgroup messages are compressed, transferred to your computer, then opened by a Qwkmail program (usually public domain, freeware, or shareware). Useful for dial-in terminal accounts, though Qwkmail can be a hassle to set up on the host end (it's easy to set up on the terminal end).

remote login   A system similar to telnet that lets you log in to another computer.

rlogin   See *remote login*.

rot13   Rotation 13, a method used to "encrypt" messages in newsgroups, so you can't stumble across an offensive message. If you want to read an offensive message, you'll have to decide to do so.

router   A system used to transmit data between two computer systems or networks using the same protocol. For instance, a company that has a permanent connection to the Internet will use a router to connect its computer to a *leased line*. At the other end of the leased line, a router is used to connect it to the service provider's network.

RTFM   Read the F*cking Manual. Often used in reaction to a stupid question. (Or a question which, in the hierarchy of newbies and Internet gurus, is determined to be a stupid question.)

Serial Line Internet Protocol (SLIP)   A method for connecting a computer to Internet using a telephone line and modem. (See *dial-in direct connection*.) Once connected, the user has the same services provided to the user of a *permanent connection*.

server   A program or computer that "services" another program or computer (the *client*). For instance, a *Gopher* server program sends information from its indexes to a Gopher client program.

service provider   A company that provides a connection to Internet. Service providers sell access to the network, for greatly varying prices. Shop around for the best deal.

SGML   Standard Generalized Markup Language. A derivation of the IBM GML. *HTML* is derived from SGML.

shareware   Software that is freely distributed, but for which the author expects payment from people who decide to keep and use it beyond a certain time (usually 30 days). See also *freeware* and *public domain software*.

shell   In *UNIX*, a shell is a program that accepts commands you type and "translates" them for the operating system. In DOS, a shell is a program that "insulates" you from the command line, providing a simpler way to carry out DOS commands.

signature   A short piece of text transmitted with an *e-mail* or *newsgroup* message. Some systems can attach text from a file to the end of a message automatically. Signature files typically contain detailed information on how to contact someone—name and address, telephone numbers, Internet address, CompuServe ID, and so on.

Simple Mail Transfer Protocol (SMTP)   A way to transfer e-mail between computers on a network.

SLIP   See *Serial Line Internet Protocol*.

smiley   A symbol created by typing various keyboard characters, used in *e-mail* and *newsgroup* messages to convey emotion, or simply for amusement. For instance, :-(means sadness. Smileys are usually sideways—turn your head to view the smiley. (The techie term is *emoticon*.)

SMTP   See Simple Mail Transfer Protocol.

Sprintmail   An *e-mail* system used on *Sprintnet*. Back when Sprintnet was called Telenet, the mail portion used once was called Tele-mail.

Sprintnet   A network owned by Sprint. It used to be called Telenet (not to be confused with Telnet).

talk   A program that lets two or more *UNIX* users, on the same host or different hosts, type messages to each other. As a user types a character, that character is immediately transmitted to the other user. There are several common talk programs—talk, ntalk, and *YTalk*.

tar files   Files compressed using the UNIX Tape ARchiver program. Such files usually have filenames ending in **.tar**.

TCP/IP   Transmission Control Protocol/Internet Protocol. A set of *protocols* (communications rules) that control how data is transferred between computers on the Internet.

Telnet   A program that lets Internet users log in to computers other than their own host computers, often on the other side of the world. Telnet is also used as a verb, as in "telnet to **debra.doc.ca**."

telnetting   Internet-speak for using *Telnet* to access a computer on the network.

The Web   See *World Wide Web*.

TLA   Three-Letter Acronym. What would we do without them? See also *EFLA*.

tn3270   A *Telnet*-like program used for remote logins to IBM mainframes.

Token-Ring   A system used for creating small *local area networks*. Such networks may be connected to the Internet.

Trojan horse   A computer program that appears to carry out a useful function, but is actually designed to do harm to the system on which it runs. See also *virus*.

TTFN   Ta-Ta For Now. Originally from wartime British radio, now occasionally used in e-mail.

UDP   The User Datagram Protocol, a *protocol* used in Internet communications.

UNIX   A computer operating system. Most *hosts* connected to the Internet run UNIX.

upload   The process of transferring information from one computer to another. You *upload* a file from your computer to another. See also *download*.

URL   Uniform Resource Locators. Used by the WWW to specify the location of files on other servers.

USENET   The "User's Network," a large network connected to the Internet. The term also refers to the *newsgroups* distributed by this network.

UUCP   UNIX to UNIX Copy Program, a system by which files can be transferred between UNIX computers. The Internet uses UUCP to provide a form of e-mail, in which the mail is placed in files and transferred to other computers.

UUCP network   A network of UNIX computers, connected to the Internet.

UUDECODE   If you use *UUENCODE*, you'll use UUDECODE to convert the *ASCII file* back to its original format.

UUENCODE   A program used to convert a computer file of any kind—sound, spreadsheet, word processing, or whatever—into an *ASCII file* so it can be transmitted as a text message.

UUNET   A service provider connected to the Internet.

Veronica   The Very Easy Rodent-Oriented Net-wide Index to Computerized Archives, a very useful program for finding things in *gopherspace*.

virus   A program that uses various techniques for duplicating itself and traveling between computers. Viruses vary from simply nuisances to serious problems that can cause millions of dollars' worth of damage.

VT100   The product name of a Digital Electronics Corporation computer terminal. This terminal is a standard that is "emulated" (duplicated) by many other manufacturers' terminals.

W3   See *World Wide Web*.

WAIS   See *Wide Area Information Server*.

white pages   Databases containing information about Internet users.

whois   A program used for searching for information about Internet users; it lets you see who is currently logged on to a host.

Wide Area Information Server   A system that can search databases on the Internet for information in which you are interested.

World Wide Web   A *hypertext* system that allows users to "travel through" linked documents, following any chosen route. World Wide Web documents contain topics that, when selected, lead to other documents.

WWW   See *World Wide Web*.

WWWW   The World Wide Web Worm, a system that worms its way around the *World Wide Web*, cataloging what's on there. You can then view the catalog (at **http://www.cs.colorado.edu/home/mcbryan/WWWW.html**).

X.500   A standard for electronic directory services.

XRemote   A rarely used type of *dial-in direct* connection.

YTalk   Currently one of the best UNIX talk programs. Unlike the basic *talk* program, YTalk lets several users talk together at once. It can also communicate with other types of talk program.

Index

273

Gopher to dialog box, 46
gopherspace, 258, 267
  navigating, 34-43
  searching, 47-51
Gore, Al, 258
Graphical User Interfaces
  (GUIs), 258
graphics
  inline images, 135
  newsgroups, 113-115
  viewing, 40-42
GUIs (Graphical User
  Interfaces), 258

H

hackers, *see* geeks, crackers
handles (user
  information), 167
hardware handshaking,
  232, 242
headers, 118-122
help access (e-mail deliv-
  ery), 162-166
Help menu commands
  About, 252
  About Pipeline USA,
    18-20
HGopher program, 201-202
hierarchies (newsgroups),
  103-105
history lists (WWW), 133
home pages (WWW), 134
hops (networks), 258
hosts, 258-260
hotlists (WWW), 134
HTML (HyperText Markup
  Language), 137, 259
HTTP (HyperText Tranfer
  Protocol), 259
hypertext, 130, 259
HYTELNET, 153-155, 259

I

IAB (Internet Architecture
  Board), 259
icons (e-mail viewing), 80
IETF (Internet Engineering
  Task Force), 260

IMHO (In My Humble
  Opinion), 259
Import Bookmarks com-
  mand (File menu), 58
Inbox, 68
  e-mail
    creating mailboxes,
      85-87
    offline viewing, 79-80
    receiving, 79
    searching, 81-82
    sending, 77-78
    viewing, 78
information distribution
  (finger program), 181-183
inline images, viewing
  (WWW), 135
inserting
  archive boxes, 106
  e-mail addresses, 83-85
  filter rules, 122-124
  newsgroups, 101-105
  text, 39-40, 72-73
installing
  Internaut software, 8-9
  Trumpet Winsock,
    238-243
Integrated Services Digital
  Network (ISDN), 259
integration, 26-27
interactive services, 190
Internaut, 3
  bookmarks, 134
  browsers, 131, 137
  closing, 26
  configuring, 58-62
  e-mail, 67
  filters, 117
  finger program, 181-183
  FTP, 143
  integration, 26-27
  mailing lists, 89
  management, 62-63
  multitasking, 27-28
  newsgroups, 97
  searching users, 159-160
  software, 8-9, 18
  starting, 11-18
  Talk program, 177-179
  Telnet, 151

window components,
  22-26
  see also Pipeline USA
Internet
  connections, 187-188
  service providers, 217
  shareware/freeware
    software, 197
  suites, 209
  TCP/IP stacks, 225
  Trumpet Winsock, 237
internet, 259
Internet Architecture Board
  (IAB), 259
Internet Chameleon,
  211-212
Internet Engineering Task
  Force (IETF), 260
Internet Guides and
  Tools, 47
Internet in a Box, 212-214
Internet menu commands
  Connect to another
    system (Telnet), 152
  Get files ("FTP" and
    "Archie"), 145
  Gopher anywhere, 46
  Search All Gopherspace
    (Veronica), 47
  Search current news, 184
  World Wide Web, 131
Internet Network Informa-
  tion Center
  (InterNIC), 260
Internet Protocol (IP),
  228, 260
Internet Relay Chat (IRC),
  172-176, 260
Internet Society, 260
InternetWorks, 200-201
InterNIC (Internet Network
  Information Center), 260
Invite command (Com-
  mands menu), 176
IP (Internet Protocol),
  228, 260
IRC (Internet Relay Chat),
  172-176, 260
ISDN (Integrated Services
  Digital Network), 259
ISO/OSI Protocols, 260

O

P

PLUG YOURSELF INTO...

THE MACMILLAN INFORMATION SUPERLIBRARY™

Free information and vast computer resources from the world's leading computer book publisher—online!

FIND THE BOOKS THAT ARE RIGHT FOR YOU!

A complete online catalog, plus sample chapters and tables of contents give you an in-depth look at *all* of our books, including hard-to-find titles. It's the best way to find the books you need!

- **STAY INFORMED** with the latest computer industry news through our online newsletter, press releases, and customized Information SuperLibrary Reports.

- **GET FAST ANSWERS** to your questions about MCP books and software.

- **VISIT** our online bookstore for the latest information and editions!

- **COMMUNICATE** with our expert authors through e-mail and conferences.

- **DOWNLOAD SOFTWARE** from the immense MCP library:
    - Source code and files from MCP books
    - The best shareware, freeware, and demos

- **DISCOVER HOT SPOTS** on other parts of the Internet.

- **WIN BOOKS** in ongoing contests and giveaways!

TO PLUG INTO MCP: ➜

GOPHER: gopher.mcp.com
FTP: ftp.mcp.com

WORLD WIDE WEB: http://www.mcp.com